Entering the

Ghost River

Other Works by Deena Metzger:

Fiction:

Skin: Shadows/Silence
The Woman Who Slept With Men to Take the War Out of Them
What Dinah Thought
The Other Hand

Non-fiction:

Writing for Your Life: A Guide and Companion to the Inner Worlds
Tree: Essays and Pieces
Intimate Nature: The Bond Between Women and Animals
(with Brenda Peterson and Linda Hogan)

Poetry:

Dark Milk
The Axis Mundi Poems
Looking for the Faces of God
A Sabbath Among the Ruins

Plays:

The Book of Hags
Not As Sleepwalkers
Dreams Against The State

Audio:

This Body/My Life

Entering the Ghost River

MEDITATIONS ON THE THEORY AND PRACTICE OF HEALING

c

DEENA METZGER

HAND ᴛᴏ HAND

Grateful acknowledgement is made for permission to use the following copyrighted materials: to Darhansoff, Verrill, Feldman Literary Agents for the use of excerpts from *Poems* by Anna Akmatova, Lyn Coffin, trans.; to Stephen Karcher for his kind permission to use excerpts from his book *How to Use the I Ching, A Guide to Working With the Oracle of Change* and his forthcoming book *Myths for Change: The Total I Ching*; to Simon & Schuster for the use of excerpts from *The Mythic Tarot* by Liz Greene and Juliet Sharman-Burke; to Princeton University Press for excerpts from *Alone with the Alone* by Henry Corbin; to Gillian van Houten for permission to use an excerpt from *The Elephant Cull*; to Cornell University Press for use of an excerpt from *Peyote Hunt* by Barbara Myerhoff. Full copyright information for above appears in Endnotes. And thank you to all who so graciously allowed their names and/or stories to be used throughout this book.

Entering the Ghost River: Meditations on the Theory and Practice of Healing is sponsored by Mandlovu, a nonprofit educational member organization of Social and Environmental Entrepreneurs (SEE). Mandlovu was created to support visionary artists, writers, and healers who are committed to the exploration, revitalization, and preservation of indigenous wisdom and medicine traditions as paths to planetary healing and peacemaking on behalf of all beings. Because of the global challenge of these most difficult times, Mandlovu's goal is to sustain those teachers and practitioners whose work is devoted to the generation and manifestation of new forms of consciousness.

Book produced and designed by Stephan David Hewitt.

Front cover photo: "Norway, Arctic Circle, Summer Solstice"; Rear cover top, "Masvingo, Africa"; and bottom, "Laura's Emergence." All photos by Deena Metzger.

Library of Congress Cataloging-in-Publication Data

Metzger, Deena.
    Entering the ghost river : meditations on the theory
and practice of healing / Deena Metzger. -- 1st ed.
    p. cm.
    ISBN 0-9720718-2-2

    1. Spiritual healing and spiritualism. 2. Mental healing. 3. Healing--
Africa. 4. Metzger, Deena. 5. Healers--Biography.   I. Title

BF1275.F3M48 2002   615.8'52
                                          QBI33-591

CONTENTS

Acknowledgements   ii
Foreword   by Stephan David Hewitt   iv
Introduction   vi
Entering the Ghost River   1

Afterword   by Michael Ortiz Hill   271
Glossary   275
Appendix I   I Ching reading by   277
                          Stephen Karcher
Appendix II   Speech by Congressman   283
                          Dennis Kucinich
Appendix III   The Story of the Porcupine   288
Appendix IV   Invoking the Holy Letters for 293
                          Peace and Tikkun Olam
Endnotes   305

ACKNOWLEDGEMENTS

The acknowledgements which are an author's joy to make, recognizing the individuals and community that assisted and sustained the work, are, in this case, deeply connected to the way Hand to Hand has come into existence. *Entering the Ghost River* comes out of Daré, its stories and sensibilities. My gratitude is, first, to Augustine Kandemwa with whom many of these ideas and visions were explored and verified. And then to all the people whose stories I tell and to my friends, students and the members of Daré who have entered with me into the exploration of what healing is and how Story carries it. To Daré itself and the ways in which we support each other's hearts and souls. The title and the understanding of its implications comes from the extraordinary scholarship and insight of Stephen Karcher, translator and interpreter of the I Ching, whose work directly inspired and instigated the book. And, though it is not customary, a general thank you to those who I know, but obviously cannot yet name, who will come forth in support of the book or the intent and possibilities of Hand to Hand. In addition, I wish to recognize both Valerie Wolf and Amanda Foulger who have read and critiqued the manuscript, encouraging and sustaining me profoundly, and to Ron Galbavy who offered us the benefit of his years of experience in publishing. Shelby Flint, jazz singer *extraordinaire*, has come forth as a skillful, devoted, and graceful editorial assistant, and we are indebted to her for her help. In the process of preparing the book for publication, Glen Hutloff joined us bringing his love of books, his insistent curiosity, and financial and administrative skills to our project. Emma Rosenthal, Sonya Lea, and Danelia Wild graciously offered to assist us in bringing the book to the community and the community to the book. And at the 11th hour, Jeff Mayers stepped forth to read proofs. I would also like to thank Michele Sang O'Brien, who accompanied us to Africa and was present at the meeting with the Ambassador. When she was assisting Stephen Karcher in editing his text, she introduced us to him and facilitated the extraordinary reading that led, among other things, to the writing of this book.

My gratitude goes to my beloved husband and partner, Michael Ortiz Hill. We have come to that place in our lives when we can scarcely disentangle our thoughts and passions from each other's. And why do so? This book emerges from the many gifts he has brought to me and our life, not the least of which was the invitation to go to Africa and experience the wonder of the indigenous healing tradition carried by Augustine Kandemwa. We expect that at the same time that this book is published, Michael's book, *Gathering in the Names,* from Spring Publications, will also appear. Each book written by one of us, but emerging from the sensibility and understanding honed, as occurs in so many good marriages, by both of us.

Finally, I want to speak of Stephan David Hewitt who, in a more formal arrangement, would carry the titles of editor, copy-editor, designer and publisher. Here he joins me also as friend, colleague and collaborator in bringing this book into the world and of imagining, with me, the possibilities of Hand to Hand. As this book, in particular, is both text and event, I can truly say that Stephan is the co-creator of this book and that our association verifies what is really possible among people in community.

And ultimately, my thanks to the ancestors, invisibles and spirits who, the old ones say, always sit in council with us and so, when we allow it, create alliances with us and guide us so generously.

FOREWORD

by Stephan David Hewitt

Three years ago, I wandered for the first time into Deena Metzger's home in Topanga with my friend Janet Mayhall to witness a Daré. We had little information about the group except we'd heard they talked about "spiritual ideas" and healing. I found the people there friendly and kind, not selling any particular set of ideas, simply a group of people who had come together to share, sing, drum, dance, and pray. There was plenty of good food brought by all, and a genuine spirit of camaraderie.

I didn't speak at council that first time, preferring to check out the group and its energy. Actually, I didn't speak at council for several months, but I did keep coming back. I noticed over time that the group seemed fairly diverse, representative of different classes, races, and occupations, but we were all talking about the same thing – healing. For ourselves, for the planet, for all our relations, as the Native Americans say, meaning everything on the earth around us.

At Daré – the Shona word for council – I found a focus of support in a gathering of people that allowed me, eventually, to talk about what was deep in my heart. As I told my dreams and stories, and listened to the stories of others, healing took place. Three years later, I am helping Deena to come forth with her latest work; it is an honor and a blessing.

There can be no doubt that we are at a critical point in our development as a race of beings. More and more, we are being shown the fruits of our ways, our thinking, the very paradigms by which we live – and what bitter fruits these are. Whether you consult the elder teachings of the Hopi, the Maya, the Tibetans, or the Essenes, to name but a few, they all refer to this very time of our history as an in-between time, a time in which we are crossing over to another world, another way of existence. The old ways are no longer valid. We cannot expect ourselves to be saved by a Messiah who descends from "on high"; that patriarchal fantasy only makes us separate from that power which resides within us all. Each of us shares a piece of the "Messiah," and when we come together in community, the pieces interlock. Then what we think of as miracles can take place.

There is no simple or easy way to describe what healing is. It is a non-linear puzzle, a web and maze of unexpectedly connected experiences, often seen only with peripheral vision. No matter what technologies we develop around it, it is still inherently a mystery. There is poetry, majesty, and beauty deeply imbedded within it. To examine the nature of healing necessitates that we look at the web of our cultural, political, and social structures that have generated disease. This is a revolutionary act. The word "theory" implies deductive or even reductive frameworks, but Deena's approach to theory is through Story and the revelations inherent within it.

Deena's way is deeply grounded in the Feminine Principle. That is, indirect, non-linear, dancing around a central point with a labyrinth of stories that weave their spidery web into a recognizable pattern. She suspends chronology for the momentum of meaning; each present moment in the book may be out of linear time sequence. But the stories as a whole cohere to show us a flower growing at the core. Something creative and interesting has appeared for us to marvel upon.

At the heart of Deena's gathering of stories is a fierce discipline and spiritual rigor. Her concern for the state of the world is constantly with her. She encourages us to examine the politics of our own relationships, as evidence of the macrocosm in which we live, to look at our own lives to see how the larger patterns around us are formed.

To carry one's story alone brings suffering; to share and hear stories brings healing. As we carry the stories of suffering and healing together, as a community, deep truths begin to emerge. Using the personal stories of her life, Deena creates pictures that ultimately cohere to form a life story dedicated to healing.

This is the nature of Daré. It is a field of relationships where we begin to see what we could not see from our own viewpoint alone. A place where we meet, you and I, and share our stories. Welcome. Have a seat, a cup of tea, and let's listen.

INTRODUCTION

September 11th called this book into being. At the threshold of a sabbatical, I changed direction entirely and gave more than the next nine months to writing this book on the practice of healing and peacemaking. I wrote it, as the times demanded, without inhibition, calling myself, on a daily basis, to the courage and stamina it takes to say what must be said. *Entering the Ghost River* was written during the period of shell shock that afflicted the country. Trauma immobilizes and confuses its victims, distorting their responses and behavior until the trauma is healed. Time does not heal traumas, consciousness does. As the nation tried to understand and assimilate the attack, other forces, perhaps deliberately taking advantage of the situation, or overwhelmed by fear and helplessness, began creating measures that could further immobilize the population by undermining the Bill of Rights. A line from my last book, *The Other Hand*, began repeating itself in my mind when I learned that the U.S. government is contemplating using nuclear weapons in an ongoing war they are planning: "We have taken the building blocks of creation and made a bomb of them." Terrorism from without has instigated terror within. Never before in our nation's history, not even after Pearl Harbor, has it been so clear that the voices, nature, and activity of healing, peacemaking, and council need to be called forth.

In the last years, I have been concerned with the state of publishing in America. I was raised with great pride in the freedoms associated with this country. Not a small influence on my becoming a writer is the sacred responsibility to act on behalf of justice and compassion. In the largest sense, the mandate is to search out and reveal truth in all its forms, no less the revelation of beauty than the examination of suffering. But increasingly, I became aware of the ways in which publishing is no longer devoted to the freedoms that are essential to an informed and self-governing society. It wasn't the kind of political repression that characterizes so many tyrannical governments of the modern world that concerned me earlier, but the impact of economic values that were amounting to censorship as large corporate conglomerates began to dominate the publishing arena, financially and conceptually, converting the book from a gift into a commodity. Increasingly, the wisdom and acuity of fine editors are being replaced by the no-nonsense authority of publicity and promotion departments devoted to the profit margin. What must be said is so often modified or replaced by what salesmen say will sell.

With these concerns, I often speculated on the tradition of the *Samizdat*, the mimeographed manuscripts that were secretly circulated at great risk in the Soviet Union during the time of Stalin and afterwards. Many of them made their desperate way to the West so that we were apprised of the horrors of Soviet life, creating great sympathy and support for those suffering under extreme oppression. And, within the Soviet Union, certainly they were the means through which consciousness and hope were carried until such time that a free press might emerge.

When *Entering the Ghost River* was finished, I sent it to an agent and then before she had a chance to read the manuscript, I withdrew it. Many events contributed to this, not the least of which was the threatened shredding in January 2002 of many thousands of copies of Michael Moore's book, *Stupid White Men,* that, among other things, outlined the stolen Presidential election of George W. Bush and presaged the Enron scandal and the administration's involvement in it. *Stupid White Men* was to have been published in September but the September 11th bombing and the political response of the government frightened or inhibited the publisher, HarperCollins. A huge non-partisan e-mail protest finally obligated the publisher to publish the book on February 19, 2002 without, thankfully, any of the extreme modifications that HarperCollins had demanded until that time.

Entering the Ghost River embodies work on healing that has been developing over the last ten years, and has realized an unexpected applicability since 9/11. And as the ways of healing are newly understood, so is the nature of disease, both personal and political. Given the times, I felt a great sense of urgency, but it was not only the urgency of concern, it was the urgency of hope. I saw that September 11th could also become a vehicle for deep soul searching and self-scrutiny and I saw that the book could assist us in the practice of transformation and peacemaking. The gift came through me, from "elsewhere," from the Divine, from the spirits, unimpeded, and I thought that I must offer it to the world in the same way – as a gift, and unimpeded, and with the same speed and urgency that it was offered to me. Eschewing all practical and economic considerations, I saw that I was being called, for the first time in my life, to bring a book out as a private edition so that it would not be subject to censorship or delay.

That is how Hand to Hand came to be. Originally, I had thought of using the name *Samizdat*, but friends pointed out that this carried a sense of reactivity when the feeling we want to communicate is of generosity and possibility. "*Samizdat* implies manuscripts being passed hand to hand," I said in defense, and instantly understood what the imprint was to be.

In the process of imagining this private edition, I realized that we could be creating a form and a vehicle for other independently published works – books, plays, music, performances, films – that have at their core the necessity of saying what must be said, and the commitment of the authors and the community. Hand to Hand is grounded in Daré which is one of the subjects of this book. Daré, meaning "council" in the Shona language of Zimbabwe, is the means through which healing is restored to the center of the community where it belongs. Or it is a community that coheres around council and healing. Hand to Hand restores the word to the community from which it originates, which it serves and where it belongs. The word coheres a community and the community offers the word a basis for its existence.

In the last years, I have received instructions from the ancestors and from indigenous peoples concerned for the planet on how to live an ethical and useful life: teach the pattern and put the forms in place. Hand to Hand, like Daré, comes out of this injunction.

My vision is that news of this book will be passed from hand to hand so that it will be received by those for whom it will matter. I imagine the book as the beginning of the kind of conversation or council that takes place at Daré where we tell each other what really matters in our lives, and where we are each deeply affected by the interchange and the wisdom that resides in each individual. I imagine readings or public events that will end in council so that the people in the audience will become a community through the contemplation and response to what is of deep concern to them all. A book, an imprint, a venture that has the possibility of creating camaraderie on matters of heart, soul, and our very survival. A book and an imprint that points toward and awakens hope and possibility. And so I offer this to you, hand to hand.

DEDICATION

This book is dedicated to the ancestors, the animal spirits, and the members of the Darés in Africa and North America, in recognition of the reestablishment of ancient alliances that invite healing to restore the world, our lives, and our souls.

what is the story

we want to know.

– Alicia Ostriker[1]

Anna Akhmatova, considered by many to be the greatest modern Russian poet, wrote these words in Leningrad on April 1st, 1957:

Instead of a Preface.

In the awful years of Yezhovian horror, I spent seventeen months standing in line in front of various prisons in Leningrad. One day someone "recognized" me. Then a woman with blue lips, who was standing behind me, and who, of course, had never heard my name, came out of the stupor which typified all of us, and whispered into my ear (everyone there spoke only in whispers):

– Can you describe this?

And I said:

– I can.

Then something like a fleeting smile passed over what had once been her face.[2]

1

"What is your medicine?" I was asked.
"Story. Story is my medicine," I answered.

I am feeling something of what Augustine Kandemwa must have felt when he first crossed over and entered the Ghost River from which one never returns, even if one's story is told in the way *Ambuya* MaGumbo and the Tanzanian trance medium tell theirs. They each lived under water in the village of the water spirits for seven years and then they returned to the world of the living as healers, carrying the spirits with them. One day Augustine was the highest-ranking officer in charge of education for the police force and their families, and the next day he was a healer. He very reluctantly gave up his pressed uniforms to take on dreads, skins, and snuff. People began to come to him with their physical and emotional disturbances. The animals began to speak to him. He had visions. The ancestors came to him in his dreams. A dream bird led him to a stand of trees on a sand spit in the middle of the river where he was instructed to gather herbs that could be used for healing. He found the sand spit near Big (Victoria) Falls and gathered the herbs and they did have the healing powers he had been promised. He saw his own shoes walking on the waters of Lake Kyle as if he were standing in them. People from everywhere in southern Africa came to consult him because the spirits spoke through him. These are the words he says when he speaks about God: "I am God's hands. I am God's feet." He has offered himself to be one of the bodies of God, and housing the spirits is the means through which he fulfills this offering. Once he acted on the dreams that had been assaulting him, he began to live among the spirits in the same way that he lives among his family, his community, and all those who come to consult him; he cannot return to his former life.

He lives among people, but he is called to conversation with beings of other realms who are often invisible to those to whom he ministers.

Those who come to him for healing may also be suffering from distress or illness in the way Augustine suffered when the spirits were calling him forth. Or they are suffering the way he sometimes suffers now when the pain of his people or the world is too much for him and he knows that he also is being called even further into initiation so that he can carry what he must carry. Within hours of our second meeting in December 1998, he fell into my arms weeping; he had not, until this moment when Michael and I had arrived, had anywhere to place his grief. He speaks of this state as "the spirits being heavy" upon him. When he sees this in people, his healing work is to bring them into alliance with the call that is coming from Spirit. Being in relationship to the spirits is the essential purpose of initiation. Sometimes one heals the body and sometimes one calls the afflicted one to initiation.

My husband Michael Ortiz Hill and I returned to Zimbabwe and Botswana in August 2001. During our stay, several Americans and Canadians came to Zimbabwe to undergo initiation with Augustine and ourselves. Located in Bulawayo, Zimbabwe's second largest city, we traveled to some of the sacred sites as well as to wild animal preserves. So it was that six of us from North America were involved in a parallel story when the world as we know it changed forever. On September 11th, we were in Masvingo, the great 15th century ruin of the Shona Empire.

At the time when the planes hit the towers, seven of us – Augustine, Michael, myself, Robin Wilds from Canada, Chuck Madansky and Wilderness Sarchild from Massachusetts, and Laura Bellmay from Connecticut – were engaged in fierce ritual work.

Two stories intersected in that moment: a story streaming toward destruction and a story streaming toward healing. It is this point, this intersection of stories, the cataclysm, the possibilities, that is the subject of this piece. Two stories, separated by geography but not by time, becoming one story or shattering into a thousand broken shards. We are all in a story, this story now. What story led us to September 11th? What story can lead us away?

There is a silence that is the heart of God. And there is another kind of silence that kills. We were shattered when we came home from Africa, but also we had been restored. We had been broken down, we had been reconstituted. Story can do this; it can take the sharp slivers and the shards and organize them into a light. This is a book or it is a letter or it is a long conversation. A memoir, a series of stories, a meditation on despair and beauty and hope. A book of healing. A communication with the spirits. Words. Words that are or are not created from the Holy Letters. An invocation. An act of alchemy. A prayer.

I had not intended to write this book, but within days of returning home it had insisted itself. Or the spirits said, this is the time to write of such things. Write about Story and the way it can cohere the world. Write about Healing. Write about Initiation. About peacemaking. Write about stepping forth, about saying, "Yes, this is the time. Yes, here I am." Each day, I fought it and each day, I acquiesced. The spirits said we should speak with each other, we should open our hearts. We have come to this. Our lives are at stake. Our children's teeth are set on edge. Everything we love is threatened. Still there is that silence in the heart of God from which creation like an avalanche of white water endlessly pours.

On September 15th, Michael and I went to Sinai in Egypt with Augustine and Simakuhle, his wife, before returning to the United States. Michael had met Augustine in 1996 when, also following a dream, he went to Zimbabwe for initiation. Integrated into Augustine's world and into Bantu culture, Michael was introduced to Daré, meaning "council" in the Shona language. Daré is the gift that we received and brought to North America as a way of offering healing to individuals by bringing healing to each other, by healing community through gathering together in alliance with the ancestors and the natural world, and by telling each other in council the important stories of our lives. All the stories becoming aspects of one story that sustains us in these dark times and helps us imagine that we all may have a future.

Because Michael was welcomed so deeply into the spiritual healing center that is Augustine's home, he began to devote himself to sustaining this African community. Of all this we will speak later in detail. Or perhaps this entire manuscript is a description of, an homage to, and yes, an invocation of "Daré mind." "Daré mind" is both new to western culture and a return to the oldest non-hierarchical, peaceful, and ecstatic forms of the Pleistocene that existed around the fire circle ten thousand years ago and that we carry, indelibly, in our genetic code.

Augustine is renowned in southern Africa as a *nganga* and Simakuhle is a dreamer and trance medium. A Shona man, Augustine was first initiated by a *nganga* of the Ndebele people. The Shona and Ndebele are traditional enemies who have warred bitterly in the last hundred years; Simakuhle is of the Ndebele line. So the marriage between Augustine and Simakuhle is an act of peacemaking as the first initiation was that Augustine received.

The work we did at Masvingo proceeded from a visit to *Ambuya* MaGumbo, to receive her insight and wisdom. "You must live close to the earth; you must plant things," the *Ambuya* had told Robin, who was (but the *Ambuya* knew nothing about her) suffering in an apartment in Toronto where she longed for the natural world. Within a few months of returning to Canada, Robin moved to the country, where she could have a garden as the *Ambuya* had insisted and where she could live out more fully her great love for the natural world. The *Ambuya* also recognized Chuck and Wilderness and the implicit partnership that existed between them and saw that Laura would have healing power in her hands. And then the *Ambuya* asked us to provide healing for her and her partner Zou and in doing so called us forth into new lives by recognizing and validating capacities not necessarily honored at home.

Inspired and encouraged by the *Ambuya*, we visited the Great Enclosure of the Queen and the Cave of the King so that we might learn through ritual work and the visions that often accompany it, how we might, each in our own way, carry a greater measure of caring for the world. We were thinking about leadership and responsibility in what we had agreed then were extremely dark and dangerous times. How might we serve community given the current circumstances? Laura Bellmay had been undergoing chemotherapy after a recurrence of breast cancer. She was fighting for life but also trying to understand the nature of healing and how it might accord with her political and social concerns. We were trying to shape our lives by thinking in terms of actions that would have integrity in all the worlds, personal as well as political, material, and spiritual. Laura was thinking in terms of gestures that would be healing for her and for her kin and community.

At the exact moment that the first tower was struck, we were at the *omphalos*, the sacred ritual center of the Great Enclosure of the Queen. Wilderness was weeping wordlessly and inconsolably. Laura was overwhelmed with grief, inexplicably bombarded by images of devastation. We were before the ruins of a 12th century stone tower with its peak sheared; but where the dark scars of fire and ash might have been once, ferns, vines and moss are growing.

*   *   *

Story is an essential structure of mind and an active principle, a living narrative structure, coherent and beautiful. Sometimes we tell the story, that is, "what happened," but that is the least of its functions. Story gathers and integrates the elements of event and imagination, reflection and image into a point, the bindu or the infinitesimally dense particle that birthed the entire universe in the Big Bang. When it opens, meaning emerges in a flow or explosion of light and understanding. We don't know the entire story until the moment when all the parts are gathered, resonant, coexistent, and then revealed. Only then and in that moment. Every story is like this. And we live countless stories simultaneously and sequentially. Perhaps, ultimately, we are each a story, a dynamic relationship of elements, its own unique shape resonant with larger stories that form the universal grid from which we emerge. These larger stories continue to shape our story as we mature and remain the focal point toward which we are ultimately drawn. The bindu at the beginning and the omega point at the end. And between them all – possibilities, but within our own shape.

Story is given and made. It is offered to us and we are constantly creating it. This essential tension is part of the paradox or several paradoxes which each of us, knowingly or unknowingly, has been given to hold, to dance with, to explore for her or his entire life.

September 11th was such a point in time. When the internal structure of such a minute particle is violently disturbed, an explosion of vast dimensions can occur that will blaze in all directions, affecting the past and the future. A billion stories that had converged rushed away from each other to form a new universe. I/We do not know all those stories; I know only the ones we were living and the shock of the collision. We could only make out the planes and the towers coming down in the wild chaos of that terrible final meeting. Perhaps the planes and the towers collapsing were emblematic of all of those billion stories and that is why the destruction was so enormous, the effect upon all of us so extreme, and the consequences still reverberating. The larger story became one story. It became a global story although we are aware that it was understood differently by different people.

Perhaps there are alternatives. Coexisting stories in hundreds of languages that can also move into our hearts and the places of grief. If we are given a choice to follow any one of those stories as I am now, trying to be faithful to that opportunity of choice, then mindfulness demands that we choose carefully the one we follow for our survival and our redemption. Mindfulness demands that the story we choose to follow and serve is the one that serves all of our souls and is the one that contains a future, an entire future history of the planet, the planet thriving, all its creatures fulfilled.

All of this is to be considered so we can address this question: What new world can emerge from such a moment?

story!

*   *   *

I am trying to tell you a story and to reveal the nature of story at the same time. A story isn't a linear event. It weaves and hums. It goes out, it circles back. A story is…. It is organic. It develops. It lives and it dies. Perhaps it is a living thing. A divine gift. The map for the soul. Let's not approach it in the old ways. Let's not presume to capture it or control it. Let's try to understand it on its own terms. Each story is particular, composed of many particularities. It never happened before. It will never happen again. A story is created from the events of our lives but it is choreographed elsewhere. An invisible hand reaches toward us from "over there" arranging, ordering. Our task is to meet it. Sometimes the hand offers elements we could not gather ourselves – a dream, a sign – that becomes part of the story, that can even be the heart of the story.

You – yes, you, the one who is reading this – you will bring something to this story. Or this story may enter your story and you may become part of it and it of you. What will come of all of this? Who will we become through this meeting? We can't know. We will see.

*   *   *

Spiritual work is based on the premise that worlds can be brought into being outside of the linear activities and consequences of daily life, outside of cause and effect. Story is the configuration where many events and different realms intersect or where a field of associations is set aquiver through the relationship of one to the other. We can walk in many worlds at once – a true healing gesture has integrity in all worlds – and activities appropriate to one realm may be undertaken on behalf, also, of all the other realms. True relationship is not linear so much as resonant.

So, people praying at the same time with open hearts may radically affect the course of events, and the patient, who the doctors expected to decline and even die, may mysteriously live, but for no visible cause. But more has occurred in addition to the patient's improvement. Coming together to pray is healing for the community. Recognizing the possibility of Spirit's intervention restores the soul. The act of prayer/focus/intent creates an atmosphere of calm that is beneficial for the patient and kin. And, as Michael who is a nurse often comments, the community's solidarity and love of the patient inspires the nursing and medical staff and assures them of the worthiness of their most difficult work. They are then also inspired to act generously on behalf of the patient, and perhaps then, by empathy or sympathy, on behalf of other patients, particularly those who are alone. This is a complex healing event and also a good story. Then why not approach healing the planet in this way?

*   *   *

On September 11th exactly at the moment that the planes struck the towers, we were engaged, as I said, in fierce ritual work of initiation on behalf of healing an individual and in order to take on responsibility for the community at large. Each one of us was at that moment being initiated dramatically as a healer beyond what we had each ever imagined. It is my hope and prayer that by recognizing what occurred for each of us then, and by finding the common story that emerges from our efforts, we can follow that story forward into a real future in which all beings are sustained.

*   *   *

Initiation. It is not so much a beginning as the word implies but the activity that allows one to step through a door into a different world. Initiation doesn't teach so much as provide the means to become someone else. The experience tunes you to the reality of a cosmic order you may have glimpsed but without entering. Now you are of it. But in the process of initiation one often sheds, like the proverbial snake, the skin of the past life. Entering into a personal and dynamic relationship with Spirit may be so drastically different from the life one has lived before, that one feels completely undone before one reconstructs a viable self and way of life appropriate to the new reality. If the initiation holds, we never go back to the old forms or the old reality; we are now incapable of doing so. We have been reconstituted so that we can live now in this different universe, our entire system attuned to a different set of laws.

In 1969, I stood before an audience of over two thousand people in a college gymnasium. This was an initiatory moment that came about during a harrowing period of political persecution. I didn't think of it as a ritual moment then, but in retrospect, it clearly was. And I certainly didn't think of that moment as mediated by the spirits, for I was an activist involved in political and social action and had no idea then of the ways in which the spiritual life and its relationship to community can be coherent with all aspects of our life, including, or especially the social and political.

In what became an important academic freedom case, I had been fired from a tenured teaching position for teaching a poem I had written to an English class in a community college. It was a time of great struggle for civil liberties and civil rights in the middle of the protest against the war in Viet Nam. The English lesson had been prepared with particular care because its subject was free speech, pornography and censorship – a tricky subject in tense times. I was trying to offer my students a considered example of the ways that they could distinguish the values inherent in a work of literature from those that are degrading. The last Supreme Court decision, the Roth decision[3] on pornography, had dealt with the intent of the publisher. I assigned an unpublished poem of my own so that the students could wrestle with this; I knew my intent and I believed it could be derived from a careful reading of the poem. Careful reading, the way of explication, was also what I was teaching. Now I was, as my attorney David Finkel said, "offering the English lesson to the people of the state of California."

The students and faculty who were supportive of me organized a rally on my behalf, attended by two thousand people. I was a very shy woman and I came to the podium trembling. As I walked those few steps from my seat, I was aware of thinking, "This moment will change my life. Either I will be unable to speak, will stutter or remain silent, or, somehow, I will speak well and so I will become a public woman and my life will be changed accordingly." There was a tiny interlude, outside of time, in which I knew that my fate was not in my hands. Something else was moving through me and I did offer myself to it. Until I heard my own voice speaking with growing confidence, I had not known what the outcome would be.

In 1972, the California Supreme Court ruled unanimously in my favor and I was reinstated to my teaching position. But that was not the critical moment. The critical moment was stepping to the podium and recognizing that the shy, introverted woman was being undone and another woman was being born; my own preferences were irrelevant. ⨯

Initiation. It is not as simple as the gods calling you forth and you responding: yes. Initiation also includes breakdown, and, only long afterwards, reconstitution. ⨯

A synchronicity occurred at the time that always puzzled me. My husband, Reed, and I had agreed to separate and the day we had chosen was June 1, 1969. It was on that date, also, that I was officially fired according to instructions directly received by the community college from Governor Ronald Reagan himself: "Get rid of that woman!" It was as if the universe had conspired to break me down completely. My entire life collapsed in shambles. My marriage was undone; my family life, my children were shattered. I lost my job and could find no work. My friends took sides. After intense deliberation, it became clear that conscience required that I fight this in the courts. A new community college board was to take office for the first time on July 1, 1969. The board members were deeply divided between liberals or progressives and conservative extremists. The Right saw this case as an opportunity to take control of the schools. Jerry Brown, soon to be governor himself, had been elected to the board and saw this case as a political opportunity to make himself known – and he was right.

The political climate was such that I was exposed to public calumny and derision. Political persecution does not proceed politely as you are moved through the court system, but is enacted viciously through the media and in the public arena. It breaks you down in every conceivable way. Nothing remained of my life as I knew it. By the time the California Supreme Court unanimously ruled in my favor, I had entered another life and their decision barely affected me, though it was affirming and important for the community. I had become someone else living another story with the moment of speaking at its core. This event was not the initiation I would have chosen. It was not the fierce but benevolent activity of the teacher or healer on behalf of the student's soul. But it called me and I went.

September 11, 2001. The towers collapse. We are devastated. An opportunity in the rubble. Not to reconstruct the old forms. But to construct something new. Something that is healing for the world. What might it be? Will we do it? Or will we retaliate and continue the cycle of violence that comes from us as much as from "the others"? What is Spirit asking of us? In Zimbabwe, we were asking, "What does it mean to be a peacemaker? What is healing?" Then the planes hit. The questions became urgent.

This is not the initiation we would have chosen. But here we are. How are we going to respond?

*   *   *

While many of the events chronicled here occurred before September 11th, this piece is being written in the shadow and aftermath of that date. The question of what it means to be a healer has taken on new urgency and power. And the nature of healing has expanded to include, necessarily, the healing of the community and the world at the same time that we are considering the healing of an individual. We must stop separating one from the other.

In the modern world, the work of the healer focusses on the realm of the personal. The herb woman, the energy worker, the medicine man or woman, the shaman, the one who lays on hands, the physician, homeopath, chiropractor, body worker, trance medium, dream teller or psychoanalyst, indigenous practitioners like the Navajo Singer, *yataali,* hand trembler and star gazer, therapists of various kinds from many different traditions – all have devoted themselves to curing or reducing the effects of illness, to easing pain, listening to the soul and extending the life of individuals. Some of these practitioners, though they are concerned with the individual, recognize also that disease often occurs in the interface between the individual and the world.

At a conference on Navajo sand paintings, a Navajo anthropologist told Michael and me the following story. He was studying at the University of Arizona and was interested, but skeptical of, native ways of diagnosis and healing. He had had a rash on his neck for a long time but could not find any effective treatment for it, so he used his illness as an occasion to consult a Navajo diagnostician, a hand trembler, as I recall. "The rash is a sign that you have offended the Red Ant People," the healer said. "Isn't that true?"

The anthropologist was stunned. It was indeed true but he hadn't recognized it. Some weeks before, he had thrown a sleeping bag down on the ground only to realize that red ants were surrounding his bed. He poured gasoline in a circle around the sleeping area and set the ants on fire. The lesion followed quickly.

After a diagnosis, the Navajo community will gather for a Sing. The patient is placed in the center of the Sand Painting that represents the moment in the mythic story corresponding to the circumstances of the disease. The Sand Painting is executed perfectly. The songs, chants, prayers are recited perfectly. The perfection of the natural order is restored. Patient, myth, community, natural world align again. Healing results.

I did not ask what offering the anthropologist himself made to the Red Ant people to make amends for his violation, but I am certain that he made them and the offerings were substantial and appropriate. The practice, so essential to healing, of making offerings, contains the dual goal of expressing gratitude and righting wrongs, to make amends for ways that we may have offended or disrespected someone, the spirits, or the natural world. The afflicted one brings an offering to the teacher or healer. The offering must be related to the story that the patient is carrying or to the relationship between the healer and the patient. The personal element is very important here. The offering itself is part of the dialogue from which the path of healing is revealed. Healers or teachers make offerings to the spirits or the birds, whomever or whatever they rely on for assistance. This does not replace an exchange of money but a fee in itself does not contribute to the healing story that is being enacted.

My house is full of gifts and each gift has a story. Almost nothing in the house is decorative in the usual sense but it is adorned with the sacred and symbolic objects that I have been given. When I look around, I see how I have been woven into the fabric of a community but I also see that by recognizing these gifts each day I am keeping relationships and healing stories alive. Once met and joined in a healing event, we are never separate again from each other. Bell's theorem postulates the continuous relationship of particles that once joined, retain a mysterious connection no matter how far they travel from each other. Connection is one of the principles that heals the diseases of alienation.

The Navajo tradition embodies the understanding that illness occurs when one has, albeit inadvertently, violated the natural order, has offended the community, the natural world, or the gods. Health results from restoring beauty, or order. Learning about the Navajo way, I was confirmed in my understanding that there is an intrinsic relationship between the health of any individual and the nature of their interaction with the planet, the nation and the community.

Here I would like to tell a story of the consequences of violating the natural world. It is a story that emerged at the deathbed of my friend Hella Hammid who had kept that story a secret for over sixty years. But it is a long story. You can find it in the Appendix as "The Story of the Porcupine."

*   *   *

Western dualism keeps these concerns separate, but in 1977, breast cancer brought the two of them irreversibly together in my body and in my mind. Even as I dealt personally with the disease and investigated my own psyche to find a healing path, I saw that I must consider, equally, the political causes of cancer and the cancerous effects of our politics. In order to heal, I had to be aware of the ways in which toxic substances – the effluvia of modern life – produce illnesses, and also the ways cancer imitates political systems. After much reflection on the nature of cancer gleaned from medical texts, I saw that cancer in its growth pattern resembled imperial or colonizing systems. It was as if I could not fully understand the politics we were involved in until I knew it in my own body. This was more than metaphor, more than analogy, more than an imaginative path toward healing. Rather it seemed to me that the very same disease appeared one way in the human body and another way in the body politic; it was the same disease, though not recognized as such by either physicians, their patients, or government, though it hurt, debilitated and destroyed in the same ways.

And being that the same disease manifests in different ways in different systems or levels, it might be possible to discern healing interventions that reach directly to the disease in all its forms. One gesture for all its materializations. One gesture of such integrity that it impacts the physical, emotional, social, political, environmental and spiritual realms. This is one way of working. We will have to research, experiment, and practice so we can become adepts of one-pointedness.

Here is another way of working: One may be diagnostically skilled in one realm but not skilled in another. One takes the principles and patterns of one realm and applies them metaphorically to the second realm to see what might be possible. You may not have political savvy, but if you know how cancer works, it may inform you politically. Or the reverse, you may be politically astute and this may give you insights as to how to respond to cancer. This is one way I am thinking about September 11th. I do not know how, and do not have the skill or power to heal the political and economic circumstances that led up to and are the results of the impact of the planes or the collapse of the towers. But I know something of community and how to move ritually in the world of healing, and I have been deeply informed by the work we were doing in Masvingo. My task is to see how these experiences translate into viable political forms or activities. Working analogously is one of the ways I am proceeding here.[4]

*   *   *

What healers have known and many medical practitioners have forgotten is that sometimes the best instruction comes from one's own experience in one's own mind and body – the way of the wounded healer. I did not know when I had cancer that I was being initiated as a healer. Spirit knew what I could not know then, that, in a short time and thereafter, my life's work would include tending those suffering with life-threatening illness.

Spirit calls us in surprising ways. Sometimes one doesn't recognize its presence until years later. Healing doesn't always look like the outcome we hope for or expect. What we think is healing may not accord with Spirit's activity on our behalf.

When I had breast cancer in 1977, the surgeon advised me to have a breast implant immediately. He would leave a fold of skin loose and slip the implant in. Surgery was scheduled for Tuesday and the implant on Friday. The biopsy of the tumor had been performed under full anesthesia. The mastectomy required full anesthesia again. Reconstructive surgery was the third incident of anesthesia. When I awakened from the surgery, I was still flat as a boy. I was undone but also aware that an amazing thing had happened. Unprecedented. After they had opened my chest again, a freak electrical storm hit the city and the electricity failed in the hospital. Though there was an emergency backup system, it did not service the autoclaves and they could not sterilize the implant. It was not possible to schedule another surgery in the near future. I had to wait at least six months and then begin again; it would be a different procedure then and would, the surgeon assured me, take several months instead of a single surgery. Now the surgery would proceed in stages, leaving me asymmetrical for many months. In the meantime, I lost interest. Then I met a woman who had a small arrow tattooed on her back. She told me that her tattooist had covered the scars of three women who had had mastectomies. And so I had a tree, a bird and book inscribed on my chest. But that is not the end of the story. My attorney, David Finkel, told me how relieved he was that I didn't have reconstructive surgery. A dear friend of his had died of a recurrence of cancer on the exact site of the first tumor. An implant would hide such a recurrence. And years afterwards, it also became clear that the materials used in the implants were exceedingly dangerous. Better to have a tattoo and a long life.

Just when *Tree*, the journal I kept at the time I had breast cancer, was to be published, I met Hella Hammid. She was an exceptional photographer who understood the necessity of an image that would be inspiring. The photograph she took of me bare-chested with my arms raised exultantly to the sky, became the Tree or Warrior Poster. It has been in circulation for twenty years, appearing also in various books, on book jackets, in journals, periodicals, newspapers and films, nationally and internationally. The original publisher of *Tree*, Peace Press, was afraid of putting the poster on the cover or even in the book. But years later, the second publisher, Wingbow Press, finally acquiesced after two prior covers. Now, North Atlantic Books, the third publisher, has designed a truly beautiful book with the image from the poster prominent upon it.[5]

One day, I received a letter from a man: "It is not only women who have to deal with breast cancer. If one in four women will have breast cancer, one in four men may well have to face it with them. Now that I have seen your poster, I am not afraid. I will be able to love my wife through the ordeal. Thank you."

When I learned that the autoclaves had failed, I fell into despair. Certainly, I didn't feel loved by the gods in that moment. But now I know, of course, that this was the moment of their greatest love. An electrical storm of such magnitude is rare in Los Angeles. Perhaps my life was saved. A story takes a long time to be completed. What seems to be the end may not be the end. We often know nothing in the moment. When Spirit intervenes it is not only on our behalf. We do not always recognize how we are being served. Sometimes we believe that we are being cursed. That is because we are as yet unable to see how our fate is woven inextricably. Sometimes we cannot see the relationship between our welfare and the welfare of the community as a whole. When Spirit acts, one gesture can serve the individual, the community and the natural world. This is one of the signs of the presence of Spirit.

*   *   *

I interrupt the copy editing of this text exactly at this place to respond to a letter I just received from St. Paul, Minnesota. The woman writes, "I am trying to make some decisions about reconstructive breast surgery or

not surgery. I need some *art* to help me. I hope the poster is still available."
When I call, she tells me that her younger sister was just diagnosed with breast cancer also. Once again, I wonder about the plague that has descended on us and how we can meet it. Some years ago we worried about breast, ovarian, and uterine cancer, but now we must also be gravely concerned with prostate cancer. Is there a way to meet these plagues without changing our culture and society entirely? I don't think so.

*   *   *

One day I knew I was a healer. In the same moment, everything became possible. In the same moment I understood that healing was both a forbidden and sacred calling, an illegal activity.

I did not train to be a healer. There is no professional training. There are long apprenticeships to a healer or medicine person and there is the mysterious training that the spirits sometimes offer, as in the case of Augustine or many people who find themselves suddenly overwhelmed with gifts and skills they could not have imagined years before. It is most common for someone to marvel at the fact that they seem to have healing in their hands and also to be anguished by the physical and emotional turmoil that often accompanies the advent of such abilities. Those who recognize the gifts when they appear are wise to seek out a guide to help them learn to work skillfully and ethically with what has been given. Humbleness is essential. The gift of sight into someone's body or psyche must always be balanced with a true respect for the range of one's inevitable unconsciousness. It is not uncommon to become inflated by the wondrousness of the gifts given and to be blinded by one's vision of oneself. Any assumption of infallibility or absolute certainty can do great harm. We do not want to exchange the too-often authoritarian stand of modern medicine for equally authoritarian stands of healers. Healers can do as much harm as medical practitioners, especially if they suffer from similar arrogance. Often new healers reveal what they "see" in someone's body or what they believe or dream, and there can be severe negative consequences. The images given to us are not necessarily to be taken literally. They may well be to guide us in working with the client, offered to us in a language we understand, that may have entirely different meanings for the patient. And also, the images may be false. Much more than an image or insight is necessary for a diagnosis or treatment plan. Caution and skepticism are indispensable companions here.

Healing requires ethical exactitude. That is why it challenges us. Healing cannot coexist with blind obedience to a guild or affiliations or alliances with pharmaceutical firms, health insurance companies, profit-making hospitals or other business interests. I recently received a journal on alternative healing in the mail that was clearly financed by advertising from health food and vitamin companies. The writers were all recognized and respected health practitioners. But this journal was not more trustworthy than standard medical journals financed by pharmaceutical companies. Vitamin manufacturers cannot be assumed to be more honorable than drug companies. Each such journal is beholden to commercial interests. Here is the dilemma: If the journals aren't underwritten, they will probably not exist. But underwritten, they are influenced by the advertisers. The ways in which research has been altered and influenced by pharmaceutical underwriting is a subject of great concern at the moment. How can the world of healing avoid the same pitfalls?

Healing also requires recognizing what psychology, medicine and society keep secret. The ways in which culture is killing us, mind and body. The healer must feel free to say, commercial interests endanger your health. Or more importantly, war is not good for you. The government that is experimenting with anthrax, for whatever "defensive" purposes, is not acting in the interest of your health.

Social activist Fran Peavy,[6] who has been working with women in the refugee camps of the former Yugoslavia, lights a candle in a small metal candleholder on a shelf next to a vase of flowers. It is made from an ammunition shell. A new desperate cottage industry in Kosovo, a community trying to recover from war. The shell is coated with depleted uranium. It is radioactive. We used such weapons in the war against Iraq. We are seeing the consequences for the children there. What diseases will come from this in Kosovo? It is alleged we will use such weapons in Afghanistan. As healers, are we not called to consider this? And when we do, are we not outlaws?

The healer looks for the causes of illness and seeks to ease them. The healer cannot look away from the causes of illness that are endemic to our society. She or he goes back to the wisdom ways of the old ones that have been repressed or abandoned. Of course, modern life is threatened in the way that healing undermines or transforms disease. Healing threatens disease and in the modern world we are the disease. To heal ourselves individually we have to heal ourselves socially and politically.

What does this look like for me?

No known road. Only stories. What is needed? Can the need be met? What story is the disease telling?

At Daré, Dei tells us that she is a massage therapist suffering from carpal tunnel disease. She had a well-paying job in a large spa but now she cannot work and has no money. More importantly to her, she knows that she has a real gift in her hands and she cannot offer it. This hurts her deeply. Later, in a private session, she brings me a gift of two Asian pears and a small box of chocolates. "They are to delight you when you are tired," she says. When she asks about a fee, I reply that she can pay me when she is earning money again and has paid her debts. I do not believe the platitude that the healing work doesn't have meaning for the patient unless they pay for it. Everything changes if healing is primary and the means are secondary. Everything changes.

If I am not in a caring and respectful relationship with the person who is suffering, if I do not respect the depth of their suffering and the ways that it impacts every aspect of his or her life, then the healing connection is contaminated. One form of respect is recognizing when the illness or discomfort is a sign of Spirit calling someone forth. It is so important not to pathologize the consequences and extremity of the inbreaking of Spirit.

My heart goes out to the one suffering. She feels it. Her heart goes out to me. I hope for healing. She hopes I will be cared for and sustained. We appreciate each other's situations and needs. We help each as we can. The reciprocity of healing affects the economic wound that festers at the core of our society.

Dei and I sit side-by-side talking a long time while I hold and stroke her hand. Working with the symptoms of her swollen hands, we tease out the larger story of the ways in which her gift was always prevented from flowing freely from her to others. Finally, I ask her what it was like to be a black woman working in a spa that largely serves wealthy white women. How had she been received? She flinches imperceptibly. "It was as if I was a slave. I wasn't seen. They didn't know or care what I had to offer. The spa insisted on a routine that could be accomplished in a specific period of time. This stroke and then that stroke. Rote movements. We were never in relationship." Dei and I are in a story about carpal tunnel syndrome and repetitive motorized motions, and we are also in a story of racism. We are in a story of the way that people are dehumanized through the repetitive gestures of mechanized labor and a story of the ways in which systemization can corrupt the essence of a relationship. The disease is not only personal; it is political. The disease is also spiritual. Dei is being asked to use her skills in ways that are more consistent with the needs and nature of community. Healing is not a commodity, it is a gift. Dei is not a rich woman. She cannot survive without making a living. Still, it seems to me that Spirit is demanding that she use her talents differently.

I suggest she begin working again, gently, doing only what she can without causing herself a great deal of pain. I suggest that she work on her friends and her family. "Ease your mother's aching feet. Help the friend with the aching back. Offer what you can when you have the intuition that you can bring healing to them. Only work on those who see you and your gifts." She feels inspired. We have eaten the pears together but she insists that I save the chocolate for myself.

She calls me a few hours later. "I remembered something. It does not seem possible, but I completely forgot this," she says. "The last morning I worked, the director of the spa called me into her office and offered me specialized training that would give me more skills and allow me to earn more money. I had determined that I would be leaving the spa very soon because I felt like a machine there, but I forgot this in the flattery of the moment and I accepted the offer. I worked that entire day even though my hands began swelling severely. I had to place them in ice water between patients. I worked eight hours without a break. That's how they book us. One client after another. My hand did not improve when I went home and I was not able to return to work."

Dei returns to the next Daré. Two months later, her health has improved. She is beginning to use her hands again but in accordance with her heart. Her life is changing. "Abundance is everywhere, is everywhere," she says handing me more money than I had asked for.

*　　*　　*

Healing. I came to this place unexpectedly and, simultaneously, I understood that everything in my life had led up to it, that there had never been and would never be anything else.

This place is the crossroads. It is where one meets the gods. The gods who take one across. Almost every culture recognizes such gods or spirits who appear when one is about to step off the cliff into several dimensions at once. These gods are also related to healing because they are the gods who assist in bringing the worlds together, in making things whole. People have recognized and honored these gods, these spirits, these energetic configurations that open the way to different ways of being, larger ways of understanding: Eshu Elegba in the Yoruba tradition; Tehuti, in the Egyptian and esoteric; Hermes and Hekate in the Greek; the sacred letter ‎ו Vav in the Hebrew that is the pathway between the earthly and the Divine; various angels, including the archangel Michael, who open the way to the world of Spirit.

These deities who travel between and reconcile the worlds have a close relationship to the weavers, those who create connections in their ways, knitting the diverse threads of reality into the cosmic order. Here we meet Spider Woman, the Native American deity whom Augustine has taken into his pantheon as *Ambuya Buwe Buwe* in the Shona language. Westerners know her as Athena, the Olympian divinity of wisdom and weaving, whose other name might be Arachne, the spider goddess who weaves the world into existence. She embodies in her chthonic nature the weaving, measure and severing which is the work of the Moirai, the Fates: Clotho, Lachesis and Atropos. Athena did not spring fully grown out of Zeus' head despite the myth, for she is the Greek embodiment of Neith as the ancient Egyptians knew her, the great lady, the queen of the gods, the secret, unknown and all pervading one.[7]

These are some of the names that human beings have used for millennia to identify, praise and align with the divine activities that bring the worlds into coherence. These are not entities, you understand, neither apparitions nor demons, but vibrant, intelligent, interactive cosmic principles which inhabit and create the universe. They are faces of God, aspects of the Divine that we can approach and somewhat understand, for we cannot approach or know the whole. They are vast and particular, both wave and particle, the annunciation of and the very activities that wind us into the story and call us forth. To create alliances with these deities, to become vessels they may inhabit like living temples, to become the means through which they enter the world, is to enter into the domain of the sacred. We become the vessels for the living stories from which beauty and healing may yet emerge to save us.

*   *   *

Through cancer, I was being educated about the ways of illness as both private and public events. My mind went back and forth between my own fate and the fate of the community. Afterwards as a healer, I knew I must never give my attention only to the individual circumstances of those who consulted me; it was right and proper to be equally preoccupied with the state of the world and at least two of the century's chronic and life-threatening diseases: fascism and war. Nevertheless, time and again professionalism required that my political preoccupations be set aside or sublimated to what is considered the foremost task of easing individual pain and prolonging life. Most of my patients understood that both preoccupations needed to be addressed but they didn't see the intrinsic relationship between them. And then there were the precedents: to be a professional, it seemed, was to set aside most of what one knew and to agree not to investigate the social and political causes of illnesses. To be a good patient was to burrow into oneself and concentrate on one's own symptoms while determinedly, sometimes even protectively, ignoring the fate of those who were suffering alongside.

*   *   *

There is no precedent in modern medicine for addressing the political, physical, and the psychological simultaneously, nor for including spiritual and environmental concerns as essential to diagnosis and treatment. The medical doctor and the healer are trained in entirely different ways and by entirely different teachers. The extent and difficulty of professional training makes the very essential task impossible to address. The doctor has not been taught that his or her task is to care for the world; but this is the responsibility the doctor is called to. It would help if the healer or doctor knew the undertaking of healing, how impossible it is to fulfill, how it may take a lifetime to learn to carry what must be carried, if ever. Still, the problem is not that the healer is not trained as a physician, it is that the physician is not educated as a healer.

A Siberian shaman came to the United States about ten years ago in the company of an American woman who had been his translator and assistant for many years. She was being trained to take over his work when he died but she was uncertain that she could undertake this. His essential ritual task was to carry and tend the souls of his community. Nothing in her own life here had prepared her for such a responsibility. Ultimately she declined the honor and the burden.

We have a responsibility to those we heal. This is what the technician does not always understand. People might think it is the reverse… that the one who is healed is in the debt of the healer, but, actually, it is also the opposite. Once we attempt to heal someone, we have taken them on. Through the intimacy of having helped to reverse the course of a disease or having helped to save a life, we have created an irreversible bond. Now we belong to each other. This is what the Siberian shaman understood as fundamental to his role, but it is not evident to us that it is a part of the territory of being a healer.

Here is something else to ponder: Our culture does not teach us how to meet the physician or medicine person properly. If healing is to take place we must enter fully into the ritual of healing, whether we are going to an indigenous healer, chiropractor or a medical doctor. We do a ritual to receive healing from a healer and that ritual creates a relationship through which such an exchange becomes possible.

Daré member Carol Sheppard approached the surgeon at the threshold of the operating theater. "I know," she said, "that you are very skilled in the work that you do but I would like to ask you if you would also be the healer with every gesture." With that request, she invested the surgeon as a healer. In other language, we can say that she called the healer in the doctor forth, that she initiated the doctor as a healer. Ritual reciprocity is part of the healing process. An exchange of gifts. It is not only the physician's responsibility to cure, we must meet the medicine person with our efforts.

Carol's proposal was accepted. "I can do that," the surgeon responded. Carol, again, prepared to meet the doctor as someone willing to carry the mantle of a healer. But she couldn't rely exclusively on the physician. The scheduled surgery was for cervical cancer but her physicians would use the opportunity to take a biopsy of her liver. Her bloodwork had been strange, and there were two ways to account for it: either she had liver cancer or her liver was healing from Hepatitis C. Given the possibilities, she prepared herself as fully as she knew how, spiritually and emotionally.

In Daré while Lisa Rafel and Danelia Wild sang into her body, she had been taken by the presence of one of the wrathful deities of Tibetan Buddhism. Astonished by the presence of that spirit, we followed the choreography of her experience with music, drums, didgeridoo, flute, voice. For us, it was the inception of music Daré, which became a monthly gathering using music and ritual improvisations for the healing of an individual. For Carol, it was equally remarkable. In the midst of feeling incapacitated by illness or exhaustion, she was vitally inspirited. And then she began the process of living on behalf of her life, gathering a team of friends and healers around her. She went into surgery praying while a prayer circle was constituted around her. The surgery was performed. It was entirely successful. When they did a biopsy of Carol's liver, there was no cancer.

*   *   *

Look, what I am trying to say is this: to be a healer in this country is an underground activity. The healer must often act secretly and develop subterfuges in order to extend her love to the world and do her work. A healer can't be trained in the manner of a technician. Skill and success don't depend on knowing when to give the right herb in the right dosage. What is required is original in every moment and the success of the work depends almost entirely upon an open heart, the willingness to enter the unknown, the ability to listen, and the great caring and responsibility that the healer dares to cultivate. And if everything is motivated by the three great loves – the love of the patient, the love of the world, and the love of Spirit – one cannot respond to one without carrying the others.

About love, what is it? Well, it isn't something that comes from any form of training. Love, compassion, kindness, openness, mercy, and yes, beauty. There is the basic combination without which we cannot heal, without which we cannot be healed. How do you cultivate them? Every tradition has its way. That is the core of the culture's wisdom. But in the modern world, these ways have become obscured and belittled. Even prohibited. Sometimes you have to crawl on your knees and beg for the opening of the heart.

*   *   *

One person cannot teach another person how to heal. But we can tell stories.

One of the members of our community has just been diagnosed with cancer. When we speak about healing as opposed to medical treatment, when we ask how Gary Davidson is to meet this moment, we do not only speak about therapies or about fulfilling his personal dreams. We ask about the gifts he has been given and how they might be offered to the community. He knows that his healing is not a personal affair. His healing and the healing of the community are two views of a single event. Kidney cancer. "Having kidney cancer," he said, "means that my body is in the same state that the wetlands are in."

"You said it, I didn't," his wife replied. But they both thought of the Ballona Creek restoration that is going on in Los Angeles, finally, after years of habitat destruction and pollution. His physician might not understand that the necessity for him to amble down to the creek to do what he can on behalf of the water fowl or turtles may be as essential to his recovery as chemotherapy. But doing so may be part of a protocol that will save his life.

Kidney cancer = wetlands

Thinking of healing the community as a corollary of healing oneself is not entirely an altruistic act. At one moment, his wife Danelia Wild confided to me that she wasn't certain that her husband could heal his condition. "I'm not sure Gary can do this," she said. In her mind was a history of pain and suffering she wasn't certain he could overcome. My response was to ask her to remove Gary's name from the statement and say: "I'm not sure *one* can do this." I wanted to take the onus from him as I was aware of how difficult a task lay before him. It wasn't that he, personally, couldn't heal it, it was that most likely no one could without the active intervention of Spirit, or what we call a miracle. Several days later, she said, "Yes, it is true no one can heal such a condition. No *one* person. It requires an entire community to heal such a condition." And the community receives healing also when it is involved in the process.

As I copy edit this manuscript, Gary is undergoing comprehensive tests to see if the kidney cancer has metastasized. For several weeks, several members of the community have sung and toned with him, systematically applying their knowledge of the beneficial effects of vibrations in the hope of reducing, eliminating or transforming the errant cancer cells. One of the women, Asia Leone, came to Daré two years ago because she was suicidal. Suicidal and unable to sing, though she has a most lovely, lilting voice. One day in a welcoming ritual at Daré, Gary gave her his precious amber bear as a talisman. After awhile, she found herself singing in the group. And then when Gary was ill, she offered her voice as a healing instrument. Her life has possibility now. Gary also is not as precarious as before. He who could not sound a note before, begins singing. He begins to revive his knowledge and practice of Reiki. He picks up the Japanese shamanic tradition of the sword that has engaged him for years. He coheres and calls forth a healing community around him.

Why and how does this occur? Because healing involves changing one's life sufficiently that the circumstances within which one lives are healthy and life-giving. When Michael and I introduced Daré to North America, we spoke of "returning healing and caring to the center of the community, where it belongs." To think of the physician as carrying an intelligence that arises out of the communal mind is different from falsely valorizing him or her as most unusual, most special, most distinct. Many developments in modern medicine do not necessarily serve the patients or the physicians who practice it, particularly the tendency to atomize rather than integrate. Who is this stranger upon whom my life depends? Who is this patient whose very life is in my hands?

Healing is mutual and interactive. Any one individual who is suffering a disease such as cancer or environmental illness, is also carrying it for the community, or as a member of the community. Their suffering reveals what is awry in the country at large. Few illnesses, these days, are personal affairs. When we were not so destructive as a species, we may have had the luxury of personal deaths, but no longer. But also this may never have been the case.

Twenty years ago, I led a workshop for women with breast cancer and their husbands. I asked the women and their partners the same question I often ask someone who is consulting me: "Why has *this illness* in particular, come to *you*, in particular, at *this time*, in particular?" The men had to bring the same scrutiny to their psyches as did the women. The premise we were working from was that breast cancer had afflicted the marriage body and while the women were carrying it, it was not theirs, *per se*, in the way that the woman carries the child for the marriage but it is not only hers.

The gift of western culture is the understanding of the nature of the individual, but it fails to understand the intrinsic dynamic interrelationship and interdependency between one individual and all the other individuals – the world they form together. September 11th and its aftermath made plain our common jeopardy. When we are liberated from the negative effects of the privatization of illness or disaster, we no longer suffer the shame and isolation that are its corollaries. One way to think about an illness is that the community is afflicted through the suffering of a particular individual. What is important here is to feel the common affliction, not that one or another of us has luckily escaped but that our suffering is occurring there, in this body that is a part of the larger body of which we are a part. Healing, then, must be concerned with the relationship between the parts. The effect of this is that the community can offer healing in return to the person who is suffering for and healing also on behalf of us. They are a part of us, like our own hand, organ, or cell, damaged and in pain. Let us ease what ails us and restore ourselves. The ill person is a member of the body politic and we suffer and thrive together. Healing occurs within a field of reciprocity. Suffering is eased within the context of kinship.

This man, Gary Davidson, can no longer procrastinate serving the community (that may, for him, consist only of great blue herons and amphibians) by thinking he must develop or heal himself first so that he can make a proper offering afterwards. No, he must make the proper offering that will summon the healing into himself as the vessel from which it will spill out toward others. He becomes the conduit and that is what will prolong and grace his life.

The process of healing and the essence of story are similar. In order to heal, you do not look to see what you can acquire or accomplish for yourself, you look to see who and what you are in relationship to. In order to understand the entire story, you do not look where it is going or the point it is making, you look for the relationship of the parts to each other.

One of the consequences of the way the community has gathered around Gary is that he can no longer identify himself as an outsider. Feeling lonely and alienated was central to his being. Then he became ill and the community gathered. Or rather, they were there before, but he hadn't been able to acknowledge it. Now, their presence and caring is undeniable. Loneliness and alienation had been making him ill; he had always known this. But he had not known how to break through the wall to others. Illness came. It broke him down, as it does, as it is meant to do. Caring flowed through. Love, as well. Community replaced the barriers he had set up to protect himself. Community took on that work. In this particular case, the healers who worked with him knew each other and worked together so the concern and attention that came toward him was seamless. I had prayed that healing might truly come through all of us so that, together, we might learn more of its true and full nature. Gary rested in the various configurations of community. He was sustained by it and is looking for ways to reciprocate. From being in a lonely and static state, he has entered the dynamic field of reciprocity and this is positively affecting his health and those around him.

Danelia, his wife, had an astonishing insight. "A cancer cell – the ultimate stranger, outcast. Cancer, the quintessential wayward cell out of communication with the community of the body." Heal the life and see what healing comes from that.

Some months earlier, when I was thinking, once again, of the relationship between western medical practices and modern warfare, I saw how each came out of a common mindset – that of the enemy that had to be vanquished. What healing might come from another frame of mind?

Instead of killing the cancer cell might we be able to convert it to being a functioning member of the body community again? What had caused it to change – environmental assault, unbearably stressful conditions, other violent disharmonies? What might restore it? Here again I see the value of bringing a single healing gesture to the body and to the community. Restore the cancer cell to its own original nature. I know that we don't know how to do it, but it seemed important to ask the question and create a field of inquiry and experimentation that has integrity with the mind of a peaceful society. Healing and mindfulness as coordinates. Danelia, who had been researching the relationship between sound and healing, says that such thinking is already in the air in experiments with light. But aside from the more academic research and experimentation, she is seeing the vigor that is newly surrounding her husband.

Bring the isolated and lonely one back into community; perhaps the cells of the body will begin to follow suit. Learn to think like a healer. Each thought can heal a situation by reconfiguring it. The condition is changed when it is relieved of the pathology imposed upon it and so is itself again.

When a healer is called forth by Spirit it is not only to affect the physical or emotional body of any person. Healing takes place in a context and for healing to be complete it must heal the individual and the community at the same time, for if it does not, the illness or distress will certainly arise again. To that end, the healer seeks out the gesture or response that has integrity in every area of the ill person's existence. Illness is not a discrete event. It arises from and exists within the context of a life lived in or alienated from community and relationship. Healing, the same. We never were, but now it is obvious that we must not identify ourselves as fundamentally isolated from each other or outside the order of the natural world. What has always been known by indigenous people, has become justly clear in the last few months to us: no single individual on the planet no matter how remote his or her life, just like no animal, no elephant, no lion, no wolf, no sheep, no element, no drop of water, no ripple of wind, no bacteria, no virus, no place on earth can be isolated from, is safe or protected from, the consequences of each and every action taken by each individual in the modern world.

*   *   *

Everyone affects everyone else, that is the first part. The effect can be positive – that is what we are working toward – but these days because we are not so conscious, it can also do us harm. In the realm of harm we are affected by other kinds of beings that we have created, aliens really to the natural world, who are outside the net of all life, its inter-relationships, its reciprocities, its mutualities. Strange beings, let's say, like corporations whose only interest is to develop and be prosperous at all costs and who have no innate moral code to which they must adhere, nor any sense of aligning themselves with the ways of being in the places where they are transplanted and determined to grow. Metaphorically, such entities act like cancer cells. In trying to understand how to live with integrity, we must begin to make distinctions between that which is within the natural world in its largest sense and that which is alien to it. For example, that which really makes us ill or kills us, may not be the bacteria itself that is hunted down and identified as the culprit, but the individual, government, or organization that isolates, reproduces, and stockpiles such bacteria, changing its nature from a creature that lives in the recesses of the soil to one that travels, against its will, in envelopes to strange locations it could not possibly imagine or conjure on its own.

Healing mind or indigenous mind meditates on such distinctions and phenomena. Woven into such a schema particular to these times, let us begin by being conscious of each other as relations and so move with compassion.

Whether we find ourselves in the modern world by choice and affinity or through grief and default, we are affecting and affected by everyone and everything. North Americans outside of the native traditions have never fully known this. We have been disdainful of the reality of the web of all life. We have not understood the beauty, meaning and implications of what is called the jeweled net of Indra. We do not know what we are imposing on the world from the way we live our little and historic lives. We do not know we are imperialist and invasive, avaricious and power hungry. Naïvely, we really think that we are only good; after all it is "us." Now we are learning the consequences of our behavior through the shadow of connection. Until this century, the web was about life; now it looks like it may be about our collective death.

*   *   *

I was deeply gratified when I met Augustine to learn that he was as concerned with the suffering of the world as he was with the suffering of his individual patients. When he treats the patients who come to him from all over southern Africa, he addresses their physical ailments, the state of their soul and the political and social conditions in which they live. I had not expected that the particular, even eccentric path of Spirit and healing that Michael and I have sometimes had to retrieve from indigenous traditions, or just plain-out invented, would receive such confirmation.

Michael met Augustine first, recognized their twinship[8] and drew me to Africa. The time that this piece focuses upon, August and September 2001, was my third visit. We had worked together during my two earlier visits and we had, in the fashion pioneered by Michael and Augustine, all done initiatory work with each other. This seemed the direction we would go again on this visit. But then there were dreams of something more. Predictions of the advent of another kind of spirit. Not the healer of the individual so much as the healer of the collective. An awesome spirit. A peace-making spirit. We wondered how Augustine was to meet this moment and possibility. And then we were together on September 11th and the role and responsibility of being a healer changed drastically. A healer became someone who acts on behalf of the community and calls on the spirits to enter and act through her or him for the sake of all beings. A healer scrutinizes the moment and asks what action or response would reflect "goodness" in this moment. A healer might be someone who brings peace to his or her patients and his or her patients might be anyone or everyone in the world. A burden, a challenge and a hope. And why hope? Because the healer knows that he or she does nothing but become the vessel for the movement of divine kindness and goodness on behalf of everyone into the world.

In 1986, fifteen years ago, I saw that I was being led away from the assumptions, values and ideas of the culture that had nourished and educated me. It was with as much surprise as gratitude that I had written:

> The girl I was did not imagine she would become the gray
> wild-haired witch of the hill. Speaking the languages of beasts
> and trees was not how I imagined my life.[9]

I am still startled by the trajectory of my life that has brought me to dreams, healing, animals, initiatory work, and now, perhaps to peacemaking, sometimes working alongside and in partnership with native healers, and sometimes in collaboration with so many different people with different skills and concerns. A vision that I had once of a luminous net that united indigenous healers and visionaries across the globe is coming into being. The vision was not surprising to me, but its realization is.

2

Story at the threshold. December 1997. Michael and I were in the airport hotel in Johannesburg, before our flight to Bulawayo the next morning when I would finally meet Augustine, whom Michael had now known for two or three years.

The phone rang and I answered it. No one was there. It rang again. Again no one was there. The third time, I heard a man's voice: "Are you Deena Metzger?"

As I answered, I was astonished that someone had been able to find me in a Johannesburg hotel. Michael and I had relied on a taxi driver to recommend lodgings. Even stranger, the deep voice and inflection belonged to an indigenous man from somewhere in South America.

I asked, "Who could possibly know me in Johannesburg?"

Ignoring my question, the man asked if I would carry the book made from the BBC film by Alan Ereira and the Kogi people, *The Heart of the World.* The Kogi, a tribe from the remote highlands of the Sierras in Columbia, had come out of centuries of seclusion first instigated by the Spanish invasion and colonization in order to warn their "Younger Brothers" of the ecological devastation of the planet. I had seen the film years before and was in agreement that these times are urgent and require us to change our lives and minds. I did not know that a book had also been written.

"Will you teach the pattern? We have identified the pattern," the man said, "and we have used it and it is effective."

"What is the pattern?" I asked, trying to remember the details of the film, wondering if he was referring to something more than the establishment of harmonious relationships with the natural world. I wanted to ask specific questions and I also wanted to describe the pattern as I imagined it, but I couldn't find the exact words.

Then I said, "A friend of mine is with the Kogi Indians." I was also mystified that I would receive this phone call while my friend of forty years, Victor Perera, a journalist, who has written about the Lacandon Maya, was possibly with the Kogi at that very moment. I had not thought about the Kogi for several years, since I had seen the film, except when Victor had called to tell me that he was returning to the Highlands. It had been a great honor for him to be received by them for they had formally closed the doors, again, to all visitors. But hearing of his work with the Lacandon Maya Indians of Chiapas, *The Last Lords of Palenque*,[10] and that he had received the teaching of Chan K'in of Nahá, they trusted that he might be able to encode their vision too. They had asked him to translate and distribute their sacred teachings so that they might be available in the manner of the Popul Vuh. Had he not had a completely debilitating stroke from which four years later he has not recovered, he would have written the book.

I spoke with nervousness and confusion. The man remained silent, disinterested in anything I said or asked. I quieted myself.

He spoke. "There is little time. If this contact is right, I will get the book to you tomorrow, Friday."

Still troubled by details, I began to review my plans for the next day then realized that all my plans were meaningless in the face of this possibility.

Then the man asked, "What will you pay for the book?"

"Pay?" It seemed an absurd question. "What do you want," I asked, "a measly thirty dollars? If it is what you say it is, I will give my entire life to it."

I was deeply unnerved as I hung up the phone. Immediately I awakened, as unnerved as I was in the dream, or more so. I did not, could not, believe it was a dream.

*   *   *

This is how Story heals. It shows us the way, especially the way we are afraid to walk.

It was our custom, when we were in Zimbabwe, to tell each other our dreams each morning. How sweet it is to wake up and know that you will begin your day by meeting in a circle in the Daré hut, among the bottles and baskets of herbs, animal carvings, books, skins, weavings, pottery, sculpture, to listen to and tell dreams. This is the most important activity of the day and you will not know what to do or how to be until this sacred ritual occurs and the ancestors come forth and whisper in your ear about the right way. And you know then because of those who are sitting in the circle and because those who have gone before you, your dead are there also, that, really, you are not alone. And even if you never see Augustine again, you understand the illusion of separation; you can rely on his coming to you in your dreams if you are in need, and that he will teach you how to do the same, though it always surprises him that his spirits travel so far.

I believe that it was in the company of Augustine and his community that I fully understood that dreams are not necessarily for an individual, but that the individual may well be dreaming for the community. Psychology with its emphasis on the individual outside of community (which is a different understanding from the individual inside the community) has unwittingly separated us from the understanding of dreams as both guiding and cohering a community. Psychological analysis is predicated on the belief that the dream originates within the self and is the expression of unconscious but intelligent internal processes. When, however, one believes that the dream is sent by the ancestors, as Augustine's people believe, then one can make a smooth transition to the idea that the dream is sent by the ancestors on behalf of the community.

To think that this dream had come to me especially and for myself would have been to aggrandize the self in ways that would undermine the very nature of the dream communication. The dream happened to come through me. I was the vehicle but not the destination. The dream was for the community. It belongs to them. To any who are willing to receive it. To you.

Accordingly, dreaming is at the very core of Daré. We end the Daré by recounting dreams that have come through us for the community. We take the dreams home and contemplate them as if they had come through each of us. Unprecedented connection results from living with and being guided by the same dreams. We have come to recognize that one way the ancestors are holding us is through the dreaming and that we are receiving necessary wisdom and encouragement this way. Dreaming together and for each other, we are each being transformed.

In such an environment of mind, I told Augustine the Kogi dream about "the pattern" and the *Heart of the World*, the second day we were there. He believed that this was propitious. After meeting Augustine, I realized that Spirit had clearly brought all of us together to create alliances that might contribute to the well-being and the healing of the world. I did not feel that our meeting was either casual or personal.

But it is not easy to believe in the reality of invisible forces weaving webs of connection. No evidence is sufficient enough to convince us. One recognizes the presence of the invisible and then one forgets. Born into western culture, we do not have a worldview to hold these events or make sense of them. Which means that a system like that of western mind that may be coherent and effective within itself is, willy-nilly, destructive to ways of being and knowing that are external to it. It cannot contain them and so by default, it negates them. That is why initiation is often accompanied by breakdown. The old structures must come down because they are inadequate to contain what is being revealed.

Sometimes the breakdown is instigated by physical illness, but that is not the essence of the event. Something happens in the disease process that is not the impact or effect of the disease itself, and we are altered sufficiently to perceive reality differently than we did before. An indigenous healer might explain it this way: The disease can be more than the physical symptoms. And it can be more than our emotional response to being ill, the pain, fear and limitation that is engendered by it. Disease can dissolve our assumptions. It can be the doorway through which something new enters. Not information, but a worldview. We enter into a distinctly different but parallel universe. In order to do this, physicists suggest, we have to go through a wormhole. Sometimes, though, the way through requires total dissolution so we can be reconstituted on the other side according to the different laws by which that universe is governed. These laws are, like the laws of our world, fully coherent and everything must harmonize with them. In this world we do not live harmoniously among the invisibles. But in a parallel universe we do. The parallel world toward which we are being called is a world where the laws include all beings according to their needs and nature. As a shorthand we can call this an ecological universe in which we thrive alongside everything else.

Sometimes disease is the catalyst that breaks down the old structures so that new ones may be established that can encompass the new reality. Meeting Augustine was such a catalyst for me. But I had been prepared earlier. I had undergone the breakdown of the old forms again and again. I had been reconstituted in mind and soul again and again. Political trial had done it. Cancer had done it. Profound meetings with indigenous minds had done it. Friendships had done it. My marriage had done it. Dreams had done it. Being a writer had done it. And now this. The Kogi.

Some day I will add, "Writing this book broke me down." This is difficult to write. A different way of thinking without vocabulary. A different paradigm. But the new paradigm doesn't have language yet or the language that is used doesn't carry the meanings in the old paradigm. But, we can't wait for the language to be developed.

I tried to understand the dream in a way that was compatible with western thought. But the only rational and convincing explanation confirmed the reality of their communication. We were in the field of intent. They had intended communication. Not necessarily with me. Not necessarily in this form. But somehow their intent had translated into this dream at the threshold of a meeting between Michael, Augustine and myself. An alliance. This alliance expanded, instantly, to include being guided by the Kogi.

But including the Kogi meant that it included others. A complex world was coming to be. Alliance upon alliance. Alliance was the healing. Without anything being said, the dream knit various people and stories into a new and larger story. The story became a map. A description of the territory. A set of directions for exploration and activity. A pattern. As this ever expanding and unifying story reflected my life/our lives back to us in new ways, we each understand that we were being guided and held by a great intelligence. We understood even if we didn't understand.

What follows is part of the map that opened for me even as a different map opened for each of us, created as it was through our own individual histories and associations. Where the maps coincided or where they were parallel was the shared territory that we could walk together.

Including the Kogi, the dream created alliances that, for me, included Victor Perera who had been alluded to. Including Victor, it included the Lacandon Maya of Chiapas, Mexico. It included Chan K'in, though he is on the other side. So it included the living and the dead. I/We found myself/ourselves in a complex web of associations and relationships. One way of speaking of it is to say we found ourselves in the domain of Spider Woman or Grandmother Spider, *Ambuya Buwe Buwe*.

Ah, my friend Victor….

In July 1998 when Victor was felled by a stroke, I did ritual work on Victor's behalf that I would not have dared to do had I not already met Augustine. My initiation had occurred through initiating Augustine. The healer in Augustine called me forth to be a healer on his behalf and my entire nature and life changed accordingly. The work I did then for Augustine was based in part on my studies of Kaballah. Among other guides, the Hebrew Letters led me, showed me how to proceed. Augustine cleared the path between himself and his estranged family and as a consequence the path between himself and Spirit was cleared. His own tradition had not offered Augustine forms for an unmediated relationship with whom he/we called The One Without A Name, but the Letters had opened that door. Jews often refer to the Divine as *HaShem* – the Name. Referring to the Divine as The One Without A Name both honors the tradition and permitted Augustine freedom to follow the path designated for him. Augustine's profound and idiosyncratic intelligence seeks out and embraces wisdom from whatever tradition he encounters, though his own work with others is based upon the *Ngoma* of the Water Spirits and also the ways in which Spirit or the various spirits speak to and guide him directly. A profound conversation was occurring in us composed of the insights of various traditions. We would each be deeply rooted in the mother language or tradition but also informed and empowered by whatever wisdom came our way. Augustine had always felt deeply connected to the Judaic tradition and began, after our work, to recognize the qualities he would celebrate in various of the Jewish Holidays. This is not different from his longing to be initiated by Native Americans and so even the appearance of the Kogi in this dream enlivened his heart.

For my own part, working with Augustine and gaining some modest facility to communicate with the spirits taught me something more about the nature of healing. This encouraged me to act on Victor's behalf in ways I never could have imagined earlier – a strange mix from different traditions that were appropriate to the moment.

When writing his remarkable book, *Last Lords of Palenque*, Victor had spent much time in the company of the great elder of the Lacandon Chan

K'in, who has recently died. It was perhaps the deepest alliance of Victor's life and it was on the basis of this work that Victor had been invited to visit the Kogi.

From my journal, August 1998:

I don't know where Victor Perera is now, what is the nature of the place between the worlds some call the Bardo where the living reside until they pass over the holy rivers to the land of the dead. These rivers are difficult if not impossible to cross in either direction and so it is said one must wait for the Sabbath in order to fully die or fully live.

I went down into the underworld, the way I have been taught by dreams and by allies, living practitioners and kind spirits to work on behalf of his soul. I met Chan K'in there, the Lacandon Elder who gave his vision and wisdom into Victor's hands when Chan K'in saw that the end of the living world was close at hand and he was powerless to protect it. It is not easy to look into the eyes of a dead man without being blinded by his light. There are injunctions against talking to the dead but I did not heed them because of the urgency of the matter. "Assist Victor so that what is best and necessary for his soul and this earth be accomplished." I wanted to leave then but he held me with his eyes, so that words I was afraid to say blurted out. "Do not abandon us now that you have died and Victor is paralyzed. Despite your grief, do not turn your back on us. It is not yet time to relinquish the trees to the fires which have, I know, started up everywhere."

The stroke that felled Victor was so severe the doctors insisted he would never walk again and adamantly discouraged any hope we might have for his recovery. They assured us he would never be able to take care of himself in any way and advised us to make arrangements accordingly. They did not think he would walk. Their certainty damned him. Important members of his community began to believe he would not return to the world of the living from the Bardo where he was trapped. They began to treat him accordingly, and he, then, fell into their despair.

Stroke was the medical diagnosis for his illness but perhaps there is another way of looking at it also. Just before his stroke, Victor had been writing about the history of genocide against the Highland Maya of Guatemala at the end of the twentieth century. Their plight, like the plight of the whales, had caused him unbearable grief. Many times he had felt completely alone in his struggles on their behalf. The last lines in the journal he had been keeping at the time he had the stroke were, "I had thought there would have been more of us."

Victor's despondency was justified. The community's "reasonable" assessment was not. For almost six months in the last year, after having been given another death sentence by yet another set of doctors in the convalescent facility, he was living with a woman whom he met and came to love. They are not living together now, but he is living a real life. His speech is difficult, but he can make himself understood. He reads. He listens to music. He engages in relationship. He is alive.

A world being repaired – what Jews call *tikkun olam* – through the dream of the Kogi, unifying living and dead, human and non-human. A dream bringing us all into a real and effective alliance that is not dependent on cause and effect, time and space. Including Victor, the alliance also included the whales to whom he devoted himself his entire life. The grief that he expressed when he was able to make his thoughts known again in words was his inability to finish his book on whales. We are waiting to see if the faculty of the writer will return to him. If not, one idea proposed is that several of his associates who have also written on the whales would each in his or her way write a different conclusion for the book. Another version of alliance and cooperation. What I might call Daré mind, but what Victor might understand as cetacean mind having studied for many years the particular and most generous intelligence of these beings of the sea.

In this moment in Africa as we were puzzling the dream of the Kogi, it was clear that the web of *Ambuya Buwe Buwe* had integrated the animal world into the universe of spirits, the living and the dead. I was aware that the presence of whales was implied not only because Victor was connected to Whale, but because the whales had appeared to me.

I am flooded with associations. Story demands that some of them be articulated here so that we see the ways in which a story, a world is integrated and constructed. We see then what wholeness is. The worldview of interrelationship that the Kogi are calling us to hold. The connections that exist in the human world that parallel the profound connections that are fundamental to the ecological systems of the world.

This is the way the whales came to me:

Nature writer Brenda Peterson took me to visit three beluga

whales confined in an aquarium at Point Defiance Zoo in Tacoma, Washington. We visited them; we visited with them. One of the consequences was *Intimate Nature: The Bond Between Women and Animals*[11] ultimately edited by Brenda, Linda Hogan and myself. It came about through an intervention on the part of the whales.

After some minutes in the aquarium watching two whales (whose normal range covers thousands of miles) circle and circle endlessly, I became aware also that in a far corner, a third whale was drifting listlessly after the death of her calf. It was untenable to remain an observer. Some intimate activity of compassion was required. Instinctively, I placed my lips against the glass to hum to the whales. After a few minutes, the two belugas, Shikku and Inuk, began swimming back and forth behind the glass wall. Brenda joined in the humming. The song entered the water.

Soon it was obvious that the sounds we were making did touch, perhaps entered, the whales in a precise and substantial communication, as if our sounds were hands. Modulating tones, according them with our thoughts, we were both touching the whales and speaking with them through our sounds. Children passing through the area stopped, fascinated. We brought the children into the humming. Soon the entire gallery area was ahum. After thirty minutes when Brenda and I were again almost alone before the glass, the two whales began sounding back to us and I was physically aware of the sonar entering my body. "Now the whales are imprinting *you* with their sonar," Brenda said. I wondered what the consequences might be. Over time, there were many and the book was one of them.

The whales have been calling out for assistance. I answered when I heard the call, as did Brenda, as did Victor. Such responses not only connect us to the animals, they connect us to each other. Shared consciousness created an even deeper bond between Victor and myself after having been friends for many years. A bond informed by this other species. A bond that included another species. The alliance that manifested, then, between all of us, now visibly included cetacean wisdom and the devastation of the cetacean community.

Victor's presence in the dream awakened many other memories and associations that were pertinent to this shared moment with Augustine. I was aware that Victor's work on behalf of the Highland Maya of Guatemala who had been systematically persecuted and murdered by a variety of political and military forces would be deeply appreciated by Augustine who had lived so many years of his life under the brutal conditions of apartheid in Rhodesia. This was exactly what Victor had been working on when he had had the stroke. One way or another each of us in the room had experienced one or another face of censorship, apartheid, limitation, colonization, war. We entered into such a conversation in which we articulated our common knowledge of oppression and our appreciation of the beauty and wisdom that was being annihilated. We were grief-stricken but simultaneously we were sustained by each other's company.

This is how it happens. The luminous net. Are these connections always there but we are blind to them until something brings them into the light? Or are we creating something new? We stand at a nexus, and the lines of connection move through us. This is how a world comes into being. It is hard to believe but then we find ourselves woven into it. Again and again. Each time it surprises us. Each time we doubt. Then different lines move through us. The web gets thicker, more solid. Miraculous, really.

Here is another way of speaking about it: We found ourselves in a story.

*   *   *

What do you do when you find yourself in a story? You remember that the story is a gift from Spirit. The story is not of your own making. It is the dynamic imprint of Spirit upon your life. So what do you do? You look to see the map that is being laid out before you. You see where the story takes you. What actions are necessary to complete the story, to live the story out to its fullest, most beautiful completion? You step into the story. You live in it. You live it out. Fully.

Several weeks after the dream, I left for South Africa. Michael and Augustine saw a documentary in which Native American people spoke about apocalypse. It appeared on the one television channel in Zimbabwe. Most unexpectedly, the Kogi were one of the tribes featured. "The pattern," we all agreed, had something to do with creating a web of connection, a circle of relationship. At the very least, Daré is a consequence of this meeting as is all the work Michael and I are doing to create relationships between Africa and non-African healers or initiates.

Knowing we were in a story encouraged us to take the dream very seriously, as if it were not only a message from the Kogi but from Spirit as well. We were inspired to enact all possibilities of connection, relationship and alliance on behalf of the earth and the indigenous wisdom that protects it.

The Kogi did come in the dream. I didn't dream about them; they came in the dream. The dream was like the vine bridge that the Lacandon lowered in the wilderness in order to meet their western contemporaries for the first time. It was a real event. A visitation. When I returned from Africa, Victor (before his stroke) told me that the Kogi used to meet holy people from different cultures in their dreams but that the destruction of the planet is so extreme now they only meet each other. Even after he said this, I still believed that my dream was a true visitation, not because I am a holy person but because it was my experience the next year with the elephant, The Ambassador, that other beings send out calls on wide nets, SOS, and some of us are willing to hear and respond. I have no other way to explain these two events. It is a question of receptivity rather than instigation. In these two instances, I answered the call as best as I could.

The story is complex. This is one of the points of origin of the story that I want to tell that came to a culminating point on September 11th and then continued on its own trajectory. This visitation in a dream and the relevance of dreaming altogether. Indigenous mind reaching out through me to other indigenous minds. A way of seeing returning to its rightful centrality and relevance. Stories are complex in that they exist over a period of time and space that is far greater than what we consider to be the territory of "what happened." The field is larger in time and also in space. They encompass many realms usually ignored. In this instance, the dream. A story that is entirely outside the dream realm is an amputated story. This moment in the story when the Kogi come forth refers also to the very beginning of the western colonization of the world. South America, South Africa, the same devastation visited on earth, human, and animal. It speaks also to the power of the indigenous mind. Even at the point of greatest fear and diminishment, the Mamas, as the elders are called, reach out across continents to a western woman on her way to meet one of their allies and get her attention.

Western mind... power... communication... technology. Things are not as they seem. Here are other forms of power and communication but they require absolute integrity and devotion to the planet. They cannot be co-opted. They are not for sorcerers. They are of the whole, for the sake of the whole. They are the means of the net for the sake of the net. They are the means of alliance for the sake of alliance. They are of the earth for the sake of the earth.

"The pattern works. What will you pay for it?"

The Kogi came in a dream to emphasize what they had spoken of in the film. The ways of the "Younger Brother" are destroying the world. They speak simply: Cease and desist.

On September 13th, the last night we all spent together in Zimbabwe, Laura, Robin, Chuck, Wilderness, Michael, and I watched *The Heart of the World* with Augustine, Simakuhle, and their entire family. At different moments, one or another of us wept for the desolation of the vision and for the beauty of their devotion, for the ruin of the planet and the natural world and the lucidity of their wisdom. When the film ended, Augustine turned to Michael and myself with gravity and hopefulness: "Can you contact these people? Can we go to see them? We must tell them, they are not alone." Story elicits this response.

* * *

As I write this we are in a war. The war is further devastating the environment, but that is just the beginning of it. It is not a new war. We've been involved for years in one way or another. It is truthful to say we are responsible for it. We established the Taliban and also the Taliban organized itself in moral reaction to western culture. We have instigated what happened there. Directly and indirectly. The minefields, the women in burkhas; we are not innocent here.

Other devastations are planned. We are not changing our ways. There has been no attempt, despite the constant rhetoric, to understand the "other." In response to the death of thousands of innocent people, my/our country is causing far more death and far more disruption. A universal madness drenched in violence has taken over us and the rest of the world. This is the kind of war that may not come to an end. This may be the war to end all wars but not in the ways we imagined or hoped since the 20th century. This may be the war that passeth understanding. This may be the end.

What is a healer's response and responsibility in such a moment?

*   *   *

I want to speak of grief. Not anger or outrage. Not what they did and what we are doing. Not how they attacked us and how we must destroy them. Not how this war may totally destroy our freedom and therefore our country. None of these. Grief. One word. War. Another word. But do we understand them yet?

There is something missing here. I do not know if I will be able to speak of it. Every language has its possibilities and limitations. If I were a Russian poet, a woman watching Stalin in, let's say 1936, noting how the fearful darkness gathers at the folds of her skirt, I could speak of this but I do not know how to speak of it in the language given to me. Perhaps that poet didn't know how to speak either.

> But in the room of the banished poet
> Fear and the Muse stand watch by turn
> And the night falls
> Without the hope of dawn.[12]

These words were written by Anna Akmatova but I was not thinking only of her when I wrote down her words. Perhaps the hypothetical poet I was imagining was struck dumb before the incomprehensible, before the ways the language was distorted, before the ways in which those in power spoke about the greater good as they committed the greater evil. As a poet, she may have been driven mad when language was used against itself. When Stalin and Hitler spoke, the poet knew that language and truth were defiled, when meaning skidded out of the words as those in power distorted the truth entirely. We must all become poets now.

The variations between "our side" and "their side" are few. Essentially the language and passions are the same. President Bush and the Taliban use the same rhetoric. God, according to everyone, is on "our" side. Each one is convinced of it and so fights his holy war against the unholy ones. Oh, it is a grievous situation. It has probably never been worse.

When I used to read about the French Revolution as a child, I often wondered whether it was possible to survive during a reign of terror. I now know beyond doubt that it is impossible. Anybody who breathes the air of terror is doomed, even if nominally, he manages to save his life. Everybody is a victim – not only those who die, but also all the killers, ideologists, accomplices and sycophants who close their eyes or wash their hands – even if they are secretly consumed with remorse at night. Every section of the population has been through the terrible sickness caused by terror, and none has so far recovered, or become fit again for normal civic life. It is an illness that is passed on to the next generation, so that the sons pay for the sins of the fathers and perhaps only the grandchildren begin to get over it – or at least it takes on a different form with them.[13]

Two years ago, my students and I read *Hope Against Hope* by Nadezhda Mandelstam. These words, above, are from that book. I feared but didn't know then for what national fate we were being prepared.

A false cheerfulness and manipulated fear surrounds us: Continue with your life. There may be a terrorist attack! They will die and we will live. Civilian casualties are inevitable but our soldiers will be invincible. Over 3000 civilians were killed in the plane bombing of the World Trade Center; we must stop such attacks from occurring again. 3,500 civilians have been killed as a result of the bombing of Afghanistan, their deaths are necessary. Collateral damage. The President advises: Go shopping! What kind of President is this? What is this life we are to continue? Is it really a life?

These words are where we must meet, these and the love that carries a healer forward so that she wants to fold whoever is coming in the door into her arms; "There, there. We will see it through." We will see it through together. Whatever it is. The dead in the twin towers. Our loved ones. The already crippled, broken further under new bombs in Afghanistan. Their loved ones. The terrible hunger that is coming this winter. The dreadful conditions in the refugee camps that will be yet more intolerable when the snows and rains come. The jobs lost in this country. The hungry in this country. The people on the street corners. Our citizens. Many of them veterans of the other wars we perpetrated.

*   *   *

Healer training: Meet everyone's eye on the street. If you meet a beggar, stop and have a conversation with that person. Offer him full respect and dignity. Recognize the full level of her suffering. The fate of the beggar … and the sacred interchange that is possible. Do not look away. Look each other in the eye.

Lisa Hughes was a woman who carried beauty and intelligence with dignity and heart. She lived in the mountains north of Los Angeles, her house situated along a stream that cascaded down a waterfall that she and her husband Ron Galbavy had constructed, bringing down huge boulders from the hills. Her dream was to create a place of retreat for women who could be healed by silence and the natural world. Once when the Dalai Lama was in Los Angeles, she had taken the vows of the bodhisattva and started doing Tonglen practice: Breathe in the pain and suffering of the world, acquaint yourself with it deeply as it resides in your body, transform it and breathe out peace. It was not, for her, an abstract practice; it softened her and deepened her. Her son-in-law was a Viet Nam veteran who loved guns and war. A Confederate flag hung over his mantle. He had had a motorcycle accident and was crippled by it. A disc jockey before the accident, he could no longer do the work he had loved. She did not know what had initiated the violence that shook him continually. Was it his wretched childhood, or the wretched war, or the accident? Facing her grief, she realized that she had taken on Tonglen so that she might ease her son-in-law's suffering. In the privacy of her own peaceful house, she could meditate on his behalf, but that was only the beginning, the way in which she readied her heart to do the real work. Disturbed by his aggression and violence, unable to distinguish that which came from his injury and that which came from who he is, she invited him to the house to sing with her and make music. They began to take hikes together with the children. Without dogma, she brought the beauty that had been banished back into his life. The task was to see who he was without judgment. The task was to meet his eye.

One day, she confessed to the women of the healing circle who were training with me in the ethical, creative, and spiritual aspects of healing, that she was agonized because she and her husband were in great debt. She had mortgaged her house in order to help support her only daughter, this son-in-law and the children. And now she couldn't meet the debts. Daughter of a wealthy family, she was humiliated by her circumstances. In a small voice, she revealed that her grandfather was one of those who had leapt from the window in his commercial offices when the stock market crashed in 1929.

That morning, a potter and glass blower had come to my house early to give me a gift. It was a blue glass bowl that she had blown herself. A beggar's bowl, she said. A beggar's bowl.

And why had she brought me a beggar's bowl? Ah yes, I was wondering how and when I would tell you this story that I have repeated in my classes.

The Buddhist teacher Jack Kornfield speaks of being a beggar in Asia. It was part of his study and training. The beggar/monk serves a profound spiritual function for the community. He or she allows us who have something in the moment to offer it to another. The beggar calls forth our generosity.

Calls forth. This is the essential phrase. The dynamic of a vital society consists of each of us calling the other forth even as the spirits call us forth. Need calls us forth. The cry of the infant causes the mother's milk to flow from her breast. A stranger who might also be nursing may find her blouse wet from the hunger cry of a child she doesn't know. The mother wants to feed the child. She wants to give of herself. She wants this. It is who the mother is. The mother. Munificent. Bountiful. Overflowing. Kwan Yin with her infinite compassion. Artemis of Ephesus with her many breasts. And there are wondrous tales of fathers left alone without hope or help who have developed milk to nurse their starving infant. We are called forth to become who we might not dare to become otherwise. We are called forth into our most vibrant and generous souls. We are called forth to meet our souls.

The dance of calling each other forth is central to Daré. One person is suffering and asks for healing but in the next instance that person, sustained and eased, offers healing to another. This exchange is often mediated by the spirits who are calling the wounded one forth to be a healer. Chiron, the great teacher of the ancient world, became the great healer because he had a wound that could not heal. There is no hierarchy in this story. The wounded one is not pitiful. The wounded one is walking a path and if we are fortunate we can assist her or him on the journey and we can recognize our own loss in the exchange. The wounded one can bring us healing.

But let us return to the beggar. I had been speaking to my students about the sacred activity of the beggar as Jack had described it. That night, Nalini Chilcov, who lived in India and Pakistan when she was studying Buddhism, described the still beauty of the early morning. The monks sitting in meditation. The dawn welcomed with prayer and chanting. Then the monks walking silently among the villagers, knowing that their entire existence depended on the generosity of the community. Putting themselves fully in the hands of strangers.

And then I told this story, my beggar's story. The one that astonished and awakened me. Why do I call it "my" story? If I had only one story that I could tell, this is the story I would offer to the community.

I had been in San Francisco to give a lecture and workshop on Story. Wanting to speak of Story in new ways, I could not depend on my old notes. I knew that if I found the right story to begin the talk, everything would follow from it. But, I couldn't find the right story. That morning I had been reading an article on healing by Dr. Joan Borysenko. Under desperate circumstances, she prayed to the four Archangels on her patient's behalf and often healing came. I felt desperate. I had, myself, in the past, prayed to the angels. Seated in a sidewalk café, I lowered my head and prayed to the four Archangels, Michael, Gabriel, Raphael and Uriel, for a story that I might offer to the audience that would open their hearts. When I finished praying, I noticed a beggar weaving drunkenly down the sidewalk. He was holding a bottle of beer under his threadbare brown serge jacket as he went from table to table asking for money. As he approached me, I quickly ruminated on whether I should support his habit, but realizing that he had lived his entire life without my counsel, I gave him some money and met his eye. "God bless you," he said, warming me with his blessing. Here was the sacred exchange, mere money given for the sacred blessing received. He went on past the next tables and then turned to me from some distance.

"Would you like me to tell you a story?" he asked.

I gasped. "Yes, please. I would like you to tell me a story."

"Do you know what General Patton said when he was fighting in Africa?"

"No, I don't know what the General said."

"He said, 'Lo, tho I walk in the valley of the shadow of death…'"

The beggar's voice trailed off and he turned away. Then he turned back and caught my eye again. "Lo, tho *I* walk in the valley of the shadow of death…"

And then, having made certain that I understood that we are all equal before death and the Divine, he disappeared.

So many cultures have stories of the appearance of the angel disguised as the beggar. The beggar as angel. The angel revealed through our response and recognition. The angel, then, always present in the beggar, but we have to recognize it. Beauty in the eye of the beholder. I had been the beggar and he gave me the story. And now you have it. May it sustain you as well.

Beggar's Bowl

And so Lisa Hughes took the blue glass bowl and went from woman to woman in the circle and begged from us. "Help me," she pleaded. It was not easy. "What can you give me in my need?" We each searched our poor and limited selves. Might we have something of value to offer a friend we loved – who loved – so deeply? Who was the beggar in this situation?

The next week, Robin Moriyah Colaine came to our circle broken-hearted over the devastation of the land, the trees, the animals, the destruction of the natural world. Desperate, she picked up the beggar's bowl and went to each of us. On her knees, she pleaded, "The world is in need of healing and I am incapable, please help me." By begging, she recruited us into the necessary work on behalf of the world. She called us forth. And that is the origin of the beggar's prayer that is at the core of Daré.

*   *   *

The war proceeds. I awaken from strange dreams in which I am trying to bring healing to the world by mysterious means I do not even understand. The sense of having struggled all night in another dimension. It reminds me of Augustine who sometimes awakens exhausted because, in his words, he has been struggling with evil spirits all night.

Perhaps it is because I read an article by John Pilger in the London *Mirror* before I went to sleep. It was sent by a friend who recently moved to New Zealand because he cannot bear living in the United States. Two nights ago, on a billboard before an auto supply place on Reseda Boulevard I read the sign, "America, Love it or Leave it." These words are fundamentally un-American. I cannot love the America that is being distorted through violence and false patriotism. The propagandists are using patriotism to gain and retain power. It is an old way. The Romans knew it well. Hitler and Goebbels reinvented it with the help of filmmaker Leni Reisensthal. A woman, I want to say. A woman! A Palestinian woman just blew herself up in Jerusalem, took an old man with her and wounded others. The first woman suicide bomber. We have come to this. She was so desperate. She had been an ambulance driver. She could not bear to see another Palestinian child killed by the Israeli Defense Forces. My people. This is what the holocaust and the death camps and the ovens do to a people; they turn a people to unprecedented violence. And the Palestinians are being driven mad accordingly. And the Afghanis. And the Somalis. And perhaps us Americans as well. I like to think we do not have as much cause to act in the way we are acting, that we have not enough cause to act as violently as we are acting. But we cannot measure suffering. We are the children of the 20th century. We invented The Bomb. We dropped The Bomb. Our grandfathers had their minds destroyed in World War I and our fathers in World War II and Viet Nam. We are crazed too.

*　　*　　*

1-30-02
Bush's Colder War And The New "Red Scare"
By John Pilger *The Mirror* - London
www.johnpilger.com

Last week, the government announced that it was building the biggest-ever war machine. Military spending will rise to $379 billion, of which $50 billion will pay for its "war on mass slaughter" and for "military operations" – invasions of other countries.

Of all the extraordinary news since September 11, this is the most alarming. It is time to break our silence…. Donald Rumsfeld, the Defense Secretary, says he has told the Pentagon to "think the unthinkable."

Vice President Dick Cheney, the voice of Bush, has said the government is considering military or other action against "40 to 50 countries" and warns that the new war may last 50 years or more.

A Bush adviser, Richard Perle, explained. "(There will be) no stages," he said.

"This is total war. We are fighting a variety of enemies. There are lots of them out there . . . . If we just let our vision of the world go forth, and we embrace it entirely, and we don't try to piece together clever diplomacy but just wage a total war, our children will sing great songs about us years from now."

. . . .The next American attack is likely to be against Somalia, a deeply impoverished country in the Horn of Africa....

Somalia.

Musician and filmmaker David Sonnenschein stops beside me after running in the hills while I am meditating overlooking the meadow that is the coyote run and boundary between my small house and the state park. He hands me a small coin that he found on the windowsill by his bed when he returned from Brazil. "No one has been in my house. I do not know how it got there." He is perplexed, perhaps a bit unnerved. "You take it. You will know how to hold it." I cannot refuse him though I don't know how to carry this too. The coin is silver and the size of a penny but it does not have the weight of American coins. On one face of the coin is an elephant. That is why he gave me the coin. On the other side are the British Coat of Arms, the lion and the griffin. The words encircling the elephant read: "XXI century. 2000. Food Security." On the other side, around the coat of arms, it reads, "5 shillings. Republic of Somalia."

I place the coin at the base of the candle that is on the altar above my desk, next to the Shona sculpture of Chaminuka, the Shona spirit of peace making, and the Shona sculptures of elephants and the Ibis bird as Tehuti. "The Ibis bird, whose head Tehuti wears and from which his name is derived, symbolizes the heart, the center of the mind and intelligence of Tehuti. Above all, Tehuti is divine intelligence, the universal mind with all of its powers of speech and creation. As 'scribe of the gods,' or in particular, the 'scribe of Maat,' Tehuti formulates all the words of creation and records them in the Akasha, or universal memory. But his word only has power when he is together with Maat, who is the Cosmic Law, which is the same as saying when the mind is centered in the heart."[14]

I do not know if the elephants can help us. I do not know if the Somalis can help themselves, let alone help us. But in my grief, I have no choice but to pray that what we cannot achieve alone, we may achieve in concert. In concert with the despised.

Five shillings from Somalia speaking of easing hunger becomes a holy object. If we cannot stop ourselves as a nation or as a species, perhaps in concert with the natural world we may be brought back to the heart. I pray this. It is a gentle prayer. But my heart is not gentle.

I am tortured by words in John Pilger's article:

Donald Rumsfeld, the Defense Secretary, says he has told the Pentagon to "think the unthinkable."

Vice President Dick Cheney, the voice of Bush, has said he is considering military or other action against "40 to 50 countries" and warns that the new war may last 50 years or more.

Is someone drunk on the bloody wine of Revelations from the New Testament? Are there those who are trying to bring about the end of days? Do they think Apocalypse will open the Kingdom of Heaven? Are these drunkards our President and his associates?

February 17th, 2002. A congressman finally speaks out. Barbara Lee voted against war appropriations and today Dennis Kucinich spoke forcefully against the reign of terror imposed by George Bush, the man he calls the unelected president. [See his entire speech in Appendix II.]

I try to stop my mind from entering into dualism. Us and Them. The Them can be Al-Qaeda but it can also be the current government.

But I must not engage in such dualisms. I cannot indulge such language. If I do, there is no difference between those who make such wars and those who suffer them, between me and them. How interesting the paradox. Not wanting to be of them, I must not separate myself from them. Yes, there must be a way to see what is occurring without creating the dualism that emerges from the epithet of "enemy."

I take a cue from Lisa Hughes with whom I shared a common birthday and who died two years ago in September. Under such horrific circumstances, breathe in the suffering and rage and breathe out peace. Can I do it? Can I breathe out peace?

*   *   *

What is lacking in the book I am writing is the love that I carry and cannot put down. Do you want to know what is the ongoing grief? I am so angry that holy books have brought us to this that it sometimes isolates my heart.

And the President advises us to go shopping. The healer must hold all of this. She may not close her heart for a moment. "There, there." She may not look away. She must bear witness. "There, there." She must know what it means to bear witness. How one is with the pain, feels it in her body, is in equal jeopardy with the patient. "There, there. We will see it through."

*　　*　　*

What carries a healer forward when she has no license because there is no license to be had for what she does, when the training for the license that theoretically covers her work undermines the basic principles she is pledged to uphold? When the other available licenses do not cover the work that she is called to do? And when one cannot and must not license the sacred work of the most ancient human traditions? What carries her is something in the heart tuned to the invisible voices who guide her and speak of goodness and a desire to comfort those who are completely bereft. What carries her is a song that comes at the edge of the wood or just where the stream cannot be distinguished from the bank and it hums the connection between one world and another. Then when someone dies or cannot breathe for the pain of living, she sings it under her breath and the prayer enters the room, a small light in the absolute darkness of grief.

When the Havasupai people were undermined by a terrible flood, Golden Bear hiked down the very steep and very long road to the bottom of the cliffs of the Grand Canyon in order to assist them. She did what she could for a people who had lost everything. When she had finished her labor she went to the river and prayed that the songs the people had forgotten would be given to her. How can you bring healing if you have forgotten the songs?

Valerie Wolf had a dream in which everything was coming to an end because we had forgotten to sing the songs that sustain the world. The dream reminded her that the Divine needs our songs as much as we need to sing.

*　　*　　*

Poet and analyst Marc Kaminsky went to the corner of his Brooklyn street and offered to sit with the firefighters who tried to put out the inferno in the towers. It is possible to speak of grief in New York where the air is still full of smoke because you breathe in the dead. A vertical city to be excavated in order to bury one's own in sweet ground that is free of ashes. But here I look out at pine trees and the clarity of sky and also know that there is no place on the planet that is free, any longer, of ashes. It is hard to imagine that what might be coming here will be no different than what others have suffered everywhere in this century for a hundred years: war, poverty, state terror, oppression, hopelessness. We film in primary colors and so, of course, we do not understand our fate. Ananke means nothing to us. Nor the three pitiless women, the ancient ones, spinning, weaving and snipping.

On the way to the post office, I saw that someone had turned a little wooden hut into a flower shop. It was a young Persian woman. In the back room was her mother in a dark coat with a scarf on her head. I greeted her but she didn't answer.

"She doesn't speak English," the young woman said uncertainly.

"She speaks Farsi," I said recognizing something in her face or posture. "Welcome, may you be fortunate here. It will be good luck for you to have started such a business here in these times. We all need flowers to survive." The name of her shop is Peace Rose.

Two deeds at once. I was able to welcome a Muslim woman in a time of terror and buy flowers for the clerks at the post office who, unexpectedly, are also on the front lines.

What is happening is so large, how can one find a sentence or paragraph to meet it? Let's put it this way. I want to break your heart.

*   *   *

I have done this before. When I had cancer, for example, and took a typewriter to the hospital and wrote two journals, one for me and one for you. I wept, then, in both journals and then, even though I didn't think I knew how, I began singing. But now the fact that we are bombarding an innocent people who cannot free themselves from the terrorist we are seeking out, sometimes turns my heart to stone. And a stone heart is not the heart of a healer. A stone heart does not belong to a singer.

In 1996, I went to the Arctic Circle in Norway twice. Once at the winter solstice and once at the summer solstice. I spent ten silent days alone in the absolute dark and then ten days again in the absolute light. This is how I marked my 60th birthday. I wanted to prepare to be 60. I wanted to bring everything together so that the rest of my life might be an offering to the world. One of my prayers was that I would receive a spiritual practice that would fully sustain me so that I could do the work that needed to be done. What did I receive? A chant. A chant came to a woman who could not sing then. But devoting myself to the chant, I learned to sing. When someone is ill or broken, I can sing to them and the song and my voice eases them now. And also the chant sustains me. So I received two gifts. The first was the gift of having a prayer directly answered and the second was the gift of song for myself and others. A healer needs a song because the spirits respond to music and beauty. When one sings with an open heart, the spirits often come.

Gary Davidson and Danelia Wild knew each other for almost twenty years before they married. In all that time, he did not know that she had a magnificent voice. Some of us in my writing class knew because of the way she sometimes sang when we were celebrating someone's birthday. She sang and I did not then. At the very first Daré I stood behind her and whispered in her ear, "Pray with your voice." Something released and song burst forth. Now she is devoted to the relationship between music and healing and is on her way to being a sound healer. Song and music return the world to harmony. Research done on the relationship between sound and healing often emphasizes the effectiveness of the human voice to restore the body and undermine illness. Song heals through restoring the cosmic order and it heals by calling the invisibles to be among us. When shaman Amanda Foulger picks up the drum or the rattle and begins to call the spirits, it is also her voice and her devotion to the song, the fullness and love that is her voice, that creates a sacred space around us.

Originally, my intent in writing this piece was to try to communicate the way of healing to those who have, like myself, been born into the world view of western, rational mind. I wanted to chronicle what it means to be taken by the spirits into their world and how one begins to work with them or have them work through one for the sake of healing. I wanted to speak of what it is for a western woman to have become a healer. How miraculous and incomprehensible it is. I wanted to describe the realm that one must enter and live within when the spirits come to one in this way.

I wanted to speak of Story and the way that Spirit enfolds us in a story to assist us in finding the one path between our lives and Spirit's intent. I wanted to speak of the way that the healer and the afflicted one collaborate in carving the story out of the unlikely rough ore that is a life so that what was obscured shines brightly enough to show everyone the way.

But the intent of this piece has altered. For as engaging as it might be for a woman to describe the internal experience of the ways of the spirits, I feel compelled also to chronicle my search these months for the way of the healer on behalf of the planet. I recognize that my own training as a political activist is being modified to include the spiritual activity of the healer. I am hoping to learn how one calls on the spirits for the sake of a planet ravaged by war in the manner one calls on the spirits on behalf of an ailing individual.

When Michael and I returned to Africa in August, I had imagined this trip as a preamble to a sabbatical. It was my intent when I returned to continue working on a novel, *Doors*, that I had started some years ago and to begin a memoir that was to be entitled, *Story Totem: Journal of a Village Healer*. I had hoped to understand the ways in which I have been called by and through Story to a unique relationship to community, to a hybrid between a healer in the modern world and an indigenous medicine woman. It would have an exploration of the nature of Story itself as a collaboration between Spirit and woman or man, from which meaning emerges as fate, understanding and path. It would have been my story but it would also contain the stories that had called so many people I have worked with into creating their lives according to the call of their souls. That book may never be written but if I have the skill, this one will cover some of the same territory or it may supercede it. Sometimes history intervenes. Sometimes we cannot do what we want to do. Sometimes our lives are not about our own lives. Sometimes we cannot follow our own will, inclination or bliss because we are being called to meet what we have been prepared, without realizing it, to meet. Sometimes our lives are about meeting history.

At some point in the last years, when it was reflected back to me that I had become a village healer, I realized that a village healer needed a village and that part of the healing task was to cohere such a community that would exist in time if not always in space. Once at a retreat in the Santa Cruz Mountains with Thich Nhat Hanh, I had suggested that because of the unusual joy and camaraderie that arose among us as we practiced sitting and walking meditation, we had become the First Floating American Sangha. I am not certain that that Sangha actually existed after that week. I am not certain that we cohered into a community. I think, rather, that the name was appropriate to the moment and then that moment passed. But the name remained in people's minds. It became an idea with potential. It began to manifest in people's thinking. It may have been premature as a fact but it was not premature as a hope.

To think of oneself as a village healer in 2001 is to recognize relationships that carry the ethos and consciousness of community, whether or not we live in the same neighborhood. To create a web of interconnections that are voluntary, dynamic and dependable is to enter into a new form of social relations that by their possibility heal some of the ills of loneliness and anomie that have afflicted our culture in the years following World Wars I and II.

*   *   *

Coming to Africa and meeting Augustine and his family and community affected me profoundly because we lived with him in his house according to his ways for several weeks on each occasion. Inevitably, we entered into another way of being that was both strange and familiar. In Bulawayo, Augustine has re-imagined a tribal form, Daré, meaning "council" in Shona, in an urban setting. Healing is ongoing and meets the moment. Those who, in the moment, have something to offer are called forth and given the opportunity to meet those who in the moment are in need. In any moment, the relationships change; donor and recipient are, over time, indistinguishable. If I have a gift with nowhere to offer it, I am deeply deprived, as deprived as the one who in the moment has a need and no one meets it. No hierarchy then of those who suffer and those who don't and certainly no investment in being among those who inflict suffering rather than those who suffer it.

I did not strategize the forms of my work that have evolved naturally in the past years. There have been so many influences and circumstances that have brought me to this place. Michael's original passion that led him to Augustine was certainly a factor. We recognized that the healing community or Daré, that is fundamental to Augustine's work, might take root in its own way in North America. This took our lives in an totally unexpected direction. In this endeavor, we were probably also influenced and cautioned by Thich Nhat Hanh's explorations to discover the face of American Buddhism, and so recognized that Daré cannot have a single face. Wherever it occurs, it will reflect the needs and gifts of that particular community. One must trust the intelligence and caring of the individual members of the community to hold the cultural form in ways that are essentially meaningful to themselves, without transgressing the basic principles of Daré.

Daré needs to be experienced and lived in order to be known. Still, there are certain principles that are fundamental to it.

The strength and essence of Daré is in the circle and its intelligence. Council is its heart. And in council one always strives to speak from the heart and allow the spirits and ancestors to speak through one. Wisdom comes from the combined voices and presence of everyone who is participating. The purpose of council is to seek answers from the community that we can't find ourselves. Asking and addressing a single question coheres the community.

Daré begins by calling in the spirits. Everything depends on this. The invocation allows Spirit to inform the participants. It creates a field of knowing and remembering. Daré also centers on telling dreams and receiving dreams as gifts from the ancestors to the circle. Council and dreams are channels between the world of the living and the world of the invisibles.

Music is another essential element. For thousands of years it has been the way that people have called Spirit and that Spirit has made itself manifest. So, in the Daré in Los Angeles as well as in Bulawayo, the voice and the drum as well as other instruments are essential components for invocation as well as healing.

Daré is for the sake of healing, but we don't presume to say we know what healing is, how it occurs, or even how, always, to recognize it. Sometimes one is the healer and sometimes one is desperate for healing. Sometimes the two activities are one in the moment. Healing is, thus, an interchange, the dynamic of giving and receiving.

Everyone is welcome and welcomed in Daré. Everyone is listened to and heard without judgment. This generous mind is not easy to attain, it takes time, practice and dedication. Welcoming, praising and blessing are the core of it. Daré is the place where each person's individual genius, intelligence and particularity is sought out, acknowledged, and called forth.

And finally, Daré is composed of all the members of the community, living and non-living, visible and invisibles, the humans and the non-humans, the people, trees, birds, animals, stones and elementals. When all the beings gather, Daré comes to be.

These are some of the basic principles, but it certainly isn't a check list. Daré emerges when people gather, some familiar, some strangers, with the intention of manifesting in the moment a community in which such principles are vibrant and alive. Each gathering, then, is different as it responds to those who have come together, their joy and suffering, and as it responds, of course, to the circumstances of the times. When we leave each other, we are different because we have allowed ourselves to be altered and because we are carrying Daré mind into all our other relationships. But, all of this comes about because everyone who comes is deeply committed to and engaged in the ongoing process of exploring how such a way of being might come about.

* * *

It is ten o'clock at night, January 2nd, 1998. We are getting ready to go to bed. It is pouring rain. There is a knock at the door. It is a young man. He has AIDS. He is worried about his lover. He couldn't begin to afford medication even if it were available in Zimbabwe; he has no money for milk or vitamins that are all his doctor can prescribe. Augustine looks to the North Americans who are in the room. He wants everyone to use his or her gifts on this young man's behalf. We offer him a cup of tea. We cannot provide medication or money and we cannot heal him. But we can help him meet his fate. We can try to imagine ways he can, before he dies, assist others. We can help him refrain from infecting others. We can help him recover the warrior spirit of the Ndebele so that he has a stance with which to meet the disease. Healer Patricia Langer from Canada teaches him an energy yoga that she modifies to be consistent with his tradition. He will make himself a shield to keep his spirits up. We can help him extend his life. We can help him die with dignity.

He practices this yoga. He determines to teach it to his lover who is also infected. He begins to contemplate ways that he can bring strength to the community of sufferers around him. Suffering brought him to the house; strength and generosity carry him back home. Just because he is devastated physically and will probably die soon doesn't mean that he has nothing to offer those around him. The ailing one becomes the healer.

A healer does not judge, as a physician must, the immediate consequence of the treatment. Healing may take a lifetime. Or it may begin and complete itself in an instant. Healing practices, if right for the individual, become life-long habits. Healing is good for you. It is beautiful. It is a way of life.

Healing may not resemble cure. The activity of the healer calls the patient into a different life with different assumptions and healing emerges from this. At its essence healing is a practice, a spiritual practice, that engaged in on a daily basis creates a life that may mitigate the symptoms, may help keep illness at bay, may itself heal.

Daré. People come without making an appointment, knowing that Augustine's door is always open to the afflicted. The community gathers regularly, and also when there is a need, or when there is time and occasion to celebrate. Sometimes people come from far away, even other countries, and stay until they feel relieved or until the days of initiation are over. These are people who cannot afford a hotel or a restaurant. They have made the long journey because their lives and their souls depend on it. On Saturday nights, when most people are off from work, they gather at Augustine's Daré to sweat and for *ngoma* (drum) ceremonies to call the spirits for the sake of healing and wisdom.

During my second visit to Africa, Augustine's son George was visiting with his wife and baby girl. He had, like all of Augustine's children born to his first wife, been estranged from his father who was feared in the family for his un-Christian ways. But George had come home and was standing alongside his father in the ritual work that Augustine was doing. We were all so very grateful for even this small healing. One night while singing in the sweat lodge, George was trance-possessed by an old grandfather spirit. Augustine recognized the spirit that was temporarily inhabiting George's body by the posture and mannerisms that George assumed, the words he used, the cadences of his speech, and, finally, by the spirit's announcing his own name. This was a spirit that was familiar to Augustine but he had never dreamed that his son would be privileged to carry him. Trance-possession is considered a gift and honor. One never knows where the spirit will land, or on whom. One does not ask for the spirit to come, one simply makes oneself available through purification and devotion. In this instance, if there was a causal element, it might have been the seriousness with which George stood alongside his father, trying to serve his spirits, humbly assisting him, learning from him, honoring him. This reconciliation had taken years. The grandfather spirit called us all out of the sweat lodge and into the Daré room. There he spoke at length to Augustine about the necessity of going to Harare and doing whatever he could to come into relationship with his estranged community. Though the distance in the family had not been caused by Augustine, he was required to take responsibility for healing it. The spirit was firm with Augustine, but also reassuring. If he followed these instructions, the family would be reconciled over time. Anyway, the spirit asserted, the family needed Augustine's wisdom and skill. George spoke for a long time. Then he collapsed. Afterwards, he could recall nothing of what he had said. But Augustine and the community remembered. Augustine did make the journey back. Last week, when we called Bulawayo, the telephone was answered by Patience, Augustine's second oldest son who had come home to work the farm so that he could earn some money for his father's community and for his own household.

Trance-possession, like dreaming, is a way that the ancestors enter and protect the circle of the living.

A common longing for community, for healing, for connection, for a real and spontaneous relationship with the spirits superseded any sense of strangeness I may have felt when I first came to Zimbabwe. But really, the moment I came into the house and had a cup of tea with Simakuhle and the family, I found myself at home in ways I had not been able to imagine. A deep sense of home. A coming home.

3

From the beginning there were more resemblances between Augustine and Michael and myself than I had ever anticipated. Augustine was born into apartheid and the Christian tradition and so he was born into western mind, but it didn't fall away when apartheid was finally defeated when he was in his thirties. When the spirits called him, they still had to tear him out of the world that had formed his thinking and sense of reality. And they had to integrate him into the world of his ancestors. When Augustine became a healer, he was initiated into the *Ngoma* of the Water Spirits.

Sometimes I ask Augustine: What are the water spirits because I do not understand – I have a monotheistic mind. And so does he. So, then, what are they? "They are one of the faces of God," he says wryly, knowing that I recognize the title of a book of poetry I wrote, *Looking For the Faces of God*.[15] Sometimes he says they are the highest form of spirits. Sometimes he says they are like angels. Sometimes he says they are the living waters of life.

Initiation was not a consequence of following his heart's desire but rather was, for him, originally, a sign of his defeat. The spirits had been as he puts it, "so heavy upon me," that he had become ill in body and mind and finally he capitulated to the demand of Spirit though he had hoped to be able to live out another kind of life. When he went into the water for initiation, unlike the times that Christian ministers had tried to baptize him, the waters parted as smoothly as the Red Sea and he was able to slip into them with the ease and grace of a fish.

Michael and I were also born into western mind. And if, being Jewish, I wasn't born directly into the Christian tradition, I was certainly born into Judeo-Christian thought; no one who lives in a Christian country like the United States can escape from its assumptions and presumptions. The suppositions are often subtle; we are not aware of how deeply we are influenced, our minds shaped by them.

For years, working with individuals or teaching, I have been speaking about the presumption of pathology that pervades psychology and modern medicine. The reason we consult a medical practitioner and the way he or she responds is based upon the idea that something is wrong. It has to be fixed. A cause or agent of this wrong has to be identified. There is an enemy. Root it out.

This is not the way a healer thinks. Something is disrupted. It may have a meaning. What is the story? Where are we being called? What is Spirit asking of us?

Cancer is a wayward cell, Danelia Wild understands. Don't kill it. Bring it back into the fold. Transform it. Its nature has been distorted. If we think this way, we see that the cancerous cell is a victim. The first victim. Not the enemy but more appropriately an object of compassion.

The therapist looks for the flaw. The complex. What is wrong. A society obsessed with what is wrong, how to fix it, oneself, improve. Obsessions.

Michael and I were at the launching of a Daré hosted by Elenna Rubin Goodman in Oakland. People were gathering and Michael was, as is his habit, holding the oracle: What is the gift that you bring to this moment and to this community?

Not, "what is wrong?" Not, "what is the wound?" Not, "why can't you act like everyone else?" or "why can't you act like me?" But: "What is the unique gift that you are?" A community is transformed when there is a presumption that everyone participating is a gift to everyone else. When illness is recognized simply as interference with the giving of the gift. When the society is transformed so that each person is honored appropriately to who she is, who he is. When there is not an external standard by which each individual is judged but rather there is a constant effort to search out the unique and unexpected qualities that are inherent in each individual. Everything changes from this sleight of mind. Everything.

After that Daré I understood the great travesty that is imposed upon our minds and hearts by the doctrine of original sin. The lie that there is an essential flaw in our nature. How this has pervaded, influenced and distorted everything in our culture, has falsified our lives. How it has led us here. Where we are. In hell.

Story. Where you begin determines its ending. Begin with sin, you end with sinning. It's the inevitable trajectory. Begin in peace. Begin with a different sense of human nature. What will come of it? Where did we go wrong? What stories regarding the nature of human beings existed before this one took over our imagination? Let's go back to the other stories. Let's begin again. Let's end elsewhere than where we are. Let's undo the world we have created. Let's live another story out to an altogether different conclusion.

Augustine says Spirit wants to heal. Augustine recognizes that the ancestors want to assist, not haunt us. His major work is not to exorcise spirits but to teach us how to make a place for the ancestors so they can be at home and do their work. There are times when a spirit has to be exorcised but in that process a place is found where the spirit can properly reside.

> At the beginning of my second initiation, [Michael Ortiz Hill writes in the *Whole Life Times*] I awoke from a terrifying dream: late night in the San Fernando Valley facing off against a huge black man in the employ of a white gangster, both of us armed with crowbars and covered with blood.
>
> When I told Augustine the dream, he laughed. "That was a good workout. I know that spirit well. He is a slave that your ancestors kept."
>
> Augustine proceeded to do ritual work on behalf of Michael and the spirit.
>
> For perhaps three seconds, I was that black slave, enraged, humiliated and absolutely powerless beneath the master's whip. And then – gone.
>
> Augustine continued, "That one will soon be back in his village, and he will be greeted with a feast because a warrior has returned and will protect the people. Now climb in the water and pray thanks. Now your spirits can be free."[16]

*   *   *

We heal the ancestors so they can heal us. We make amends. We create an altar. We live according to the sacred. Paul Shepard, one of the visionaries of our time, recognized this.

> Prehistoric humans…were autochthonous, that is "native to their place." They possessed a detailed knowledge that was passed on from generation to generation by oral tradition

through myths – stories that framed their beliefs in the context of ancestors and the landscape of the natural world. They lived with a "sacred geography" that consisted of a complex knowledge of place, terrain, and plants and animals embedded in a phenology of seasonal cycles. But they were also close to the earth in a spiritual sense, joined in an intricate configuration of sacred associations with the spirit of place within their landscape. Time and space as well as animals, humans, gods – all life and nonliving matter formed a continuum that related to themes of fertility and death and the sacredness of all things. During prehistory, which is most of the time that humans have been on earth, the dead and their burial places were venerated and mythic ancestors were part of the living present, the dreamtime ones whose world was also the ground of the present. Ignore them as we will, they are with us still."[17]

Prehistory. The Paleolithic. The Pleistocene. Why not start there and see where that trajectory will lead us?

This is how Paul Shepard concludes his masterful book, *Coming Home to the Pleistocene:*

What we can do is single out those many things, large and small, that characterized the social and cultural life of our ancestors – the terms under which our genome itself was shaped – and incorporate them as best as we can by creating a modern life around them. We take our cues from primal cultures, the best wisdom of the deep desires of the genome. We humans are instinctive culture makers: given the pieces, the culture will reshape itself. [18]

One difference between Augustine and myself is that when I was torn out of the modern mind, I had no access to those ancestors and indigenous traditions that held different understandings into which I might be integrated as a healer. There was nothing beneath my feet except a certainty of a great spiritual intelligence with which, if I were careful and devoted, I might be connected.

Or at least that is what I thought. It didn't occur to me then that I could claim as ancestors those who came long before the Hebrews identified themselves as the Chosen People. That I could go back before Abraham, long before Abraham, to find my ancestors and origins.

I was deeply into this book, had written most of what you are reading and beyond, had been thinking deeply about where the sacred story that might heal us could begin when I was given *Coming Home to the Pleistocene* as a gift. I read this book with rapt admiration and gratitude. It is with my own wry smile that I recognize Paul Shepard as an ancestor. "Is it possible," I asked Michael who gave me the book, "that I am trance-possessed by Paul Shepard? Is that what you had in mind, my beloved trickster? Of course, I never met him, but is his spirit helping me write this book?"

"The spirits and the ancestors want to heal," Michael answers.

"I promise not to blame him for any flaws."

"Always a good practice," Michael responds, laughing. "But, you know that Shepard was probably trance-possessed by the old ones, himself," he paused, "as you are."

*   *   *

Between the Tree of the Sun and the Tree of the Moon flows the underground Ghost River that interconnects the two, according to Stephen Karcher, a translator and interpreter of the I Ching. This is the home of the souls. "This world is not only populated by humans, but by the souls and the ghosts and spirits. Between heaven and earth there is no place the *guishen* do not exist."[19] This is why we are transformed when we drink of the Ghost River.

> HEXAGRAM 29 THE PIT, GHOST RIVER, *KAN*....
> Pit is the sacrificial pit at the Earth Altar and the underworld waters that flow through it, the Ghost River that connects the Sun Tree and the Moon Tree, the axis of the world, and opens the gate of destinies through which souls enter the world.... In action, it represents a critical moment that requires courage and determination in face of great fear engendered by the presence of the ghost world. It confronts and dissolves obstacles, venturing, falling, and moving on.

> The ghost world.
> There is a connection to the spirits.
> Hold your heart fast! An offering brings you success.[20]

According to Augustine, it is when we are separated from the ances-tors and the spirits that we experience water spirit disease. The symptoms of this disease vary – moodiness, lability, stomach problems, a sense of alienation and disconnection from one's community and the world at large, excruciating empathy, being undone by one's responses to the suf-fering of the world, a history of tragedy and mishap, bad luck, money trou-bles, money easily made and easily lost, vivid dreams and daydreams, extreme visionary activity that is often both dramatic and incomprehensi-ble, social awkwardness, not knowing how to deport oneself in the world, and general instability and dislocation caused by disconnection from the spirit world.[21] I have watched Augustine move through a crowd of strangers, sometimes on a city street, and identify someone with water spirit disease. When he comes upon someone who is suffering, he never fails to stop to greet or converse with them. Often a brief conversation establishes rapport between them. When we travel with Augustine, we always forget to schedule time for these unexpected interchanges, but they always occur, on the street, in a restaurant, in a hotel lobby, on the train. Years ago, when Michael and Augustine were looking for a house for Daré, Augustine saw that the East Indian real estate woman was suffering deeply. Even she responded gratefully to his ministrations. Only after her soul was eased, was Augustine able to concentrate on the practical issue before him. Stranger or not, Augustine does not hesitate to inquire about the person's dreams or his or her emotional state, offering insight or rec-ommending a path of healing. He is able to identify those whom the spir-its are calling to consciousness and alignment with an accuracy similar to an X ray revealing a broken bone.

September, 2001. We had taken the train from Bulawayo to Victoria Falls. Michael, Chuck, and Augustine were in one compartment while Laura, Wilderness, Robin, and I were in another. In the men's compart-ment were travelers from Zambia where a powerful indigenous healing tradition still exists. Augustine's impulse to bring questions to the soul set the tone and soon the Zambian men were revealing the pain and suffering they were experiencing. During the course of the evening, he recruited both Michael and Chuck to work alongside him and together they brought them enough comfort that the Zambians spoke to others. Soon there was a line outside the compartment. All three worked indefatigably through the night. Augustine can work this way because he doesn't cate-gorize it as working. Pains alleviated. Hearts restored. Family problems identified, untangled, resolved. Tarot cards read and interpreted. Herbs offered and dreams decoded. A suggestion of how to proceed, what offerings to make to the spirits, what path to follow. Reminders to follow the ethical life, for its own sake, and because unethical practices are often at the root of disease and disquiet.

A woman had approached Augustine because she was suffering from various physical ailments. She could find no rest and no relief. He asked her about her dreams and her life story. After speaking together for a long time, he realized that she was the niece of a trance medium who had died some years before. The medium had been a fine healer and her family had become quite wealthy through her work. When the medium died, her husband kept all the wealth without redistributing it to her birth family and their relations, as was the custom. The afflicted woman was one of the living relatives who had received the benefit of the medium's success. Augustine advised the woman to make amends by appeasing the spirit of the trance medium whose birth family had been treated badly.

This is the kind of ancestor work that Augustine recognizes as essential. We are not only responsible for our own lives but for the lives of our ancestors who have gone before us. Prayers, Masses, Kaddish said for the dead during a period of mourning have this goal in common, to ease the soul and spirit of the dead. Augustine has taken it further and I have followed his example by asking my students to take responsibility for the activities of their ancestors and, when appropriate, to make amends. The consequences of the deeds of the dead affect all of us even unto the seventh generation. Therefore, it is our task to see if we can bring remedy, for ourselves, and for our successors. We will see how this played itself out between Valerie Wolf, her dead father, and myself later in this manuscript. But in the meantime, it is important for all of us to know that we are not innocent. We ask the children of the Nazis to make amends for their parent's deeds and for the deeds of Hitler and his followers and those who were governed by him. We have to examine our own souls and the souls of our fathers and mothers. And then we must make amends.

A student of mine, D., discovered that the infertility from which she suffers may be caused by hydrogen sulfide gas seepage in the vicinity of her beautiful house from oil wells that may not have been properly capped. Or perhaps there is no way to cap them as hydrogen sulfide is known to disintegrate the concrete casings of oil wells over time. The Kogi warn us particularly to refrain from taking minerals out of the earth, from taking the bones out of the body of the Mother. Who knows what they understand that we do not?

How is it that we are able to live? Without blood we cannot live and without bones we cannot walk.... When they dig into the earth and take its gold it is the same thing. Down below by the sea there was a lake and there were many Mothers there. They have drained the lake and they have dug into it to take petrol. One day the river itself will catch fire. Gold has its own thought and it can speak. It is a living being. They must stop stealing it. If they take all the gold the world will end. The Mothers of the banana trees, of all the trees and of all the birds, they have all been stolen. They are cutting off the flesh of the Mother's body.[22]

D.'s inheritance is from her grandfather who made his wealth in the early days of the oil business in Texas. The children suffer the deeds of the fathers, however unconscious or unaware, unto.... The children, then, are the ones who may redeem the deeds. What is the proper offering that she can make on behalf of the ancestors and also on behalf of the unborn child she hopes to bring into the world? D. once told me that she felt from the beginning that buying a home built on a reclaimed oil field was somehow meant to call her as a healer to reconcile with the land.

The African woman understood that the soul of the trance medium was distraught over injustice. Her birth family was impoverished and the family or clan she had married into was thriving. Greed. The niece was innocent of any of these transactions; she had not even thought of them before Augustine had elicited the story from her; still she was suffering the wrath of the ancestors. She did make the proper offerings. She redistributed her money. She healed, body and soul.[23]

In the morning, the line outside Augustine's compartment reformed itself. Once again Michael was working alongside Augustine with the oracle, the tarot cards, and Chuck Madansky was using his knowledge of herbs and psychology to assist. As Augustine says repeatedly, "Spirit wants to heal." Spirit will use all the means present to bring healing. A great healer is not only someone who is very capable but is someone who gathers around himself all those who carry healing powers as well. When the web of healing is large, miracles can occur.

*   *   *

SPIRIT WANTS TO HEAL!

Augury extends the realm of healers from the living to the dead, the ancestors and the spirits. It assists us in negotiating the world where invisible and visibles, humans and non-humans coexist and interact. Through the activity of divination, the power and wisdom of the other world reaches across the divide to meet the moment. Augury, divination, dreams, signs, synchronicities are the means of the ancestors; they are the common language through which they communicate with us.

The Catholic Church and many Protestant denominations are largely opposed to divination. When it is efficacious, they say it is because Satan is speaking. Judaism is not as adamantly opposed to divination as the Catholic Church and many Protestant sects, but it has its anxieties. In the Old Testament, King Saul, the first King, had all the witches killed. "You shall not suffer a witch to live." Once, however, this edict was followed, the King himself wanted to consult a witch so she could raise the prophet Samuel from the dead to tell Saul his fate. The King promised the Witch of Endor immunity from his edict if she would raise the dead for him. She did. Samuel came. He said that Saul would die in battle. And he did.

A few years ago I ran into the contemporary witch and seer, Z Budapest, whom I hadn't seen in many years. She is a descendent of a long matrilineal line of healers, diviners and herbalists. She spoke of the persecution she had suffered from the Los Angeles police force that had arrested her for reading the cards accurately. Z said her cat had warned her in the way familiars can communicate to adepts like Z. Though instructed not to read the cards of the woman she later discovered was an undercover agent, Z ignored her intuitions. The police woman had told Z a true story about her daughter's illness; she had not fabricated a story for the sake of the police department. Z couldn't refuse healing to someone even if it endangered her. Z read the cards well. The daughter healed. Z was arrested. The police officer? I am not certain that I remember the end of the story, but I would like to believe that what I think happened, did. As I recall the story now, the police officer resigned but was obliged to testify against Z. Finally, it was exactly Z's skill and accuracy that condemned her. Over time – too long a time – Z was exonerated.

There are laws in many states against divination despite the constitutional injunction to separate church and state in our country. Christian thinking has penetrated our minds so deeply that government does not always discern the difference between religious and secular thought. A true democracy reflects the larger wisdom, the entire spectrum of understanding, that emerges from all the different perspectives gathered in the nation. When people become afraid they act to narrow the possibilities, when it is exactly the expansion of mind and heart that will protect them.

For many Christian people divining or healing may only be done in the name of Christ, and even then it is suspicious. Most aboriginal peoples would not limit healing powers to one mode or way or god. In these realms, as well as in other realms, our aboriginal ancestors recognized the fingerprint of the Divine in diversity and divination – healing being no exception.

What often characterizes meetings between different healers is the delight in the display and exchange of healing ways. Each individual demonstrates his or her ability to move skillfully in the invisible realms and in the waters of the Ghost River. A healer will have a medicine bag, real or figurative, what the Navajo call, *jish*, that represents or contains some of the range and specificity of her or his powers, energies or skills. It points to the healer's allies and her or his ability to read the signs, invoke spirits, enact healing or protection for an individual or the community. The I Ching and the Tarot cards are means that have managed to survive despite the general disdain in western culture for things marvelous and strange. Some healers are dreamers, some can read the signs of the natural world or are exceptionally skilled at interpreting events or reading the past or the future. Indigenous medicine people may be said to carry the medicine or healing power of a particular animal or one of the elementals. When I was assisting Annie Kahn, a Navajo herbalist in making a fire, she commented that I carried fire medicine and then later in the evening also rain medicine. It is the task of the healer or medicine person to develop his or her particular gifts or sensitivity to the language of non-ordinary reality. Because each may be an adept in a certain area and no one capable of the whole, it is always advantageous for healers to work together and let the spirits choose who and where and how they will enter on behalf of the community. And it is also interesting when diviners work alongside the healers, in the ways that the Navajo separate the roles of the diviners from the singers.

Most people who have healing gifts have come to understand deeply that it is Spirit that is bringing healing into the world through the individual. The healer is merely a conduit, albeit a devoted one. Divination is a collaboration with the invisibles. And, in the manner that Augustine enlists anyone and everyone around him to enter into the healing arena, divination calls the spirits into the circle as well.

As we stepped off the train, Augustine was approached and reproached by a Zambian woman who had not had the time to speak with him and wanted to meet us at the Falls so that she might receive healing from him. It broke our hearts that we had to go on and we agreed to meet her at the hotel or at the Falls before we went into Botswana – the border closing within a few hours. We never saw her again and we prayed that she might find a healing path for herself.

It is not that Augustine heals so much as it is that he finds the way of healing the individual can walk. Healing is not a passive activity. We accept the activity of the healer on our behalf, but we must meet it with our own actions, with the ways that we will live our lives. Western medicine does not ask us to scrutinize our souls. This is a great lacuna. Western medicine does not ask us to change our lives.

Take a pill
+ keep on
doing the
same!
No
Change.

Psychologist Diane Broderick expressed her helplessness with her patients. "We do good work. Healing occurs. But then they go back into their lives and get infected all over again. Sometimes I feel as if there is no point in healing, if we cannot change the basic conditions from which the diseases emerge."

*   *   *

"I sat by the river of Jordan and wept."

We were talking about the water spirits. Sometimes there is a drama that involves water in order to bring an individual into another state of consciousness, into a deeper understanding of reality. Sometimes we enter into symbolic activity in order to mark or facilitate such a moment of transition. There were the two different mediums I met who each, independently, told me that they had lived seven years in the river. Sometimes the spirits orchestrate a theatrical moment that might involve water. But it may be anything; let us not be literal minded about water. The spirits arrange to speak to us in a story that we will understand.

Because Augustine was raised in the Christian tradition, he understood baptism and so it spoke to him. Or, as Michael has described in his book, *The Village of the Water Spirits*, baptism was originally a way of affiliating with the spirits that were indigenous to Africa. Africans did not find Christianity as alien as they might have because of the bridge of water. Augustine responded to water first as an African and then as a Christian and then again as an African. When Christianity fell away from him, he was left with the substance of his original tradition – that of the water spirits. He saw through the three ways of knowing: the way of the old ones, the ancestors; the way of Christian doctrine and the teachings of the Old and New Testaments; and the way of the spirits as it was being revealed to him. Then he came upon the common thread. "And the spirit of God hovered over the surface of the water." He was freed to return to his original heart.

To do the rites of any particular religion, you must do them from within the religion. But from a spiritual point of view, the rites do not connect you to the religion, they connect you to God. To which God? In the language through which I am coming to understand such things – to the God who cannot be named who shows one face to you and another to me. But God is God.

*　　*　　*

My intent here is to map the territory that has received me and the territory to which I have returned. I want to find words that will serve me to understand what must be understood. When *Ambuya* MaGumbo returned from the bottom of the river, she still wanted to be baptized in the Christian tradition, but when it was attempted, she went into a frenzy; the water spirits protested in a wild flurry of writhing, foam and desperation. The minister tried three times but it was not possible to soothe the waters. Finally, she was told that she had to remain in the territory of the water spirits. This was to be her life and her intelligence and her knowledge.

This happened in a similar manner to the Tanzanian trance medium who brought us the wisdom of an old grandfather spirit when we came to Zimbabwe for the first time. It was she that told Michael and I that our souls were not married. It shocked us as we had married three times, each time with careful ritual preparation. The first time we had married before the community, but we never mailed the certificate. The second time we had married in Costa Rica but the judge never filed the papers. Finally, in Payson, Arizona, a justice of the peace in cowboy boots startlingly similar to the pair I was wearing performed the ceremony and made it legal. The words of the Tanzanian medium stung. We felt hurt and unseen. But, this summer when we collaborated together on behalf of those who had come to Africa for initiation, we understood that she had been correct. We had had to yield our personal ambitions and ego to the primacy of the work and the third entity that is our marriage. It had taken fifteen years for us to accomplish it without knowing until recently that this was our spiritual goal. In retrospect, fifteen years is not such a long time for a marriage to cohere. Chuck and Wilderness came to Africa to celebrate their marriage of twenty years. But Spirit seemed to indicate that they were yet to marry. The path laid out before them was so filled with hurdles and confusions, they, we, often thought we had misunderstood. Only at the end of our time together did everything become clear so their souls could entwine.

Augustine himself wanted so badly to be baptized by a Christian minister into "the one true faith" but the ancestors understood that the Christian way was not the way for Augustine and they claimed him for the *njuzu* from the other side. It was only when he yielded to the old ones as they were gathered in his dream council waiting for him that they allowed him to enter the water and become the healer that he has become. Before that he was one of the highest ranking police officers in the country, but working much against his will, and then he was freely able to serve the spirits with the work of his hands and his heart.

Here is the dilemma: Gain and loss in the same moment. The spirits call to us. We are filled with Spirit but often bereft of human company. When we come home, we want to be at home with our people. We want to be among them. We want to be of them. We do not want to remain set apart. But even when we journey on behalf of others, when we come home with the gift for the community, we may remain separated from them forever because we have been in the Ghost River and it marks us.

What does it mean to enter the Ghost River? Perhaps it means that when we are called into a certain relationship with the spirits, we are required to yield to them so completely that we are actually dissolved in the waters of their consciousness and, like them, are never fully constituted as entirely separate individuals again.

Perhaps the spirits are not *in* the Ghost River. Perhaps they are the Ghost River and when we enter there they are able to flow through us the way water can flow through sand.

The Ghost River is milky white and the ancestors are white with clay, the chalky dissolve of the dead. The Ghost River is composed of the stars strewn at random into the sky by the trickster gods. The Ghost River is the issue of the milky breast of Het-Hurt, the great cow who nourishes the world. It is the earthly mirror of the Milky Way that like the ancestors lights our way. As above, so below. The milk churns and feeds us and the spirits gather around us and so we are sustained.

All the myths I studied in the past seemed to insist that one must always leave the land of the Spirits and return to the land of the living or one will die or go mad. The renowned anthropologist Barbara Myerhoff, also my dearest friend for thirty years, was my first teacher in this area; I never questioned her authority as each myth that I read supported this thesis. Or at least, that is how the myths are interpreted by scholars who are most often carrying western mind.

Barbara began her career by studying Native American cultures in the United States and Mexico. But midway in her career, it was proposed that she study her own people instead. This arose out of the nationalistic fervor of the late sixties. White or western anthropologists were criticized for creating stellar careers by analyzing and interpreting the lives of other cultures that were for the most part marginalized. But the critique was also a response to the general inability of the European mind to see the thing-in-itself without imposing its own values and understanding.

Barbara herself tried to be impeccable in this area. And it is true that the distinguished shaman, Ramón Medina Silva, asked her to record the Huichol myths so that they would survive. He feared that his culture – only a few remaining members were still able to resist the continuous onslaughts of various Christian missionaries – would soon be gone.

Barbara would tell this story:

The Huichol Indians of Tepic, Mexico hunt peyote. It is a sacred journey and the community tends the fire for the entire time that the shaman, the *mara'akame*, and his companions wander in the desert searching for the holy medicine. When they find it, they gather what the community needs for the year and immediately partake of it, the *mara'akame* for the sake of vision and the others for the sake of beauty. Sometime afterwards, as they return from the visionary country, the *mara'akame* suddenly shouts, "Run!" and everyone stands up and runs out of Wirikuta, out of Paradise. If they stay too long in Paradise, they will be unable to return to the human world, or at least that is how Barbara relayed the story to me. I remember her emphasis upon this moment, the way she shouted, "Run!" and how it impressed me.

Writing this and wishing to get the spelling right, I return to Barbara's text, *Peyote Hunt, The Sacred Journey of the Huichol Indian*. There is no reference to the flight that was so central to Barbara's story! I can only think this is because she was under the thrall of western dualism that imagines a very great division between the sacred and the ordinary. Having spent some time with Ramón and his wife, Lupe, I believe that they lived within the sacred universe, in ongoing relationship to the spirits and the natural world so that even the activities of daily life were sacraments. When they went to Wirikuta they simply went from the sacred into a special domain of the sacred, as the dualism inherent in western thought between the sacred and the secular does not exist for them.

Perhaps we should have understood this when we sat alongside Ramón Medina Silva in Baskin-Robbins Ice Cream Store after he had made a presentation at California Institute for the Arts. He was dressed in his beautifully embroidered clothes, no different here than at home, no different for a sacred activity than for the activities of daily life. All morning, he and his wife Lupe had been pressing colored yarns into beeswax to make the glorious yarn paintings that illustrate the myths that hold the stories of the true nature of the universe, moving seamlessly, it seemed to us, from one world to another. What we didn't understand is that they were living entirely in one world, that being whole is diverse and dynamic, and so they were grounded in each moment with various spirits and nature. What should have amazed us is that neither Los Angeles in the present nor the entire history of Catholic and governmental imperialism and violence were able to disorient them. The Catholic priest who had attempted to extract the myths and their meanings from Ramón as a way of both honoring and undoing Huichol beliefs had complained to Barbara that Ramón had been generous in his telling but everything he said contradicted what he had said before. One of the ways the Huichol had been able to preserve their culture and their lives was through deft and agile evasions. Another way was to live without distraction within the world of the spirits and ancestors.

Much to the amusement of the clerk at the store, Ramón insisted on savoring each one of the flavors while creating a mythic story from the tastes and colors. The story was based on the magic of separation and unity, and in the end, all the flavors gathered together as vital beings within his stomach where they went about the work of creation. As you might imagine the simple act of getting an ice cream cone took several hours.

Barbara does record a similar incident at the end of the peyote hunt:

On the way home we were all very hungry, having eaten so little for so long, and decided to stop at a restaurant for dinner. It was New Year's Day and the restaurant was pretentious though empty except for a crew of very elegant, haughty waiters, who gasped at the sight of a party of filthy Indians and gringos entering their establishment. Indeed we must have been a ridiculous spectacle – so haggard, so exhausted yet so unspeakably happy – sharing a precious secret, giddy with our invisible treasures, realizing that no outsider could tell that we had been transformed, knowing that others only saw us as mortals. Our delight only intensified as the waiters blanched and drew themselves up when we began moving tables around to accommodate our party. Ramón grew expansive and playful after his long ordeal, and the excursion to the restaurant gave him an opportunity to indulge his flair for drama and humor. When we had seated ourselves, Ramón stood and began to chant in Huichol as he "read" from the menu. To everyone's amusement he invented a fine story about the menu listing all the foods the Ancient Ones like best, and that obviously, they had been here before us and left the menus for us, but unfortunately the "Spaniards" couldn't read Huichol and therefore hadn't prepared these foods for us.

We ordered our food…. Francisco played with his silverware to everyone's amusement, and although he had never held such implements in his hands before, managed them very well by imitating Ramón. When the food arrived, the companions threw little bits of everything to the four directions and up and down before eating, just as they had done throughout the trip. Bits of egg, tortilla, butter, and melon flew through the air in a sacred hail. The expressions on the waiters' faces were truly memorable. Also unforgettable was the sign of Francisco solemnly dipping his bony finger down the neck of a bottle of soda pop and spraying it about, in the proper manner.[24]

*   *   *

We interpret myths as insisting on an absolute line between one land and another, a border that must be respected. The first time I climbed Mt. Sinai, we entered Egypt through many checkpoints that were jointly monitored at each station by Egyptian and Israeli soldiers who assured that everyone who entered also exited. The stories that sharply delineate the boundary between one world and another also distinguish the world of the living from the world of the dead. The ferry that goes from this world to the other, goes full and returns empty. The ferry driver does not disembark at the other side and he does not know the territory to which he brings his bereaved passengers who think they have lost eternity because they have lost their lives. And if one of the living somehow manages to pass into the other world or the land of the shades, she or he must proceed with great caution because the situation is perilous and it is possible that they will never return.

Western thought is always concerned with borders and boundaries, territory and fences. We even mark time, rigidly separating this hour from that hour, this day from that day, this appointment from that appointment. We can say that the process of limitation and circumscription, differentiating and maintaining boundaries and borders, is inherent to the culture and that we construct our minds and understanding around these categories. If one infringes on the boundaries, people are often shocked or outraged, they feel violated, whether one is speaking of lines between nations, between individuals or between worlds. There is no area that is free from these restrictions whether it is the organization of time, the relationship between people or the treatment of illness. Medical practitioners of all kinds divide their healing time into equal segments in order to provide treatment in an orderly fashion, assigning a particular hour or portion thereof for a particular patient's care as if one's anxiety or pain can be manipulated into a container. The issue of boundaries is essential to psychology and therapy, and is often based on whether a patient easily recognizes these arbitrary delineations – only they are not arbitrary to the therapist or the culture that has developed around their assumptions. Living in this culture, practitioners from other traditions are coerced into practicing according to these rules even though many of them recognize that it undermines their work. But one cannot practice outside a culture and one either has to create a new community governed by different assumptions or one adjusts to the existing mores. It is hard enough to be a healer in this culture; to take on the task of organizing one's patients into an intelligent community is more than challenging.

A little perspective allows us to see that the distinctions westerners hold almost sacred, certainly absolute, are really artificial and arbitrary. For someone carrying indigenous mind many of them are capricious, are essentially destructive to social relations and spiritual connections. All our recent wars have developed out of these subjective habits of mind that rigidly organize the boundaries of property, territory, and the realms of self and other. Other people do see the world differently. Nomadic peoples have suffered our boundary fetishes as have animals and other life forms. We have in what we must recognize as madness even learned how to confine and allocate water, what one might consider the freest of spirits, and I am certain that we would contain the wind if we knew how. There are all those fairy tales of winds confined in a sack that are freed deliberately or accidentally and cause havoc. These sound like teaching stories, moral tales, but they also reflect our anxiety about anything we cannot confine and contain and measure. We can see the progression from distinguishing territory to creating borders, to controlling the territory, to presuming one owns the territory. Mine and yours. Self and Other. This world. The other world. Soon the borders imply danger. The liminal spaces, the places between, the no-man's land, become fraught with uncertainty and anxiety. Ecotones that mark a transitional area, between two distinct ecological communities are often spoken of as stress lines or tension belts revealing not so much their nature as our presumptions and concerns. Because the ecotone is a transitional area it is a domain of great richness where the qualities of the two communities intermingle. But for minds trained in the necessity of distinction, such arenas can seem chaotic, and chaos, despite its ferment and abundance, is disturbing to western ways of organizing reality.

Trying to measure the immeasurable, to delineate what is always in flux, we recognize fractal systems, and their beautiful mathematics. Perhaps we can say that indigenous mind is fractal, a moving boundary tuned to light and dark, the round of seasons. It differentiates real and, therefore, shifting events, day and night, summer and winter. The act of recognition is not, however, for the sake of possession, organization or management. Neither the land nor the animals nor the spirits can belong to anyone. Rather we belong to the land, the world and the gods. We even belong to the animals when we are summoned to carry and serve the intelligence of animal spirits.

One can live in this world and the other world at the same time. That is the goal of consciousness and development. Daré or rather Daré mind attempts to restore a flow of caring and concern between people that is not packaged or circumscribed. Sometimes we look at each other and understand that the way of the healer has brought us to the activity of radically changing culture through restoring the intelligence and the ways of many old forms.

When Stephan Hewitt came to Daré it was as if he had come home. At the New Year's Daré in 2001, he spoke of *Grace*. *Grace* had settled upon him and he was allowing it to alter him. Sometimes I want to write – he was allowing it to *altar* him. Yes, that is exactly the right word. Through Daré we are *altared.*

It began with the frogs that are his totem. Frogs, like bats, are our sentinels. Fragile and sensitive, they register the fate of the planet. When they go, and their populations are endangered, we go, the planet goes. It is not a matter, as with some other species, of preserving habitat for them. They register global conditions. A few frogs in frog preserves, like a few bats in bat preserves, cannot sustain all life. Either life on the planet will be hospitable to them and all species, or life, itself, will disappear.

Like so many other people, Stephan came to Daré broken-hearted. He also came carrying dreams. In one dream, a frog spoke about the threat of extinction, saying we can't live without green, mossy places. Following this, he created a small sanctuary, a green, mossy place. A ritual gesture that eased his heart and was an offering to the world. This was the beginning of the slow and subtle process through which Daré became an integral part of Stephan's life and he became integral to Daré. Can we say that his connection reflects the ecological complexity of Daré mind through which individuals, exactly because of their distinct gifts become woven into the fabric of community?

Perhaps the council question was: How have you been called by Spirit? What were the signs? Stephan was hesitant to speak. He is a private person. But the question insisted that he address it. He spoke quietly of having been brought to his destiny, in the subtle ways that the Spirits work, by a casual encounter. Something seemingly insignificant occurs. We are intrigued by a book or an advertisement. Curious, we respond. And then some weeks, or months, or years later, we recognize that our lives are entirely different. What was a modest inquiry has become a path. Unexpectedly, he discovered he had the ability to channel wisdom from the other side. He pursued this work for some years and then he gave it up publicly. His connection with the spirits was continued privately and through astrology and spiritual counseling, but the circumstances of contemporary life demanded that he work in business and that began to subsume his life, though it left him deeply dissatisfied and restless.

Perhaps it was simply circumstantial that his work came to an end just as Daré became an important part of his life. Or… my understanding is this: Daré is a cultural form that can hold all of our gifts. Though he was quite skilled as a channel, the social and cultural framework around him did not hold it. It was an eccentric activity disconnected from the fabric of ordinary life. This is no longer true for him. And it is no longer true for the rest of us who are able, increasingly, to live our lives with integrity. Culture immerses one and sustains one. That is its function and its purpose. Healing the community demands that a vital and supportive culture be restored. A culture we can live within, like whales in the sea. Musician, sound healer, astrologer, psychic, writer, computer expert, friend, you name it, these are the gifts that have a place in Daré and the Daré community. And having such a place where he is welcomed in his entirety, is something of what Stephan recognizes as *Grace. Grace.* The shimmering, generous, open-handed gift of the presence of the Divine.

So it is that Stephan has been speaking to Gary Davidson about *Grace.* Having recovered sufficiently from kidney surgery to investigate the lymph node in his chest and lesions in his lung, Gary underwent more tests. "The tests are inconclusive," the doctor said. We did not ask what this meant. It meant one thing for the doctor, and another for us. The lymph node in his chest was reduced, without any medical treatment, by one-third. "We are in a miracle," I said to Gary.

"If nothing else occurs, the circumstances are already miraculous," he answered, aware that his life is still at stake.

Reading Gary's astrological chart, Stephan saw that Gary has an extraordinary capacity for healing. "This is the opportunity of Grace," Stephan said. "A doorway. But you must gather all your inner forces and walk through it." Ultimately, Gary will have to walk through that door himself, whatever that will mean in terms of changing his perspective and his life down to the cellular level. But the loving and intelligent presence of the community makes such a change possible. And though the image is of a deliberate step across a defined threshold, it is not, of course, so dramatic. One day we make an offering, the next day we reach out to someone we would have ignored before, the third day we give precedence to the wetlands, the fourth day we sing or pray on behalf of someone who is ill, and then, we look back and see the ways we have constructed our daily life, our allegiances and preferences, the ways we spend money and time and recognize that we have become someone else – our self. *Grace.*

*   *   *

"I was underwater seven hours," Gilbert Mpofu said, explaining that one of the signs of having become a *nganga* was his ability under ritual circumstances to breathe under water; now he intends to go home with his bushels and baskets of herbs to establish his own Daré. It was about five years ago that this Tonga man from the north of Zimbabwe, had, following the instructions in a dream, sold his chickens for enough money to walk to Bulawayo to find the healer his dream spirits urged him to meet. He apprenticed to Augustine for five years. Recently, he suffered a critical illness with a complex of symptoms that could have been diagnosed by western medicine as severe depression, chronic fatigue syndrome, but most likely AIDS. Concerned with the extremity of his fatigue, loss of weight and a growth on his chest that we all recognized as karposi sarcoma, we arranged for him to be tested at the local hospital and began to consider how and where he might be sustained in his last days.

A few days before the test, Augustine, Simakuhle, Michael and I came together in the Daré to journey on behalf of the group arriving from the U.S.. It had not been my intention to pray for Gilbert but once I found myself on the other side, it became clear that my work was to pray for him. I proceeded, in the way of the Tzutuhil Maya who, according to Martin Prechtel[25] consider healers to be spirit lawyers arguing on behalf of their patients, to fight for Gilbert's life. I do not know how long it took, but soon I felt a sense of relief as if my elaborate prayers had been received. Two days later when Gilbert came to Bulawayo, he told us that the fatigue and pain had suddenly passed from him the very night that we had been praying. He took the blood test and it was negative. The tumor was diagnosed as a fungus. He was pronounced well. Gilbert returned to the farm able to work for the first time in months. But he also declared himself ready to build his Daré hut on his own land in his village in the north. Only now that he is able to live under water is he ready to return home.

We can dismiss Gilbert's story, or his understanding of it, as merely metaphoric, ignorant or preposterous. I can dismiss the Huichols as ill-mannered and unsophisticated. Certainly that is how Europeans have diminished Africans, Native Americans and other non-western peoples. This view is insulting to the individuals and their wisdom traditions but, worse, it has justified brutality, enslavement, exploitation, murder and genocide. I would rather seek out and excise the remnants of prejudices and suspend my perception of reality to allow the indigenous stories and experiences to educate me and expand my vision of what is true and real.

The traditional western story of the journey has this shape then… the shape of setting out and returning home. But, perhaps, there is another way of structuring the story. What is the story that develops when one steps into the river and is saturated by the sacred waters so that when one steps out gleaming, water dripping down one's body, one is in the act of returning to the river, one is still within the river, one has become forever of the river, has become the river and the servant of the river, all at once.

To write this I must step out of the language and assumptions that are basic to the myth of the journey. A journey implies setting forth and going home. But I am not speaking about going out and coming back. I am trying to understand that one can enter into the Ghost River or cross over into the other country and never leave it even while one is walking here among the living as one had before. I am trying to understand what it means to walk in two worlds at once.

4

There are spiritual practices that follow the teachings, procedures, precepts and rituals that have been followed by particular people and cultures for centuries. These are the known roads. Then there are the unknown roads.

"What is a path?" I asked Peter Levitt as we were seated on a boulder tracing the well-worn pathways of coyote and deer through the sage, oak and lupine that still remain in the canyon where I live.

"A path," he said, "is where you walk, and others have walked before." I was grateful then for the company of those who had gone before me.

Now I find myself on a path that closes behind me and opens before me, one step at a time. I cannot see clearly where I have come from and I cannot see where I am going. No one can follow me here and no one has gone before me in exactly this way. Having followed precise directions and wise counsel as devotedly as I ever have in my life, I got lost and found myself on an unknown road that my soul was enjoined to follow. This has happened to others but it never happens to anyone in the same way. The practice that develops is not one of tradition, it is a practice that one is delivered to as if by the direct intervention of Spirit. It is, as all spiritual practices tend ultimately to be, essentially lonely and one must be scrupulous in determining when the guidance is coming from Spirit and when it is simply one's own voice and mind in disguise. I/We must be able to distinguish, in each moment, the difference between mass hysteria and real enthusiasm, between being full of oneself and being full of God. To worship or serve Spirit is to try to model one's behavior according to Spirit's nature. We do not pray to Spirit so that our needs may be met, our prayers answered, our desires fulfilled. We pray to Spirit so that we may be given the means to serve Spirit well and so we may model our lives and shape our hearts around the configurations of the Divine.

I was not called to the way of the water spirits in the manner of Augustine. Though I have been in close alliance with him and though my husband has yielded to Augustine's path, I have not thought of my path in these terms. It is not my path. It is another language, a foreign tongue, but beautiful, and there is much here that speaks to me deeply and has spoken to me thus my entire life. I can walk alongside it without being of it. We can engage in exchange and interchange, learning from each other, giving each other the gifts of our experiences.

What I want to say is this: Michael went to Africa and was initiated by Augustine into the way of the water spirits. I went to Africa and was initiated by Augustine but not into his tradition. Initiation does not imply doctrine or dogma. One can be initiated into a tradition and one can be initiated, that is, connected to the spirits in whatever ways they choose to appear to the initiate. A spiritual teacher must be able to discern whether a student is truly following the path that is opening before her or him. The quality and development of the teacher is essential here for he or she must be able to guide the initiate in understanding a call to a way or a tradition that is different from that of the teacher or anyone else.

*   *   *

Valerie Wolf looked for a teacher who could help her understand her dreams in their own terms, rather than from the perspective of tradition. She had made a pledge to Spirit: If Spirit would heal her young son who was going deaf from the scarring caused by repeated allergy attacks and infections, she would devote herself to a healing path. Her son began to recover. She had to keep her pledge.

What indigenous people would call a dreamer, Valerie was called by her dreams to Native American practices long before her family confirmed that this was part of her heritage. As is so common in the United States, the truth of their Native American ancestry was suppressed. Still, it was not appropriate or possible for her to become a Cherokee healer or a Nez Perce healer. Her visions were too varied, her history and heritage too diverse for her to choose one way or another. Also, it was not a tradition she was seeking, but rather the path of a healer. My task, in working with her, was to help her become that healer and to initiate her in the path of the spirits. The dreams and visions that were coming to her, the synchronicities and events that propelled her forward were all sourced in indigenous mind. I took on the work and the responsibility hoping that I could work authentically from the original place where people of all traditions meet… from a vision of essential truths of the universe toward which each path moves, albeit in its own way and language. I did not judge her experience by what I thought or believed; I have tried to follow the text of her dreams as they revealed themselves over the years. The dreams and her experience have created a little world that is coherent in its own right; it is our task to discover the intricacy of its nature and laws. We knew that we were understanding what was being revealed when the implications of these dreams, the practices and knowledge were useful to others, when Valerie, based on what she was being taught, was able to diagnose and treat those who were ill but who didn't necessarily share her world view. She was being given a worldview that was deeply related to the worldview of her ancestors, though often different ancestors or spirits come to her in her dreams, teaching her what she needs to know for any given situation. They do not necessarily impart the particulars of their tradition but the tradition inflects the teachings so that they are specific and exact. When the Ndebele grandmothers appear she knows she is being invited to a deeper relationship with the ancestors. When the Nez Perce spirits appear she is being invited to focus upon dreaming or to adopt a greater rigor and discipline regarding her practice. Who comes to her are the wise ones and each of the teachers and traditions has something else to teach her appropriate to the moment they appear. She is not being asked to live her life like her ancestors or to convert anyone else to this way. She has been given a path that has integrity for her as a healer. It is her own path, informed though it is by others. My task is to help her discern, outside of dogmatism and personal preference, the path that is being revealed.

A series of dreams. Dreams of world disasters. Gatherings of crows followed by deaths in the family or the community. Friends suffering pain or diseases before the events. Animal deaths. Dreams of being bitten or attacked by lions, snakes, bees. Environmental destruction. War against Afghanistan before it happened.

"How do I bear these dreams?" she asks. "Why do I dream these events? Why know what is going to happen, who will suffer, who will die if there is nothing I can do about it, if I don't even know until later to whom this suffering belongs?"

"To learn the way of the mind of the ancestors," I answer. "To begin to fathom the nature of the universe in which such knowledge comes to a member of the tribe. To know what it means to bear witness. To know the nature and range of suffering of all the members of the community, so that when it is possible to act, you will be acting within a context, you will act from wisdom and compassion."

*　　*　　*

Psychologist Diane Broderick was tracing the history of how she became a healer. Not her academic training or experience but the sense she had from the time she was a child that Spirit had marked her for a special relationship. In many countries, one of the sons is often given to the Church as one of the daughters may be marked to take care of the parents or to serve the Church as a nun. The question I had asked was this: If you had been born into a tribal society that read the signs and marks that surround a child, how would the community have known that you were destined to serve the spirits?

"I was born with a heart on my face," she remembered, realizing for the first time that in another culture such a mark would have been noted and treated with respect. "When I was a child, I wanted to go to Mass every morning. My mother refused to take me but I said I would go myself. I did. Every morning I awakened early and attended Mass before I went to school. It did not matter if it was blazing hot or if there were four feet of snow on the ground, I was called out.

"As I was walking to school by myself one day, I saw a vision of the Virgin Mary and fell down in a faint. As I was going to Catholic School, there was no one to tell; the nuns would not have been pleased to hear of such a revelation. I forgot this sequence of events until now."

In the wisdom traditions, the elders are alert to the signs that a child has been marked by the gods. Such a child is considered precious to the community. Had Diane been born into another kind of society, the elders surrounding her would have been careful to provide the education and training that would support and embellish her heart. She would not have had to fight so hard to find appropriate forms that would carry her loving in the world.

When a holy person dies in the tradition of Tibetan Buddhism, a monk is designated to search out the child who is the reincarnation of that holy person. When they came upon the child who was raised to be the present Dalai Lama, he was just a toddler. The little boy reached out to the vajra which had belonged to the deceased Dalai Lama and said, "That is mine."

Patricia Langer was born with a caul over her head. Such a sign is considered fortunate by those who follow Spirit and a curse by many fundamentalists. Patricia also has what is called second sight or what African Americans call "four eyes." When, as a young child, she observed that her aunt was pregnant before anyone knew about this, her grandmother had a Mass said in order to save Patricia's soul. But neighborhood people also visited her grandmother for healing and the woman secretly relied on Patricia for assistance with diagnoses but without acknowledging or respecting Patricia's gift. A photographer who can reveal the spirit of the land and an extraordinary healer and teacher, someone who can see into the body and the soul, Patricia has suffered for years from society's disdain and fear of her gifts.

*   *   *

It is the task of the orthodox to honor and preserve the traditions exactly. This is so the community has the teachings, their meanings and practices in a pure form. If no one remembers the wisdom ways that have developed over the centuries, we will be completely lost. We will not recognize an ethical path and we will not know how to meet the Divine. Orthodoxy is conservation. The great orthodox teachers are adepts who are devoted to the ways and meanings of the exoteric and the esoteric. They meet the moment through holding and interpreting scripture, liturgy, and lineage. Their teachings are based upon what has gone before and their task is to preserve continuity. They often mediate between earth and heaven, teach us how to honor the soul and live in community and, finally, how to prepare for our death.

It is the task of other teachers to cut a new path to the Divine and to refresh the sacred life. When religious observance becomes rote, as happens regularly, individuals seeking God or the Divine set out on their own. These seekers may seek out an established path other than the one to which they were born and or they may find themselves alone in the wilderness. For many the wilderness is exactly the place to find God because it is, by its nature, free of the presence and dogma of human beings. Still, the wilderness is by its nature unexplored and also wild. How does one walk within it? In the wilderness one can easily be overwhelmed with signs and portents. Spirit does speak to us but we easily mistake our own desires and hopes for signs. If we want something inordinately and the wanting creates a path, we often think that this is a Call, while often it is not. The unconventional guide has the charge of scrutinizing every revelation to be certain that it is substantial and then to help the student find the meanings and worldview that fold the signs, their nature and content, into what becomes a coherent but individual cosmology/theology. And as it can be said that most mystical and spiritual traditions, at their core, share some basic assumptions and understanding about the ways to come to and the ways one serves Spirit, so it is assumed that there will be resonance between the individual path and the long established traditions of visions and revelation. We follow different paths up the same mountain; we speak different languages for the same acts of submission to holy service and praising God.

When one's spiritual life is unconventional, one faces the difficult task of finding the ritual gestures and practices that accord with what has been revealed. Then one proceeds in her lonely way without making these into dogma for oneself or others. If one follows the second path, it is not only useful to have a teacher but, I think, essential to be deeply informed and educated, to have worked seriously within another spiritual practice or religious training prior to initiation so that one has some understanding of the spiritual life, an ethical foundation, and the means to evaluate the nature of one's experience. As in every practice, religious or spiritual, it is essential for every practitioner to step away from the smaller passions and desires of the self, to differentiate the call of Spirit from the thrall of ego. This is at the core of all religious and spiritual work.

We do not have to reinvent the wheel here. It is best to yield to the ways of accomplishing this that have been perfected over the centuries. Buddhism and other forms of meditation and contemplation provide practices to differentiate the ego from the Self in the act of opening the heart to the recognition of the intrinsic relationship of all things – or "interbeing" as Thich Nhat Hanh speaks of it. Whatever dreams and visions came to me or to Valerie, they did not replace, but actually required, the most simple, most essential act of sitting in meditation and contemplation and trying to understand the teachings regarding compassion that have been revealed and refined over centuries.

*   *   *

We need a break. A little humor. Lightness around the heart. A joke here. Or two. Laughter. Teaching stories.

In the pew before the altar in the church, or in a seat before the ark in the temple, or with his head on the prayer rug facing east in the mosque, or climbing a steep mountain, a man is praying and weeping, berating himself. "Dear God, I am nothing. Nothing. Dear God, I am nothing."

Behind him, two people overhear his seeming anguish. "Look," one says to the other, "at who thinks he's nothing."

And this story:

The abbot or abbess, the roshi or rimpoche, the rabbi, one or another priest, priestess, minister, or great teacher of a religious or spiritual congregation is brokenhearted because the community has fallen away from services and the religious life. She sees the ennui and dispiritedness that has overcome the people but she is unable to remedy it. Deeply concerned, she consults a friend who carries equal responsibility in her own religious community. The Rabbi tells her friend the Abbess that she doesn't know what to advise her. "Such are modern times. Our communities have drifted away. But there is one thing I can say: Know that the Messiah is among you."

Astonished and confused, the Abbess returns to her abbey and calls the nuns and lay practitioners to a meeting. She repeats the conversation she had with the Rabbi and looks each person in the eye. "I know this," the Abbess says, "I am not the one who is the Messiah. I am too ambitious for our community. And you know that I am often strict and impatient where it would be far better to be compassionate. Sadly, I have not developed the heart that the Messiah would carry. I am not the one."

Then each person scrutinized her heart and spoke in turn. No one claimed the honor though each would probably have acquiesced, if absolutely required, to take on such a burden. This one was too lazy. This one was too greedy. This one had lustful thoughts. This one only wanted to be in solitude. This one was too angry with people and their needs and faults.

"We do not know who it is, but as I trust the Rabbi, it is clear that we must act as if what she said is true and so we must treat each other accordingly, as if any one of us might be the one," the Abbess responded.

And so they did, seeing what was holy and good in everyone while being generous and understanding about what they now perceived as inevitable and appropriate human flaws. The new sweetness and respect between them was deeply attractive to the people in the community. It was a great pleasure to be among the members of the abbey. People came from afar for the experience of holy tenderness. And so it was that the sacred community was restored. As for the Messiah... well, perhaps the Messiah is the awakened community caring for each other.

*   *   *

These are somehow the same story. Do you see? These stories are shaped around the 0 of nothingness. And what fills this 0? The substance that fills nothingness. Form and Emptiness. The intrinsic complexity and multidimensionality of a true story – the entire universe compressed into a point – means that it can never be told once or one way, but that by its nature it requires translation into a thousand, thousand variations and explorations until its zero entirety is approached.

Faith &
Belief

*   *   *

There is such a great difference between the life that emerges from belief and faith and the life one lives without belief and without faith. Still, belief and faith cannot be made imperatives. One may try to live the life that would be lived if one had faith, but still this is not the same as the life of faith. That is, the life that is lived spontaneously within a dialogue and interchange with Spirit. And there it is. There is nothing we can do. Belief and faith cannot be willed. But when the spirits come forth, one enters into another paradigm. When they truly come forth, it becomes impossible not to acknowledge their existence. One may try. It often seems too great a stretch from what we consider to be ordinary reality to the world in which they appear in their own way, in their own forms, in their own time. Sometimes one hopes one is mad or benighted – as protection from an overwhelming and incomprehensible reality into which one is being ineluctably drawn. But after a while one cannot pretend that the spirits are not with one. There is no other logical or rational explanation for the mystifying events around one but the irrefutable existence of Spirit. And then when one sees that their appearance only carries goodness and this goodness is extended to all beings, then one has no choice except to yield. Except to express gratitude. This is the moment when one is graced with belief and faith. A belief and a faith based on one's own undeniable experience.

Journal entry, July 1998:
Nora Jamieson asked, "You are enjoining us to walk with great care noticing all the signs, omens and auguries, attentive to

symbols and synchronicities, to the manifestations of the natural world, to dreams, to memories, but you have also said that we need to be careful not to overemphasize the signs, not to be caught by them."

At first it seems to me that the signs are simply that, signs. Signs that there is an intelligence and extraordinary consciousness in the universe and that it is addressing us personally. At first, we think we are mad. Then we find ourselves incapable of refuting the revelation of Spirit. Ultimately, we yield to it. There is a Call and we are trying to understand it in order to respond.

We are trying to understand. Now we must try to understand the signs. How is Spirit speaking to us? What is the language or languages Spirit has chosen in order to converse with us? Some people are trance-possessed, others are visited by animals, some can understand the cards or the stars, others have dreams and/or visions. Books fly off the shelves, announcements arrive in the mail at exactly the right time, the phone rings and our lives can turn upside down if we allow it. This stage is learning the language.

Now we try to follow the signs. Again we have to be attentive. Are we understanding? Are we following or initiating? Are we inventing through our interpretations, are we using signs to assert and justify our own will or are we yielding?

Another period of caution. At this point we can be dazzled. We use the signs to establish ourselves as worthy or important. The signs are subsumed into the service of our ego.

No one escapes this humiliation.

Afterwards, we begin again. We try to follow the signs, paying attention to the language and the sequence in order to fathom their particular meaning, testing the consequences against the good of the world. These events are not on our own behalf; these events are to guide us on behalf of the community outside ourselves. On behalf of the natural world, on behalf of others, on behalf of Spirit.

Now we can walk without paying so much attention to the signs but following the road, being attentive to the work that is required, to the way it is enacted. This journey can last a long time. It can last a lifetime.

But sometimes we yearn for the signs again. Because we are lonely. Because we have been so involved in doing what we hope is God's work, we have come to miss God. And as we cannot experience God directly, we look for the signs, we yearn for the signs, we are bereft without the signs.

Without the signs we find ourselves in the dark night of the soul. This is where I think I am now.

In this place, there can be signs. Michael and I were returning from the first council of Elders at Ojai. We intended to stop at the beach we knew but no matter how we tried to get there, we were prohibited. No parking places, people, police everywhere, no privacy, no solitude. Dismayed we went on and then, unexpectedly, were able to park beside a lonely promontory overlooking the water just as the sun was going down behind a huge rock. The light on the water broke into a thousand colors so that the sea came forth in pale colors, bronze, copper, silver, gold, aluminum. Yet we saw that the sea was a single entity formed through the energy between the particles, not the particles themselves, the way Spirit is and inhabits the space between.

We watched for a long time, unaffected by cold, standing, or hunger, until the light vanished and it was sea again, only the sea. I thought we had been brought here. Exactly at this fleeting moment. To see this. A gift from the universe. A way of saying: We were there with you. Because of this, we brought you here so that you would know.

Such extraordinary signs but sometimes I am unable to take them in, to believe in my own perceptions. Our peoples have read the signs for thousands of years, but when we return to this script, this scripture, we are afraid that we are inflated or deluded.

M. and I were walking on the Mogollon Rim in Arizona. I was distracted by my own emptiness and distress. Try to look for signs, I advised myself and my eyes fell on a perfect circle of lichen upon the pale green rocks, and then another and then another. A narrow gray weathered trunk of a tree, sheared perhaps by lightning and so standing there like an erect bear or wolf guarding the entrance to the underworld.

Speaking then of how I have of late been attracted to the old ones, the rhinos and the elephants, we came upon a branch coiled about a knot in the wood forming the elephant's eye and descending into a graceful trunk.

Is it a worthy occupation for someone to spend her lifetime learning to read such signs the way her foreparents read them, the way some peoples sequestered from our censure still read them?

As I write, thunder, rain, and hail. Is this a sign? Perhaps for someone. For me, in this moment, it is just pure joy. I gather a small dish of hailstones and bring it as a gift to Michael who after eight years of preparation has begun writing his book.

5

I am trying to see if I was ever called by the water spirits, to see and understand Augustine's perspective and that of the tradition from which he comes. It behooves me/us to attend the original wisdom that western culture has systematically undermined. But my mind does not grasp it entirely and I encounter skepticism in myself where I would like to meet openness. So I proceed the way that I know which is the way of story. I look for the story not as I have told it ad infinitum, but as it might have been configured, only I didn't notice. To tell a story, you bring the elements together in a new way. You look to the bits and pieces that you haven't considered relevant before. You bring the elements and the raw materials and the small details, the quiet moments, what is visible peripherally together. You align events and images that were previously disconnected and then you see what you have and what is revealed.

I was born by the sea and until I was grown and left New York, I walked alone every night along the shoreline, pacing myself to the thunder of the waves breaking in the Atlantic. If there is anything that characterized me particularly as a child and adolescent, it was this quiet routine. But also I never thought about it. It was not a prominent element of my identity and yet it was at the core of my being. If you had asked me about myself, I never would have mentioned it. What I was conscious of then was this: I wanted to be a writer and I thought that writers knew how to walk. And so it behooved me to learn how to walk. But I would not have told you that I felt compelled to come to the sea each night, or how I knew that the writer walked by the sea. I would not have had the words then to explain that I immediately connected to writers who also walked by the sea. That is why I was intrigued by Eugene O'Neill and later when I came across his work,

Pablo Neruda, not only for his poetry but because he lived and walked in Isla Negra.

> Pablo Neruda, I introduce myself as the one who is behind you. I sleep under your feet and walk where you walked. Perhaps I walked to Chile, for since I learned your name, I could do nothing but walk after you. After I read your poems, I walked in my sleep.
>
> In Chile, I pursued you. When you took walks, I followed you to know how a poet walks ....[26]

When I came to Los Angeles to be married to my first husband, we found an apartment that looked directly onto the Pacific. Home alone many nights because he was a medical resident, I sat by the sea and listened to the waves breaking hour after hour. I did not know I was being shaped by unseen intelligences. I did not know that I had come out of such salty minds. These are my origins. But we rarely recognize the story being configured as we are living it. Only recently did I understand enough to write:

> The dolphin journeyed past us in dark and secret arcs. They possessed me on a beach of shells, sands of holy dead. The dolphin took me without breaking the water, without a gesture or a word. The dolphin came and I sent two women out in a canoe and someone pushed me into it. It was night. The current took us. We saw nothing. Then we did see something. A sleek black fin. Around us the soughing of breath. The sea absolutely still and breathing but for an occasional slap of belly against salt. And a black fin endlessly turning and the soughing of breath from the deep.

When the dolphin came, I was teaching at the sea of Cortez alongside Beverly Antaeus, or Hawk, who joined us this year in Africa. Master canoeist, adept of the rivers and waters, Hawk found, some years ago, that she was in need of a vision quest. She wanted to do it under someone's tutelage, but I suggested, actually, I insisted, that she go out on the river alone. She chose the White River in Colorado and Utah and set out with her dog, at a time when the river was traditionally calm. Paddling along, she came upon a spit of land that was ideal for a camp site. She made her way toward it but the dog became so wild and uncontrollable that she had to proceed elsewhere. She made camp that night at a less hospitable place.

It was not very accommodating and just as she finished preparing the site, an unexpected wind came up as the sky turned black. Within minutes she was in the midst of an unseasonable and unprecedented hurricane. Twenty-four hours it raged while she wept and prayed, broken by the power of the natural world and the power of God. A power one doesn't fully recognize when one is so capable, so skillful in navigating the rapids of all sorts. This was not negotiable. She was fully in the hands of the great powers. Then it was over. She finished her journey and when she made her way back, she passed the sand spit where she had wanted to disembark. It had been devastated by flood waters. Had the dog not prevented her from disembarking there, they would have surely drowned.

Of all the wisdom I have gained from Hawk, which is considerable, there is one teaching that has entered most deeply: when you are navigating a difficult segment of a river, you do not focus on the obstacles or you will capsize. You concentrate on the way through and that perspective will guide you to safety.

*　　*　　*

There have been moments in my life when I have been compelled to solitude. Not drawn to it, but compelled by it. The necessity to enter that ordeal has always come upon me unawares and I have not known how to explain it. I followed it, though it was difficult to do as a woman of my background. It was not wonderful. But it was not resistible either. I could, as I think of it now, tell my life in terms of these repeated forays into the solitary life. Those moments of solitude that seemed most authentic, those that reached most deeply into the core of silence when I was a young woman were always at the sea.

Today I walk the dunes. Tomorrow, I return to find my own tracks and follow them again. A friend says, "Your journey is going home again." At dawn the dunes say, "No one has been here before." Everything disappeared as a man might into your hair.

I am wandering down to water. I was born by the sea, but my father was not a sailor. I do not know how to live out in my hand what comes to me in storms. These days, I have had to learn north and bitter and fjord.[27]

As I write these words and meditate upon their possible meanings and implications, I understand how much my life has been a struggle between the expectations of family, my upbringing, education and culture as opposed to the call and understanding of my soul. (Not the expectations of these times but the demand of these times. This distinction seems important to note.) My soul has summoned me to ways of being and knowing that are alien to the sensibility of modern life, but that are indigenous to the planet where we live. I have never understood this before. I have sometimes approached these words, but I have never understood them fully. A call to the elements. To the elementals. To the sea. A call that always came with words that I found fearsome and yet overpowering – ordeal, rigor, fierce. Wet and cold words. Not my choice, but perhaps my destiny. The call of Spirit. The advent of the spirits in the ways they chose to appear to me in the beginning.

We are born here in order to know *here*, not only in order to know ourselves, not only in order to know each other. We are born to a place. We think we are born to a family or to a culture, to a religion, a race or a vocation, but we are born to a place that we cohabit with other creatures with whom we are interdependent; we are of each other. If we alter that place beyond recognition, if we build over the place until it is unseen and mute, if we destroy the place, if we kill the creatures of the place, if we poison the place, if we bomb the place to dust, then we have destroyed the essence of what we have been born to. Then we are no longer ourselves. We are monstrous then. But we do not know it. We do not know that what was holy in us has ceased to exist. We are born to a place and we die to a place. I did not know this when I was young. No one I knew knew this. Very few know this now. Very few know it well enough to change everything in their lives.

Tuesday, October 2, 2001, 1:00 a.m. The news is bad. It looks like we are planning to invade Afghanistan. The inner voices advise me not to let an invasion distract me/us from the work required to change our lives so that we do not continue to be part of a war machine.

*   *   *

Zimbabwe, bloodily carved out of that portion of the British Empire once called Rhodesia, is a landlocked country. Though devoted to the *Njuzu*, the water spirits, Augustine only saw the sea once when Richard Kimble took him to Cape Town where Augustine entered the freezing waters, embracing the waves for hours. Simakuhle had never seen the sea.

It was also for this reason that, after the North Americans left, Michael and I took Augustine and Simakuhle to the Sinai Peninsula. First we climbed Sinai, the holy mountain, and then we went to the Red Sea where Augustine and Simakuhle stayed for hours, heads bowed to view the various schools of fish in the translucent turquoise and emerald pools nested within the cobalt waters alongside the coral reef.

We were among the sacred stones that had become liquid for the sake of the sea creatures who had been given the life of swimming within beauty. The sand at the shore was white and the stones dark and musical in the tide. But a hundred yards from the pool and the hotel in both directions, there was a long line of seaweed and shells twined into plastic, bags, ropes, fishing lines, utensils and myriad bottles and aluminum cans. After I saw this, I could no longer go in the water. I wanted to go back to the hotel room, but I looked to the water and said belligerently, "Ok, if there is a large plastic bag, I will clean the beach." And there it was. One of those simple miracles. A huge black bag, larger than any I had every seen, 5 feet by 3 feet, at the least. It had apparently blown down from the houses or washed up in the tide. Reflectively, I gathered what I could so as to restore the beach. The bag was exactly large enough to clear everything between where I was standing and the entrance to the hotel.

Cleaning the beach, I was reminded of the visit I made to Tepotzlan in Mexico when Morena Monteforte was dying. One afternoon, overcome with imminent loss, I wandered out into the fields by a stream alongside the house. This village nestled into the mountain is beautiful but if you walk any distance you are overwhelmed with garbage. This once pristine enclave in the mountains is as besmirched by modern life as is every other place of beauty on the planet, including Antarctica. I came back to the house, took plastic bags from under the sink and went out to clear the stream and its environs. It was the offering I made to the gods so that Morena would either live or have a good death. I was thinking, particularly, of Hekate, the crone who stands in the birth chamber and by the deathbed. Traditionally, the offering that was brought to Hekate where three roads meet – at the tri-via – was garbage. This mystified me for many years until I realized that before modern times garbage was compost. The garbage that one brought would decompose and become soil and the new would come from it. This exactly described the cyclical aspect of the triple goddess. When I called a few weeks later, her step-mother told me that Morena had had a good death. I had made the right offering, I thought, to the right spirit.

Morena was the daughter of a prominent Guatemalan novelist and a Tzutuhil Mayan woman. Raised by her father's mother, Morena did not meet her mother until she was in her thirties when she traveled to her village, San Pedro de Laguna on Lake Atitlan. There her mother greeted her by showing her the hammock that had been reserved for her all those years. "Where have you been, *hija*?"

Some years later, I also traveled to San Pedro de Laguna with Morena, Michael and our dear friend Victor Perera who was investigating the military operations against the Indians in the area. A devout Catholic, her mother, who could not speak about either the military or the guerillas, told us all the prohibited village stories about the maligned *curandero* tradition and then, as if it were not against the Church, she let us do a healing for her to relieve the pain of her kidneys. It was an extraordinary moment, when I, a white urban woman was working alongside a Guatemalan woman in her mother's village, both running our hands tenderly along her mother's body. Perhaps without this intervention, Morena might never have touched her mother but now the woman who had not been permitted to raise her daughter was lying back in her daughter's arms. But that is another story, as is the connection or alliance between Morena, Victor and myself; another story that intersects this story and the Kogi story, enhances them and may be told at another time. I had not expected when I was the young teacher and Morena was one of my students, twenty years earlier, that there would come a time when I would be called to meet these various faces of God, in order to serve and heal the ones I have been given to love.

*   *   *

After my own mother died in December 1996, I wrote these words:

....
You must weep
from your own body
that which will wash
your own life
and reduce it to grains
of sand, glimmers,
brief and eternal lights.

By the time
you have finished weeping,
you will be dissolved
into the waters of life
which sustain us....[28]

*   *   *

Speaking of the sacred Hebrew letters, Yitzchak Ginsburgh writes that Mem ⵁ is the fountain of divine wisdom, is the waters of the fountain that ascend from their unknown underground source and it is also the waters of the fountain that flow down from above.[29] This is the same Rabbi Ginsburgh who lauds Baruch Goldstein who massacred 29 Palestinians, on Purim, February 24th, 1994, who had come to pray at the Tomb of the Patriarchs in Hebron during Ramadan. Benjamin Netanyahu, when Prime Minister of Israel, had him detained because his response to the massacre was inflammatory. How can these two seemingly opposing visions live within the same man? Is this not the dilemma of our time?

But now we return to the sacred waters to see if we can enter them as we are being called to do. We enter certain waters without being affected by them. But other waters transform us entirely. What makes the water sacred? Is it the ritual that we do? Is it our intent? Is it what we are willing to see and yield to?

Even though it is such a struggle to yield to it, when the sacred comes to us, it is not to give us power, it is so we can serve it. When we are in the domain of the water spirits, they do not empower us, rather, they break us down as they penetrate us. Then if we are fortunate, we serve the spirit that has entered us with a joyous heart.

*   *   *

One of accomplishments of the *Nganga* Project that Michael initiated was to buy a farm for the African Daré some twenty miles outside of Bulawayo. Recognizing that colonization had undermined the peoples' ability to support themselves, the *Nganga* Project is committed to sustainability. Serafina Farm is situated on an aquifer so even when there is drought there will be water for the corn, so there will always be *sadza*, vegetables, eggs and goat milk. In time there will be fruit on the trees. You bore a hole deep into the earth and then the water seeps up from the subterranean stream. This is all one needs to live. This piece of land and the waters beneath it. Andra Akers thinks the next wars will be fought over water. If she is right there will be other wars after this war for oil. But I am distracted by the moment and must turn back to this work. We know now that in one of the world's poorest countries, Augustine, his family and the community will be protected from starvation. There will be enough to eat even considering what must be shared with the monkeys who also inhabit the land.

Almost two years ago, the Serafina Trust took title to the land and Augustine became a farmer. Such land, so abundant in water, had always been owned by white settlers in what was once Rhodesia. Squatters, who were taking possession of the farm next door, made moves toward this farm but Augustine was able to have them relocated elsewhere. Augustine's white neighbor, with his small holding who shares water with Augustine when the pumps break down, was simultaneously protected from takeover. The monkeys stay and share the corn but the squatters leave. The squatters are the veterans of the war for independence in which Augustine also participated. Now Serafina Farm belongs to this black man and his community but not to the other black men and their communities. Still, thirty years ago this could not have been imagined. Some of those white settlers who took the land from its original inhabitants have had the land taken back from them. Augustine did not take the land, it was purchased for him with money from The *Nganga* Project. Michael, tracing his ancestry back, discovered he comes from a clan of slave owners. I was told by a black friend that her relatives spoke of their Jewish lineage from the slave owners in Louisiana. I had thought I was free from this karma, but it is not true. We are all being called to the scrutiny of our own lives and those of our ancestors. It is time to make amends. This belongs to the realm of the healer as much as his or her training. Righting this wrong was not our primary motivation, but purchasing the farm was an offering to justice.

The question of justice is complex. When the Europeans colonized Africa they not only made war on the native peoples, taking their territory and undermining their cultures and lives, they also made war on the land and the animals. The land war against the animals still exists because colonization has made it impossible for the native peoples to return to a way of life that is harmonious with the natural world. The elephants, for example, cannot migrate freely across the ancient routes that accord with the two hundred year cycle of trees devoured and trees restored. In times of drought, elephants dig water holes with their trunks when the familiar sites have dried up but they need to be able to move across the land to the aquifers and, as things are, they cannot always do so. They are confined to preserves or areas that do not entirely encompass their ancient nomadic routes. If the ways are blocked or the ponds are not artificially maintained, they die.

Not every government has the economic means to protect and sustain the animals; most African governments do not have the means to protect and sustain their people. Tourism is an incentive but the income is needed to restore the society that colonialism destroyed; it is not sufficient to restore the natural world so that all the animals will thrive. The governments that have been established are based on western models; they have no choice about this. Shumba, a friend, neighbor and initiate of Augustine is a career officer in the Zimbabwean military. He served in the peace-keeping force in Somalia. One day, speaking to Michael of his experiences there, he focused on the difficulties that occurred when the Americans arrived. "Westerners," he said grimly, "do not believe Africans can solve their own problems, so…" The implication was that the West was implicated in both the creation and the intensification of various crises.

It is easy to say there are too many monkeys or too many elephants or too many people. Simakuhle is the mother of eleven children. Between she and Augustine they have fifteen children. In a country so devastated by AIDS that 25% of the adult population is infected and the life expectancy has dropped to 30 years, birth control cannot be a serious consideration. In a continent ravaged by drought, famine, and endless wars and pogroms, limiting the population is not the main concern of the humans. Raising the children to know the spirits and to be generous to the community is perhaps Augustine's and Simakuhle's essential work. Still, it happens often that there are too many monkeys, elephants and people for a particular place. Or for this planet. But who is to say which beings or species or individuals are to be sacrificed so others can live, and which others are to be sustained? When the ecologies of the natural world and the societies were altered by colonization, these issues were not considered. When the Europeans left rather than live under black rule, they did not take these dilemmas with them, nor did they restore the country to its original pristine condition, nor did they give up their influence or their involvement with the economic life of the country, nor did they return the resources they had withdrawn over the decades, nor did they stop withdrawing the value of the country that is in the hands of corporations. Now the people are forced to live according to European and American standards even though they do not have the means or infrastructure to do so. Poverty and desperation is endemic and seemingly incurable. And this terrible fate is shared by the animals and all living creatures.

On one of the last days in Zimbabwe, we met with a contractor that we were introduced to in Masvingo on September 11th and then, met mysteriously when we were driving down the road in Bulawayo, the second largest city in Zimbabwe. He has now dug a well in the backyard of Augustine's Bulawayo house. Augustine, at least, has land and water now. We sustain the healer and he sustains the community.

*   *   *

We have all gathered by the little pool in which Augustine does immersion rituals. Next to it is the sweat lodge and nearby a fire pit where the stones are heated. Augustine has just finished offering each person herbs, which he himself gathered in the bush to smoke. Matthew, two and a half years old, who has been helping Augustine by passing the "cigars" that Augustine has been making from herbs and brown paper to the people who will go into the sweat, places one against the coals to light it for himself. Then he and his older brother Mosie, age three, smoke the herbs. I look to Augustine who laughs at my concern. Everyone around me is watching the children who have learned caution, skill and the sacred from their elders.

Be with me in this moment. Try not to retreat into your certainties and the presumption that you know something about child rearing that these people may not know. I say this because the entire time that I was in Africa, I found myself being "busted." Spirit busted me as I saw again and again the ways I presumed I knew something that others didn't know. Hubris and arrogance are endemic to westerners. The presumptions of western education and values and development, blah blah blah! Sitting in meditation, the Zen student gestures for the Roshi to hit her or him across the shoulder with his stick, *kyosaku*, so that she can wake up. Imperialism and colonization are based on the presumption of superiority: intellectual, moral, emotional and spiritual. We were wrong. From the very beginning, we were wrong. Let's look in the mirror and wake up.

Simakuhle's and Augustine's children deport themselves with astonishing maturity. I watch my reflex to interfere because direct supervision seems absent. I missed the fact that in African and indigenous societies, the older children properly and expertly raise the younger ones. This means that Israel, who is six, is quite alert to the needs of Mosie who is three, who in turn looks out for Matthew. As an American woman, I arrogantly think I know something despite the fact that these children are not suffering what children in our country suffer all the time. They are not selfish or spoiled. They can make entertainment out of anything. I have watched them turn a piece of silver foil, the wrapping from a candy, into a toy they share for hours. They are exceedingly helpful, intuitive and intelligent. They are not violent. They are generous, kind and cooperative. They all carry artistic gifts. From about the age of two they participate fully in the life of the community; this means that they assist with the domestic and spiritual work as well as receive from it. They are not exploited because such work is not the dreary, enervating soul and body destroying labor of industrialized and colonialized nations. This work is life giving. They are the children we wish to raise but have not.

There is an anguished cry from an adult in the water who has been brought to facing her many demons and afflictions. Augustine goes to attend her while Tenashi, his sixteen-year-old son, steps in and begins drumming. Israel and Bekkhe look up, alert, ready to assist. Israel, age seven, may also drum, quite competently, if needed. And when he drums, it is to the cheers and encouragement of his older brothers and the community. Simakuhle, who is sitting nearby on a brightly patterned zambia, that serves alternately as skirt, apron, ground cloth, wrapping, begins singing to Maria, the great mother, the water spirit, the Queen, the compassionate one.

Saturday is always Daré at Augustine's house, as people don't work they can come for healing and initiation. Augustine was doing the preliminary work of initiating the African visitors and the North American visitors at the same time. He had done the rites of purification and now they would enter the sacred pool and the sweat lodge. Earlier Michael and I worked with several of the visitors, and the North American women had been doing energy work, drumming, rattling, praying. Elenna Rubin Goodman and Barbara Borden, who were with the first group that had come to Zimbabwe in August 2001, were waiting to enter the water and had been in conversation with a group of African women about their lives. There was a commotion in the courtyard as a taxi arrived with an old man. Though a taxi is a great expense, a family who had come for Daré had sent one for the grandfather. He would never have believed that "white people carry spirits," the family said, if he did not see it with his own eyes.

*   *   *

We are called in many ways. The call goes out and often we do not respond as we do not recognize it. It passes us by. Another call comes. We answer or don't answer. And then again. Sometimes we answer but the full implication of what is occurring does not become clear for months or years. We may respond to different calls – we may think of them as passions or opportunities. They begin to coalesce. We see a pattern. We begin to wonder who we are that we should be woven into such a pattern. Then, perhaps, we understand that Spirit is weaving a web.

Here is the contradiction. The pattern is only a means through which we are called. And the pattern is specific and relevant to who we are, the work that needs to be done, the reality of the world and the nature of Spirit. Both are true at the same time.

my call to Peru

✱

Here is another contradiction. We want nothing more than to be called by Spirit and when it occurs, we are terrified and turn away. Being called by Spirit is being called home; we feel it in our hearts. A great sigh of relief echoes through our lives. We have been called, finally, and it is good. But also, we know that we are being called away from everything we have thought and believed. We were not living in a world in harmony with Spirit. We say it outright: Render unto Caesar what belongs to Caesar and render unto God what belongs to God. We hope there is no conflict, but, it is everywhere. And as the allegiance is to Caesar first and as we are not dismayed by this contradiction, being called by Spirit is often experienced as being called away from home.

I was called to the animals but that does not tell it. I was called by the ordeal of cancer – that is insufficient to describe it. I was called into the heart but that does not describe it. I was called by light and dreams, by texts offered to me I could not possibly have written myself, by coincidences and synchronicities, by grief and by illness. By a frightening but increasing ability to see a pattern cohering around someone, to see the story they were living, the holes in the story, the meaning of the story, to see into the heart, to see into the body-politic the way some healers can see into the body to see the disease hiding there. I was called by ordeal and by joy, by great loneliness in the midst of community, by knowing and by not-knowing, by the known and the unknowable, by what was visible and by the invisibles. All of these impinging until it was impossible to assume that these were the chance occurrences or isolated gifts of my own life. The reality of elsewhere became clear. The reality of Spirit undeniable. I was called and I answered. But even so, I was, as Augustine had been, as so many of us have been, anguished by what I had to turn away from in order to answer the call.

Being called to Spirit has meant that I must re-examine, step away from, perhaps even renounce my history, my tradition, the values and understanding of my culture, the assumptions and activities of my country. As Augustine had to renounce so much of Christianity, I may also have to renounce so much of Judaism, western culture and America. The violence of the Old Testament. The violence in the New Testament, Revelations in particular. The doctrine of original sin. The history of Christian violence against "the infidels" and the violence of contemporary Israel. The presumptions that these are the true ways. The only true ways. America's assumption of superiority and the world-threatening remnants of manifest destiny. We have become so dangerous.

Spirit requires us to examine what has been revealed by Spirit as opposed to what has been contrived and proselytized by men. It insists that we face the distortions and lies that have become the infallible texts of belief. It means that we must question and rebuke many of the highest and most powerful authorities; it means that we must scrutinize our own affiliations and identifications to see how we may profit illegitimately from what we hold dear. For me it means separating violence from wisdom, self-interest from compassion. It means stepping away from the delusion that there are chosen ones, that God has revealed God's self to one people but not another, that a book can be holy and still advocate violence of one people against another people, that the needs of one country supercede the needs of any other country, that we are right and the others are wrong, that we are God's people and they are of the devil, that the human is superior to the non-human, the male to the female, that the Jew, Christian or Muslim is superior, and that there can be holy wars.

Augustine has become interested in Judaism. Or we can say that an old interest is revived through what I have introduced about Kaballah. One day, I tell him my understanding of the meaning of Israelite. "Jacob was given the name Israel," I remind him of what he knows of the Old Testament, "after he wrestled all night with the angel or with God. Israel means 'one who wrestles with God.'" Therefore, I assume that the word Israelite does not refer to the Jews but to anyone and all who spiritually wrestle with God. Something close to radiance shines out of his face and Augustine's laughter is long and deep. For a moment, without knowing exactly what he is thinking, I am simply rocked by his joy. Then, it becomes immanently clear. He has always been outside the Old Testament and, worse, forever outside of the Chosen People. But now, he does not believe he has been disdained by God. He is also, as the spirituals insist, one of God's children. Beloved. Chosen, if he desires. Brought into the fold and the great luminous net of all beings.

Later, Fiso, whom Augustine is initiating, thanks me for this interpretation that Augustine relates to him. He confesses that he has felt intrinsically unworthy his entire life because he has assumed himself to be outside the circles of God's chosen ones. Unworthy because he is black and unworthy because he was not chosen. This is unconscionable. Once again, the wounding smite of western mind. Once again, the possibility of healing. I am so grateful. It was so simple. Irony: he feels redeemed because he no longer sees himself unworthy of and outside the tradition. Somehow I have brought him into the fold just as I am stepping away. Why do I think I must leave? Fiso's exclusion is one reason.

Seeing the ways in which Augustine has been deeply wounded by the Judeo-Christian-Islamic tradition, I am forced, yet again, to look at the scars that women carry because of these religions. Augustine's suffering is not dismissible or excusable. Neither is the suffering of women.

Writing this manuscript is one sign of stepping out of the assumption that a woman born into my tradition can never carry the official mantle of a dreamer, visionary, prophet or teacher. Women rabbis have been ordained in the last years, but it is a new phenomenon and not honored by the orthodox who claim to be the true keepers of the tradition. And no matter the progress, it is still not easily recognized that a woman can be a mystic. A woman is not expected to set out, honorably, on a path that deviates from tradition. A man is often encouraged to cut his own path to the top of the mountain. But a woman is not.

But one cannot simply walk away. There is too much wisdom in the tradition to deny it altogether. Just as Augustine believes Christ was one of the great healers, teachers and spirits, so I recognize that I have been formed by the ethical insistence at the core of Judaism and by the teachings of the mystical tradition.

This morning I select a holy letter to help me understand a dream. I did not expect to select ח Chet, the letter that speaks exactly to dreaming because it begins the word for dream, *chalom*. Jewish mystics and students of the *Zohar* recognize the dream as communication from God as we know from the story of Joseph the great dreamer and dream interpreter.

The dream is a gift for the community as well as a means of coming to know oneself. ח Chet also carries the meaning of wisdom (*chomah*) and devotion or piousness (*chasidut*), requiring individuals to apply their learning in ways that meet the rigorous ethical requirements of the soul.

"The dream is the word of the Divine, the teachings of the ancestors calling us to the Way and the sacredness of all life." [See "Invocations of the Holy Letters," Appendix IV.]

Tradition requires that we honor the lineage and what has been revealed. Healing also requires that we honor the ancestors while scrutinizing the harm that has been perpetrated. Tradition requires that we stay within it. Healing may require that we make amends, retain what is valuable and then walk a different path. Healing requires that I/we ask: What ideas implicit in my tradition, education and culture have led to the terrible circumstances that threaten to wipe out all of life? How can we step away? What new story is being revealed to us to follow that is not on the path to devastation? If we find the new story, can we be careful not to codify it? Can we try to prevent it from becoming the new dogma, the new tyranny?

* * *

In turning away from the more orthodox paths, a single word sustained me. Gnosis. I was inspired and supported by this path tangentially connected to Judaism that one could engage in a spiritual practice that allowed for individual revelation. Last night I was reading Harold Bloom and Henry Corbin on the great Sufi master, Ibn ʿArabī, who, stepping away from the narrow religionists, stepped onto a mystical path that was simultaneously traditional and individual.

> Abu'l-Barakāt. A profound and original Jewish thinker who converted to Islam toward the end of his life (d.560/1165) …. "Some souls…have learned everything from invisible guides, known only to themselves…the ancient Sages…taught that for each individual soul, or perhaps for a number of souls with the same nature and affinity, there is a being of the spiritual world, who through their existence, adopts a special solicitude and tenderness toward that soul or group of souls; it is he who initiates them into knowledge, protects, guides, defends, comforts them….it is this friend, this defender and protector, who in religious language is called the *Angel*."[30]

Tradition within tradition. One never leaves or never has to leave. The sages support one's particular path and one traces its trajectories by referencing those who have come before.

This was not my experience. The guides, the energies, the angels that are, for me, most often in the form of story, did not come forth in traditional ways. Gnosticism, then, as way but not a tradition. I looked to books to find language for what was ineffable but not to find a trodden path that I could follow. I would not have minded finding such a path. But, I couldn't ignore the one that insisted I walk, as into the wilderness. Nor can I lead anyone onto any path I have discovered. I can say that I have learned how to crawl through the brambles.

It is difficult for me to write this because I am a woman. Every sentence that a woman writes is accompanied by the ground note – do I dare? When a woman steps out of tradition, there isn't another underground or mystical tradition to sustain her. Only the vast unknown and the internalized assumption that she is a heretic and no good will come of it. Still, there is another question that I must ask myself: What has been lost because of timidity?

Barbara Myerhoff, bless her, introduced me to the ways of indigenous peoples. Fortunately I met her when we were twenty-one and twenty-two years old and not after she had left the study of Native American peoples for the Jews of Venice and the Fairfax area of Los Angeles. Without her help, I do not know how they would have found me or I them. But she opened my mind to their values and practices. Early on I recognized that these cultures had developed an understanding of the right relationship between humans, animals, the natural and spirit worlds, that was beyond any intelligence or wisdom carried by my tradition or the modern world. These people read signs. That is they are versant in the languages of Spirit. They look to the wisdom of other beings. From the beginning, I was humbled and inspired.

I had always thought that God speaks in many different voices and that there are as many paths to the Divine, as many gods, as many names for gods, as many creation stories, as many wisdom traditions as there are cultures in the world or beetles on the planet. The fact of diversity and ecological balance, the fact that the existence of the planet depends on upon it, was formative to my thinking early on and this allowed me to look for wisdom and spiritual knowledge everywhere but, particularly, in the old ways, among the marginalized and the despised. Ultimately, I began to understand that there is as much cause and necessity for all the different spiritual traditions as there is for diversity in the natural world. The loss of any tradition is as grave a loss as the loss of any species. And the dominance of any one tradition over others seriously unbalances the natural order in the way that a noxious weed can take over an ecosystem endangering all. We are dependent upon the pantheon of prayer.

Monday, October 08, 2001: Bombing. I cannot support the war that is being visited on Afghanistan.

*   *   *

To speak of the rights and possibilities of women at such a time is bitter. Michael met three women encased in burkhas, accompanied by a man in the chapel of UCLA Medical Center where he is a nurse. On the one hand, Michael had the opportunity to be very kind and respectful to people who, today, are the object of extreme fear and projection, and who are frequently, simply because of their origins, the subject of state terror. And so he reached out to them generously. But on the other hand, he had met three women who were required to walk in their own prisons and he was constrained from reaching out to them in this dilemma.

Photograph in the newspaper of an American soldier leading two captured Afghani fighters: They have been shrouded in cloth and look out through a small opening in the jail of their clothes. If the cloth did not stop mid thigh, we would think these are women in burkhas, but they are men in prison.

And here we are – these women do not have the freedom to speculate on their own path the way I do. It is a newly won freedom that my friends and colleagues and countless women and men that I do not know gave a better part of our lives struggling for, and then there are those who went before us for centuries. But at this moment, some of us, myself included, do hold it. This is a great privilege and also a responsibility, especially to see that such opportunities are extended to all women, especially to see that good comes to all beings from the use of the gifts and privileges that I have received.

I do not think it is my own longing that leads me on such a path. I think it is a history of coincidence between political concerns and spiritual revelations, between my vision of the unbearable suffering inflicted by religions and modern society and the possibilities I see for authentic and beautiful lives. Pain and beauty drew me forward and when it became clear, though I did not have the words then, that Spirit was calling me to the difficult and idio-syncratic labor of being a healer, I tried not to resist too much.

6

"How did you become a healer?" Valerie asked.

How did I become a healer?

This is how it happened. I was teaching a writing class in my home in response to a request from my dear friend, theatre director, Naomi Newman. One of the participants asked me if she could speak with me for an hour. I said, "yes." And my life changed. I stepped onto a path that I have been walking ever since.

I look back at my notes from that first class in 1976 and see that the questions I am wrestling with now were the questions that were in my mind then. How do we access the inner world? What are the false boundaries that are erected around our experience? What is the nature of prison? What is vision?

It seemed to me then that this was essential to rescue the authentic life from shackles and incarceration. I thought healing might result. I think I was right. Only now I have thirty-five years of experience to back me up.

Then I had cancer. When I had cancer, I learned how to heal from cancer. That is, I learned from cancer what healing is or might be. And I learned some possibilities about healing ourselves of cancer. Also preventing cancer. How we might do that.

How? We have to change our lives.

After I was raped, I learned what rape means. I tried to understand the etiology of rape; I tried to understand the rapist and the rape victim. I watched my own suffering and then I learned how to heal from rape.

A woman came to see me because she had learned that I had also been raped. "A man asked me for a glass of water," she said. "Everyone says that it was my fault. That I should know better."

113

It was terrible what had happened to her. The terror. His violence. The pain. All of it. Horrible. I listened to her for a long time until everything was said, everything carried together. I held her, of course. She wept. We wept. And then we wept for the glass of water. Between us, we did not know what was worse, being raped, or being unable to offer someone water.

"A woman," I said, "has a right to respond to someone who says he is thirsty. A woman has a right to give someone a glass of water." To emphasize this right, she took a secret name. She called herself Rachel. Rachel at the well. Jacob is looking for a wife and he comes to a well. He is thirsty. Rachel gives him water. In the mystical tradition, she is known as Rachel Weeping For Her Lost Children. She is called the Compassionate One. She is called the Womb of Compassion. *Rachmunas.* "Have *rachmunas*," my mother always said. "Have a heart. Be compassionate." *HaRachaman* is one of the names of God in Hebrew and *Rachum*, the Merciful One, as *Ar-Rahmaan* is The Most Beneficent and *Ar-Raheem* is The Most Merciful in Arabic.

If we live in a world in which we must refuse someone a glass of water in order to protect ourselves, then we must change the world. And changing the world, we heal from the rape. That is how it is. She agreed. It was not healing to have been raped and then to have felt that she had acted foolishly. She had acted honorably. Knowing this was healing.

When I was persecuted, I learned how to love and affiliate with the reviled. I learned to look at every event through every possible perspective. I learned to revise my assumptions, to revision everything.

When people were suffering, I prayed to be able to bring relief to their suffering. I did not ask what techniques could be applied to their suffering, I asked what needs to be done here, and may I be able to do it or may I affiliate with those who can do it.

When a woman said she had never eaten at a table in her mother's house, I set the table for her. We cooked a meal together. We ate it. This is not standard psychotherapy; but we did it. And she no longer feared food.

When a woman wanted to invite her dead father to a meal, but her tradition could not honor such an event, we set the table for three and poured him a glass of wine. His daughter said the blessing the way he would have said the blessing. She put food on his plate as well. We ate with the dead man.

A lawsuit was filed against a psychotherapist who was accused of having established a cult. He was, or said he was, a religious man. Orthodox. Pious. I was named in the lawsuit because I had worked, briefly, with one of his clients. He had asked her to consult with me and we had worked together for several months. I hired an attorney to defend myself as was necessary. "Look," I said, "I'd like to talk with the client. I think we can work it out."

"That is what the courts are for," the attorney said.

"No. The courts are the last resort. Like every piece of legislation, the fact of the courts represent a failure of ethics," I pleaded with her.

"It's not possible," she said. "The laws and procedures prohibit it."

"What can we do then? Can I speak with her attorney?"

Her attorney had made a career for himself prosecuting cultists. My attorney did not think he would be sympathetic. But, finally, I had an opportunity. He wanted to speak to me. He wanted to depose me. I was glad.

When he entered the conference room for a preliminary fact finding meeting, I said, "I will answer every question you ask truthfully, without an oath or under oath. There is no question I will refuse to answer." My attorney was alarmed and tried to stop me, but I continued. "But I want to be able to speak to you about what happened. I want us to remove the assumption of conflict here. You are not my enemy and I am not the enemy of your client. She came to me for healing and so I am responsible to her. Let us see how we can help her together."

At the end of the interview, the charges against me were dropped. As he was leaving the room, he turned to me and asked, "Why didn't you tell her what to do? Why didn't you insist that she free herself from the influence of this man? Why didn't you insist?"

"I spoke to her as honestly as I could. I kept nothing from her. I told her what I thought and where I thought the dangers lay. But, ultimately, if my task was to help her build confidence and independent thinking, I couldn't use my influence to coerce her. I couldn't repeat what was injuring her."

"But you could have saved her."

"No. She had to save herself. And ultimately she did. I had to have confidence in her. I worried about her but I had to trust that she would find her own independence. I couldn't be another person that had authority over her. I couldn't do that. Not even for 'her own good.'"

When a woman said she had never been mothered, we invented the aunt who might have saved her. Over a year, she spent long hours with the aunt in her imagination. She became stronger. She had ground to stand on. She could go on. She began to thrive.

When a woman confessed that her mother had accused her of causing her boyfriend's suicide by revealing her mother's infidelity, I rocked her for long hours. It took months, but then she was free.

When a man did not believe in himself, I found ways to undermine his disbelief. He became part of the family. We called him Uncle G. We needed an Uncle and he needed family. He laced the cranberry sauce with Jack Daniels and smoked cigars with my sons on Thanksgiving. We could have talked to each other one to one in my equivalent of an office for years. Professional interactions. Polite. Bounded. Careful. But, as it takes a village to raise a child, it also takes a village to heal a child. The child he had been needed a village. It would have been presumptuous on my part to assume that I could and should be able to bring or inspire healing on my own. We needed a team. We needed so much that lies outside the professional relationship, that the professional relationship cannot provide. Not instead of it, but in addition to it. Family. Interactions. Interdependencies. Affection. Cigars. I learned to be a healer by asking others to work alongside me and then by giving up the title and the label for the activity. Uncle G. taught me this.

The woman who had breast cancer had stopped dancing. Her back had been injured and she was not dancing. Then she became ill. Slowly, we worked our way back to the dance. To the reason for the dance. The meaning of the dance. She began to dance. In the dark. For her husband. For her life. The week before she moved to a rural community in Oregon, she came to the house for an annual gathering of writers and artists. She entered through the land. She danced on the land. She danced the land. She danced the healing of her body and the land.

When another man was bitter, I asked him what he loved. When he was afraid of madness, we sought out the wild beauty that had been denied. When he was afraid of exploding, we quietly honored his passions. Everything was revisioned, until the secret and hidden life, the pain and the possibility, could all come forth. And then, of course, and rightly so, he left this country and its denial of the real life. He returned to a modest house on a modest farm in a small country where he had spent summers as a teenager and then where he had worked for a period of time and he settled there. If you find your land then you go home to it.

Another woman was overwhelmed with exultation and physical intensity. Energy ran through her body like lightning. We saw that Spirit had come to her and it was going to be difficult. The story that she had been telling for days substantiated this. She was terrified and intrigued. But, we said, yield to the Divine. The sudden presence of the god can be overwhelming. One has to be able to distinguish the spiritual from the pathological. We sat with her for hours. Sometimes we were silent and sometimes we sang with her. The cello player followed the rills of her body as she gave herself over to the unbearable. We kept a heartbeat on the drum. The Divine was with her hour after hour. Her history is Celtic. We told the old myths. She was taken down in the cauldron. Deconstruction and reconstitution. Ecstasy. She yielded to it all. Later she was serene and joyous.

Psychiatrist and explorer of consciousness, Stanislav Grof, calls such situations spiritual emergencies, thus honoring the moments of spiritual emergence. The actual presence of Spirit is always difficult for anyone. God says to Moses, "Hide yourself behind a rock, so I can pass by." If we are not prepared, we can be burned up. Still, it is essential to differentiate the Presence from a physical disease and physical disease from Presence. This doesn't diminish the physical and emotional extremity one may be suffering, but it points to a different response because the cause is not pathology, it is energetic.

Kundalini is spiritual energy coiled at the base of the spine like a serpent. Awakened, it flashes like lightning through the body. Physicians who do not understand this process of initiation try to subdue the symptom. It is the wrong approach. Drugs and sedation are not called for here. The task is to honor the sacred energy while trying to learn how to contain but not suppress it. The task is to learn how to recognize this stroke of the gods. The task is to allow ourselves to be altered, even on a cellular level, by the holy touch.

One becomes a healer by stepping outside conventional understanding and recognizing the beauty in a given situation. Then one carries the courage of such understanding. One becomes a healer in the face of the extremity of splendor by allying oneself with the spirits in the form they present themselves.

A young girl had been a witness to unbearable violence. Eight years later, she couldn't walk without falling. The doctors diagnosed a disease of the pineal gland. But they couldn't find the evidence for it. She couldn't sleep. She had headaches. She couldn't function. She couldn't go to school. Valerie and I worked with her. Clearly there was something wrong but western medicine hadn't found it. The sleep was easy to remedy. We suggested that she take melatonin. It is made in the pineal gland. The doctor agreed. He should have thought of it. She began to sleep but the other symptoms remained. Finally, it occurred to us, from speaking to her, that she was afraid of going to school. The school was a violent school as are most schools in Los Angeles. Her mother couldn't afford to move and couldn't afford a private school. All the doctors and social workers insisted that she had to adjust to the situation. But after conferencing with her mother, we told the girl that we would try to help her find another option other than returning to school. Even if she got well, she wouldn't have to return to the school, we promised. She got well. Then the psychiatrist understood that the girl had been retraumatized every single day that she had gone to school until finally her entire system had collapsed. Her mother brought her lessons home for several months and the next semester she received a scholarship from a private school. She remains well.

This is not a story about how a young girl was healed. This is a story of how one develops as a healer. Valerie and I listened intently. We assumed the girl knew something and our task was to ferret it out. We allied ourselves with her. We did not try to overpower her with our knowledge. We did not ask her to conform to what was, in fact, an untenable situation and only she knew it. One becomes a healer through learning respect for the native wisdom of the individual who is suffering. And one does compromise the individual by insisting she acquiesce to impossible circumstances. Accommodating, adapting to, conforming to what is essentially unhealthy and destructive when the practitioner knows it is unhealthy, is often standard medical procedure. Political, economic and social conditions are not in the forefront of the physician's mind or concern. In contrast, one becomes a healer then by listening to the intelligence of the illness and standing by the person who is suffering.

A woman had been diagnosed as bipolar. I found the diagnosis pernicious. My response was that what was wrong was outside her, not inside her. The difference between unbearable dualism and the dance of Yin and Yang. As I saw it, such a diagnosis got her medication but it didn't bring healing. It limited her through the assumption of pathology, but it didn't bring life to the woman whose dreams indicated she was a bodhisattva even if she didn't believe it. She didn't believe it because the culture didn't encourage her to live it. So, we encouraged her. And she found ways. This is the way I saw it.

When she read my analysis before publication, she said she had seen something else. She said she had found the diagnosis useful. It gave her a ground to stand on. And along with the medication, it kept her alive long enough to reach for and come to know the real life. She and I met, she said, after she had been on medication. She said the medication had helped keep her alive until our meeting. Now it was the time for the dream of the bodhisattva to be met. And she did so.

Sometimes she still cannot bear the dark. Which of us can? Sometimes, I say, it is remarkable that any of us are still alive given the circumstances of modern life. Anyone who survives has triumphed. Any one of us can curl up in the dark and rock endlessly with the pain of the world. This is not a sign of weakness or failure. Think of it as the menstrual hut that women can repair to when the blood comes and the veil between the worlds thins and we cannot bear so much reality. So we rock. So we hold each other. So we lament together. We keen and we wail. Then we go out again.

I became a healer through being passionate about seeking out the gifts that have been given to people. I saw her intelligence immediately. I saw her heart. Recognizing these rather than focusing on limitations made all the difference. First, she healed, but second she became a cornerstone of the community. Some days she calls, and says, "I'm down today. Persephone in the Underworld. I've been called down." We say, "Bring back treasures from Hades when you emerge."

One day she asked, "Will you teach me what you know?"

"I will try," I said. "Look for beauty, intelligence, skill, any eccentric understanding, the hidden, obscured and denied qualities and possibilities, and call them forth. Don't be daunted by the individual's lack of faith in herself, place yourself determinedly against the habitual diminishment in our culture which results from competition and commercial values. Look for those that Spirit loves, though this is unrecognized, and stand alongside them. After that, it's easy."

Then Elenna called a Daré into existence in Oakland. I bought her a large urn for tea. Enough, we hope for 50 people. Better than a license or a degree.

How do we heal? We take someone in our arms. We rock each other. We pray. We lay on hands. We journey to the other world. We run energy through the body and restore harmony. We become family. We create community. We sing and dance. We weep, we wail, we tear our hair. Ultimately, there are no protocols. We tell the stories again and again until we see the path they are revealing. The story, the sacred and unique story that is at the foundation of the person's life, reveals the healing path. The story that reveals the disease also reveals the way of healing. And so one follows it.

When a woman had no place to go, I invited her onto the land. When she became feral, we praised the wilderness. When she was homeless, we invited her to live in the trailer our artist friend had just vacated. But mostly, she lived outside until she didn't. When she threatened suicide, I bargained: Give me three years. If life is still unbearable, I won't interfere with whatever you do. In the meantime, I promised I would not hospitalize her. It wasn't easy. We were both undone and redone through the relationship. We drove each other mad with fury and frustration and we also recognized each other's goodness and unique intelligence and so we called each other forth. She healed. I became a healer. I wasn't the only one who assisted her. She wasn't the only one who taught me what I know. But we were essential to each other. It was unprecedented, what occurred. If I had known what would transpire, I might not have done it. Fortunately, I didn't know. I can say the same for Daré, if I had known what would be required to bring it into the world, I wouldn't have volunteered. Fortunately I didn't know. Fourteen years later, the woman and I still share the land, with Michael, with the wolves. She was always an extraordinary writer and artist even if these gifts were sometimes buried. But now she has also become a professional landscaper. How did she learn? The land taught her. But this also – she has become my daughter.

Land, beauty, dance, music. The animals. The Divine. Following what matters. Finding meaning. Trusting each other. Bringing the errant cell back into the fold. Refusing to take part in activities that undermine the life force. Healing our lives so they can heal us and others.

Vitality. Sometimes you see the embers of life force concealed in the ashes. A little breath, the activity of a bellows, can enliven the fire. This is also the healer's task.

Healing cannot be confined to a technique nor can it be contained in an hour. Healing is acting on behalf of the whole life. Healing is doing whatever is required so that the entire life is restored. The way of healing cannot be known in advance. It is a creative act, unique, improvised in each moment. A stepping into the unknown. Calling for the spirits to assist. Acting as advised. Holding the act of healing holy.

How did I become a healer? I apprenticed myself to an extraordinary analyst, Dr. John Seeley. I watched his work with me. I scrutinized his heart. I studied the way he followed justice and compassion. I recognized the depth of his spiritual life, and learned kindness, patience and integrity from him. I learned that each moment and incident necessitated a unique response that was thoughtful, empathetic and wise. I learned to try to understand in specific the suffering that people were carrying. I learned to honor the spirits and to listen to what they advised.

And so when someone asks for healing, I offer everything I can.

And if the world requires healing, we try to meet that too. Even if we are broken ourselves, we try to meet it.

And whatever the spirits request, I try to meet.

*　　*　　*

What is the technique you use as a healer?

I don't have one. I do what is required at the moment.

What school of healing have you been educated in?

I was never educated formally as a healer.

What training have you received?

No formal training.

What guides you?

The story guides me. And beauty guides me. And the spirits guide me.

How do you know what to do?

I never know. I start out not knowing. If I think I know, I assume I'm wrong.

What then?

I pray. I don't look for the flaw; I look for the intelligence, for the meaning, for the surprising and unidentified possibilities and hope. I don't turn away from the pain. I don't separate myself from it. I let myself feel it as deeply and intelligently as I can. I don't pretend a little pill can heal it. I look for the story that has been given through the circumstances of the person's life, and then we try to go there, to understand its dimensions and shadings so it can be lived accordingly, can be lived out, can come to fulfillment. I enter the story as deeply as I can. I honor the story. I do not limit our connection to a fifty minute hour. We become part of a community. We share each other's fates. Healing comes.

Healing doesn't mean escape from suffering. It doesn't mean a long and painless life. It means a real life. It means all of it.

Oh, yes, here is a story that has to be told.

We were in Greece enacting the Eleusinian Mysteries. During the day of silence at Delphi, I had some time to go off on my own. I climbed into a bower of vines where I could be alone. It seemed to me that I heard a voice speaking to me and as she spoke I found my body being shaped to the age and tone of the voice. I was bent over as if I was an old hag. It occurred to me that I was hearing the voice of Hekate, the crone, coming through me.

"You will never have another lover," the voice said. It was as if the combined suffering of all the lonely women I knew, myself included, opened before me and enveloped me.

"You will never write another book," she continued. My world dissolved. Ashes and emptiness. The word taken from me. The word that I loved and that I had learned was healing.

"You will live your live in constant and unremitting pain without hope of relief." A long silence. "Now choose."

A long time passed. A lifetime, perhaps in twenty minutes. Like so many others I knew, I had in the past reached moments when I could not go on. I had thought of suicide. I had thought of going to bed and not getting up. I had said it was too difficult.

Barbara Myerhoff and I had developed an exchange between us. I would come into the house, weary and dispirited and ask, "Do you have a little cyanide?"

"I do," she would answer, smiling, "but I'm saving it for myself."

"Well, I can't bear it," I would protest.

"Who asked you?" she would retort.

And so I/we would pick up our burdens, a few tears, a little laughter, they go far.

I took the hag's curse seriously. Could I bear what she was prophesying? Others have suffered worse. I knew that. I was not immune. I did not think I should be privileged. But how could I bear it? Would I volunteer?

I heard my own words before I knew what I would say. "I want to live. Whatever it is. I want life. The whole ball game. Whatever it is. I'm here."

And then she laughed. That laugh you imagine the hag laughs. It is chilling and exuberant. It dissolves bones. There is nothing left after such a laugh. And I laughed with her. When I came down the mountain to join the group I was aware that I was picking wildflowers as if I was the Kore, the young girl at the heart of the Mysteries. The girl, the mother and the crone.

"What happened?" Steven Kent asked me. He and I were officiating the Mysteries together. "You look radiant," he said. "You look like a young girl."

7

September 11th. Michael and I were praying with Augustine and four North Americans in Masvingo, Zimbabwe. Afterwards, we were afraid to go to Egypt. I was afraid to fly Egypt Air which was prohibited from entering the United States until some days after regular American and European flights resumed. But there had been signs. And signs, we had to presume, were shown to us from a divine perspective that included the future, that included September 11th and its aftermath. So we were being called even more strongly than before. We had thought, abstractly, that our journey might have healing potential. Now, it seemed that we were being tested and we had to meet the test.

So it was that Augustine, Simakuhle, Michael and I went, after much soul-searching and trepidation, to Egypt, a Muslim country, on September 15th and climbed Mt. Sinai on the 17th, my sixty-fifth birthday and the first day of Rosh Hashanah, the Jewish New Year. And so it is that I am trying to write a text that speaks to the possibility of old and visionary ways of healing and knowing reentering the world, albeit through the most peculiar and unexpected circumstances.

On the eve of a world-threatening conflict among what has been called the three great religions, the four of us unexpectedly met with a Muslim Bedouin family at the threshold of our climb. Of this meeting, we will speak later, but as a result we were put in the care and company of a Bedouin boy and his camel. We ascended the holy mountain in a unison of prayer that recognized the necessary end of the heroic mentality and called for peace-making spirits to descend on all of us, to be disseminated to others bringing healing in this desperate time.

The war we hoped would never occur began after our return to the United States. The world continues on a trajectory to destruction. And yet there are signs of a parallel trajectory of consciousness in the world that is outside of violence. These two images: a plane turned into a living bomb bringing down a tower as large as a modern city, a woman praying for her life at the *omphalos* in the Great Enclosure of the Queen at Masvingo, three others being initiated on the mountain by the cave of the King and one week later, five beings, whose meeting was entirely unlikely, silently climbing a holy mountain in the starlight, praying. Different stories converging, each of which reaches back into the past and forward into the unknown. To write an esoteric text is to pray that the stories projecting viable and generous futures will take precedence and come to life.

8

When we came home from being with Augustine in Zimbabwe, I knew I was coming to meet my death. My death and our death. A question pecked its way into my heart and nested there: How does one meet her death? How shall I meet my death?

There came a mysterious answer that I am called to address: You meet your death through harvest.

You bring together everything you have learned and experienced, everything you have done, every way you have been prepared and you carry all of this forward for the sake of the community. You examine your life to see where Spirit has been calling you your entire life. You step out of self-interest, ego and resistance to Spirit. You scrutinize your life for the details, events and interactions that speak to the call or intervention of Spirit and then you step into the story toward which you have been called. What is it you are to harvest in order to face what may be coming? You become the person that your soul intended and you step forward. You meet this moment, this death.

*   *   *

Wednesday, December 12, 2001. Michael and I came home to Topanga on Monday from Pine Mountain where we have been in retreat. We came to meet a friend who managed to emigrate to Canada last year – just in time! – to check on Pami who shares the land with us and who just had her knee replaced, and to be with Gary Davidson as he enters the first medical stage of fighting for his life by undergoing an angiogram with the probability of angioplasty or the insertion of a stent.

As Gary lay on the gurney, Michael sang healing songs from the African tradition and worked with the cards so that Gary could muster the exact energy and focus to bring about the best possible healing result. Several prayer circles and ritual events had taken place on Gary's behalf and our common prayer was that he would not require angioplasty or other extreme measures before the ordeal of having his kidney removed and receiving treatment. We all joke about the maxim I always assert at such a moment: It is easier to heal someone before the diagnosis than afterwards. This isn't scientific – you can think we are just fooling ourselves – but it is practical. Diagnosis tends to reify a condition. Better to do as much of the ritual and healing work beforehand, when you are not up against the body and the mind. Often the suspected condition turns out to be milder than expected and sometimes, not often, but sometimes, there is no pathology whatsoever despite the earlier indications. In Gary's case: prayers answered. The artery is blocked but not so severely as to require any medical intervention. He will be able to withstand the surgery. He will take on the healing of this condition, at least, in a way that is not invasive.

And finally, we returned home so that Michael, who had been stuck with the needle after drawing blood on a patient dying of AIDS, could himself meet with a nurse practitioner and pick up another round of anti-retroviral medication. Returning to the solitude of Pine Mountain, late that night, I began to fall into despair. I do not know if I can meet these times as they are required to be met. I can see, I think, something of how to be, of how to act. But, I do not know if I can bring in the harvest. I know from watching my father that aging often has disappointment in it. It is not about the personal grief or joy over my own accomplishments, but rather the fear that I will not have met the potential that came with the gifts that I was given, that I may not be able to make the offerings that the world requires now.

Kabbalah teaches that there are four worlds: The worlds of spirit, idea, action and finally, the world of manifestation. Nothing matters then until that final world has come to be. And it is not a complete world unless it is inspirited, unless it carries and is informed by the other three. Form and consciousness must not be separated from each other. The fourth world, the world of formation, is the garment for the other three, and the world of Spirit is the essence of the Divine that comes into formation through thoughts and action. This history, these life experiences, this life-long training, these dreams and visions, given and received, these instructions that seem to come sometimes from the other side, this hope…. This is the time to meet the times with all of this behind me, you, and us. I can write about it, yes, but I do not see the path clearly.

Tears this morning. No surprise. I meditate. I come to the computer. I pray for wisdom and direction. I pray that these words are of use.

"If not you, who? If not us, who? If not now, when?"

Harvest. You step into the story in which you have been living and toward which you have been called your entire life. This is how I understood this ten years ago:

When I ask a gift from my death, it is that at the last minute I will be able to look back over my life and know, without any doubt, the entire story I have been living. As this final gift, all the details and events that I have been relentlessly ordering my entire life will arrange themselves in a simple and startlingly beautiful structure, until meaning – surprising and dazzling – flashes out of the dank, sticky, and entwined chrysalis of daily life. Then I will know, despite pain, disappointment, and limitation, that this life of mine has been a good and meaningful work.
....

Every life is a story.[31]

What I am doing here is trying to follow stories. The stories that converged on September 11th and the story of my own life meeting it as well. The stories that have converged to create the woman I have become. Yes, I am trying to discern the nature of the story I have been living my entire life that is composed of all the smaller stories that I have followed over the years. I have also assigned myself the task of following the very directives that I developed and offered my students over the last thirty-five years. Something like the doctor taking her own medicine. Ideas develop slowly and sometimes you are not even aware of their full nature and implication because you are also always within the world of the idea and rarely feel the necessity to step out and see it wholly for what it is. The same with a story. If one is in it, one is inevitably in one of the parts and cannot see the whole. But then circumstance demands that we step away to look. This is what has happened to me/us through the impact of September 11th.

In order to follow a story you have to see it in its entirety. But in order to follow the story you also have to see all the stories from which it is composed. Simply reviewing one's life in a chronological fashion will not reveal this. Maybe it should, but it doesn't. Chronology is not a narrative in itself. Events do not relate to each other because of sequence alone. One moves into a story and then, you know the way storytellers speak, this first story reminds them of a second story and, holding the thread so you won't get entirely lost, they tell the second story, and maybe even a third, but not necessarily each in its entirety, enough to make the association and then they come back to the original story and move forward. Or back.

A field of stories. A cluster of associations. Images and metaphors that link one story to another though these may be peripheral to the central event. Characters and personae who weave in and out of the various narratives and chronicles.

Stories are real and living. We do not invent them. They exist over there in their own dimension. Or they are a dimension in which all the other dimensions are contained. Those of us who wish to live an authentic life step into that dimension and put on the story as if it were our own, a garment that the soul wears in order to make itself known.

Almost fifteen years ago, I gathered people together in the hope that we might meet regularly in what I called "The Field." It was my sense then that the field of intelligence that might emerge would sustain us all. The same image repeats itself and repeats itself, then and now, in one form and then another. Story understood not by its conclusion but by the tensions or resonance produced by the ongoing subtle understanding of the myriad relationships of one story to other stories or events.

This is how Stephen Karcher speaks of it in *How to Use the I Ching, A Guide to Working With the Oracle of Change:*

Hexagram 2, Field. This is the primal power to nourish and give things form. You see it in the earth, the moon, the mother, the devoted servant, the mare. You are confronted with many conflicting forces. Yield to each thing and give it form. Nourish and provide for it. This can open a whole new cycle of time…. At first you will be confused by the profusion of events…. Let your power to realize things be so generous that it can carry everything that approaches. Cherish each thing and help it grow.[32]

Or this is another way the I Ching speaks:

Hexagram 48, The Well…. Resources held in common; underlying structure; communicate with others, common needs; the water of life, the inner source. The ideogram is a group of nine fields with the well at the center. The well is both a social structure that lets people communicate and help each other and a deep source of life water there for all to draw on.

Outer and Inner Worlds: Gorge and Penetrating. By repeatedly confronting outer danger you reach an inner ground where the water of life wells up.

Hidden Possibility: 38 Diverging. The inner center of the well contains the possibility of turning divergent opinions into creative tension.[33]

I am not writing this in a linear way. You are and are not witness to the process. Sometimes the prose proceeds one word, paragraph, idea after the other. We go from here to there. But then, I am reminded of something and double back. Return to the first pages, insert something, skip forward, then back. A change there, however, requires a change here. The past affects the future, but also, the future changes the past, reveals something that was hidden, uncovers a meaning or extracts a misunderstanding. Something that will happen and that we cannot predict or account for will change our understanding and concern regarding what happened previously. We cannot proceed as if we are innocent. We have to take the future into account. We have to account for ourselves. I am trying to account for myself. When appropriate, I try not to hide the signs of how this piece is coming into form.

Much of what appears here was written in October and continued through February 2002, but today, is [was] Tuesday, November 06, 2001. A few days ago, Nancy Odin of the Green Party was prevented from taking a plane to Chicago because she had written an Op-Ed piece in a Maine paper objecting to the war. And so I do not know if you will have the opportunity to read this book at the time that it will be most useful to you. I do not know if it will be able to find a publisher or whether I will be able to publish and distribute it on the web.

November 29, 2001. John Ashcroft has testified before the Senate Judiciary committee that anyone who opposes the way that the war on terrorism is being conducted, or the war on Afghanistan, or any war the President may engage in, is interfering with the war effort. He is speaking of objections to the war, to the conduct of the war, to the Office of Homeland Security, to the military tribunals for suspected terrorists, to those concerned about the violations of civil liberties. His words are obviously a threat.

A few years ago I thought of starting a publishing company called *Samizdat*. It was not a response to political censorship but to commercial censorship. Perhaps this will become a *Samizdat*. I will not think beyond this into the future because I must continue to write no matter what.

Today is Saturday, December 08, 2001, and I stand by what I have written.

Today is Wednesday, December 12, 2001. I stand by what I have written.

Second draft Sunday, February 03, 2002. I am still standing here.

Final draft, Wednesday February 27, 2002, my son's birthday. I am standing behind what I have written.

*   *   *

In early September, 1973, I was having dinner in a Cuban restaurant that Ernest Hemingway frequented. Seated across from me, under a photograph of "Papa," was a prominent Cuban novelist who had fought in the Sierras alongside Che Guevara and Fidel Castro and who had written an acclaimed novel about that time. "I am writing another novel, but I will not be able to publish for twenty years, if then," he confided to me. "These times," he continued, "will not permit it to come to light, but I can neither keep from writing it nor can I insist that it be published. It is not only a matter of my life, but also it is a matter of my life. Cuba is a different country under the embargo than it will be when we are allowed back into the family of nations."

I knew then that I did not understand the complexities of the country though I had come to Cuba, in part, to understand exactly that. Later that week, I met with an artist who held an important position in the government. The meeting had been arranged, I understood, after my own character and integrity had been well scrutinized; I could be trusted. At the end of the evening, the artist invited me into his studio where I saw the luminous and forbidden paintings of homosexual love. "In twenty years," he said, "they may see the light. Or never." But no, he didn't want to leave Cuba and, no, definitely not, he did not want the United States to interfere in Cuban affairs on his behalf. About the United States... well, the U.S. had supported and profited from the criminal regime of Batista. Things were far better than they had been then. Far better. So, he would bear what he would have to bear until... until when? Perhaps if the United States lifted the embargo, his life would improve even more, his government would not be so defensive, he would be able to paint what he loved. Things were not as simple as Americans thought they were, he said.

*   *   *

On September 11th, terrorists attacked the Pentagon and the World Trade Center in New York City. On the same day in 1973, twenty-eight years earlier, terrorists had initiated a bloody coup by attacking the Moneda, the Presidential Palace in Santiago, Chile, killing Salvador Allende, toppling the first democratically elected socialist government in Latin America and establishing a military dictatorship led by General Augusto Pinochet.

I had been in Chile in September, 1972, the year before the *golpé* and had good reason to know within ten days of the brutal takeover that it had been assisted, if not directed, by the United States. Ten years later a film, *Missing*, was made about a father, played by Jack Lemmon, who goes to Chile to search for the killers of his son, a young man who had had the misfortune to meet a drunken military officer in a bar in Valparaíso and learn from him about the attack that was taking place at that moment. The officer was bragging about his connections with the Americans who were involved with the conception and execution of the coup. I do not remember if this is exactly the story that was told in *Missing*, or how much of the truth the filmmaker was able to tell, even though the filmmaker was Costa-Gavras. I know this is the real story upon which the film was based. The young man returned to Santiago that evening and told the officer's story to his wife who was able to escape Chile. A few days earlier, the footage from the documentary film on the Chilean labor movement that the young man was working on had been smuggled out of the country. I was one of those who, with the smuggler, made a film using this footage. The first film about the *golpé*. It was made on my dining room table. We called it *Chile: With Poems and Guns* and we dedicated it to Charles Horman who was killed because of what he had innocently come to know.

We carried the story of Charles' death for ten years and the story of the *golpé* until Pinochet was removed from power. It was not that we didn't speak out; it was that we weren't heard. Almost thirty years later, international subpoenas have been issued to arrest Henry Kissinger to stand trial in a world court for his participation on behalf of the United States in undermining various governments. These subpoenas were issued after Augusto Pinochet was returned to Chile to stand trial for the crimes committed when he was in power. Still, the citizens of the United States in whose name such deeds were done, do not know what they/we need to know. May our government take heed.

New York Times on the Web
March 28, 2002
FOR CHILEAN COUP, KISSINGER IS
NUMBERED AMONG THE HUNTED
By Larry Rohter

> SANTIAGO, Chile. With a trial of Gen. Augusto Pinochet increasingly unlikely here, victims of the Chilean military's 17-year dictatorship are now pressing legal actions in both Chilean and American courts against Henry A. Kissinger and other Nixon administration officials who supported plots to overthrow Salvador Allende Gossens, the Socialist president, in the early 1970's.

> In another action, human rights lawyers here have filed a criminal complaint against Mr. Kissinger and other American officials, accusing them of helping organize the covert regional program of political repression called Operation Condor. As part of that plan, right-wing military dictatorships in Argentina, Bolivia, Brazil, Chile, Paraguay and Uruguay coordinated efforts throughout the 1970's to kidnap and kill hundreds of their exiled political opponents.

I am reminded of a fairy tale called The Goose Girl. A princess, traveling to another kingdom to be married is overwhelmed by her maidservant who takes the princess's clothes, the gifts her mother gave her, and her horse. When they arrive, the maidservant impersonates the princess and marries the king. Afraid that her deed will be revealed, she has the horse killed and mounts his head above the city gate as a warning to the princess who is now a goose girl. But each day as the goose girl leaves the city with her flock, the horse speaks: "If your mother knew what has been done, how her heart would break." The words alter and repeat themselves in my mind over and over again: If we only knew what is done in our name, how our hearts would break.

September 11th. A black day. One day the U.S. government attacks a person or a nation or a land without understanding the consequences of its behavior. Twenty-eight years later, the United States is attacked. This might be called karma.

On the 13th of September 1973, I flew back to the United States from Havana through Lima. I had been in Chile the year before and for the first time in my adult political life, I had felt hope because of the government that had been elected and the enthusiasm and possibility that was evident among the people. One afternoon, we had joined a woman at her table in a crowded café. "How do you like Allende's government?" we asked.

"I didn't vote for him," she said. "I am of another class. I didn't think Allende would be good for me and my life. I was afraid I would lose my assets." She paused, picked up the cup of coffee she was drinking and took a sip. "But," she continued with tears in her eyes, "you know this peaceful revolution changed the way we speak. We use the "*tú*" form, *tu savais*, you know. And so I am less lonely. This is what the government has done for me."

Pablo Neruda died of heartbreak and cancer a few days after the coup of September 11th, 1973 in which hope and beauty were destroyed as bombs fell on the Moneda, the Presidential Palace, and Salvador Allende was assassinated by dark forces that were financed and advised by the United States. His world had come to an end. It was insufferable. May this not be the fate of the poets and the planet so threatened at this time.

If you flew to Cuba from Mexico City in 1973 as I had, then you would have had to return through Canada or through Lima. On my flight back from Havana were the members of the Cuban delegation to Chile who were returning to Santiago after the bombing of the Moneda; they would not stay there long. Pinochet would win and begin a reign of terror. Our language would change. We would learn new words that we would never forget: the disappeared, *los desaparacidos*. There are 1200 *desaparaci-dos* in my country at this moment. They are all Arabs or Muslims. They are being held without bail. Their families do not know where they are. The government admits only that they are suspected terrorists. One of them died in jail of a heart attack. Our government said he was not tortured. We have always said, "This cannot happen here."

Early on the night of September 11, 1973, I had noticed that the Cuban elevator operator looked dazzling and had remarked on her beauty. We had become friends. Sometimes I was weary with all the political talk and meetings that characterized my visit to Cuba. Then I rode in the elevator with the women operators and we talked about what women speak about, our hearts, our beliefs, our hopes, our families, our disappointments, our fears. Restored by the intimacy and truthfulness of these connections, I was able to return to the work of creating bridges and alliances that we hoped to accomplish by being there.

One evening, we were invited to the elegant Cuban nightclub, the Copacabana. This was not my form of entertainment but it allowed the Cubans who were guiding us to take their wives out for a fine dinner and a night of music, an evening they could not afford otherwise. At one point in the evening, I left the table to go to the restroom and the other women followed me. The anteroom was large and mirrored and furnished with very comfortable chairs. We sat down here away from the smoke, music and clatter of dishes. And we spoke. From the heart. Again, as women do. Across the boundaries of culture and language and politics. We probably stayed together in conversation for over an hour and then, as if nothing had transpired between us, we rose and returned to the formal relationship that politics required.

Irina, the elevator operator, was planning to attend a party after her work shift and she had sparkles in her hair and rhinestones everywhere. It was Saturday night. She was full of anticipation of the evening ahead. After we heard the news of the *golpe*, none of us slept. The streets were full of wailing. Mourners were everywhere. People staggered through the streets, though it was not wine but grief that disoriented them. When we made our way back to the hotel, Irina was working the morning shift. Her mascara had run in black lines down from her eyes and she had not bothered to wash her face; it appeared as if she had torn her hair out with her hands. Her clothes were shredded and she had the eyes of someone who had looked directly at death. "Chile was the only friend we had in the universe," she said.

I am writing this as if it will be possible to speak out without being censored. I am writing it as if we still live in a democracy. Perhaps I have learned something in all these years about the relationship between cancer and fascism, about what happens to the soul and then to the body, to the body and soul and so to the world when one is inhibited from speaking. Cancer is a disease of the body but it is also a disease of the soul and so it is a disease of the body politic. There are dire consequences when censorship becomes a secret act within the self. Sometimes writing is the most skillful way we have to protect our lives. We can choose to write what can be published, or to write what must be said. To write what must be written even if it is not published is a great freedom. The silence that eats the soul is cancer.

9

A title for a book came in a dream in 1978. The dream itself was strange. I was looking at my palm and there were no lines on it as if I had had no life, no past, no present and so would have no future. Then a title came across the screen of my dream as if I had been watching a movie: *The Woman Who Slept With Men to Take the War Out of Them*. Images had come to me in dreams before, but this was startling enough to remember and ruminate upon for six months. I took a ream of paper and a typewriter to Mendocino and rented a cabin at Ames Lodge and set out to write a book with that title, trying to discover through the writing what might have been implied, what might have been invoked when the title appeared. This was a critical moment. It was the moment I stepped out to meet the dream as an equal. I could not guess or fabricate who or what "sent" the dream. But I knew, despite psychology with which I was well-versed, that the dream was not mine and so the title was not a gift given to me by myself to do with as I wished. I recognized the title as a responsibility from elsewhere I was to try to meet. I didn't understand any of this. Oh yes, I had believed in God as a child in the way a child believes, but then the terrible history of the twentieth century had caused me as a social activist and a humanist to look toward the human to solve the transgressions and crimes of the human. What sustained me in these times was the utopian hope that we might make a better world. I realized that ethical concerns were often derived from religious thought, but I did not think then that they came from Divinity though they might have come from the thought that the Divine exists. No matter. Whether God existed or not, the world was suffering unbearably and human activity was required to temper human activity. I had only begun a year before, through the incidence of cancer, to consider the reality of Spirit or the Divine or God. But still, having seen that the Divine did not interfere directly in human affairs, my attention went elsewhere. I didn't expect to feel the hand of God.

I am not a dreamer. I am not one of those medicine people who are uniquely blessed with frequent dreams for the community. There have been such people in all indigenous communities when the separation between the human and spirit world was not fortified from our side like the Berlin Wall. Such beings remain here and there, even in the urban industrialized, technologized world, even here. Valerie Wolf is such a one. Perhaps there are more of such beings than we/they know because the knowledge that one is not dreaming for oneself but is dreaming for the community is not current knowledge and so they cannot fully understand the nature of the blessing that has been given them. And if they are not artists, they do not know how to hold and respond to the world of images that rains down upon them night after night.

I am not such a dreamer. But I did learn over the years when the rare dream awakened me that I must understand it and follow its instructions. I learned this, as I have learned most of what has been essential to my life, in idiosyncratic ways. After I had written two novels, I fell into despair about ever writing anything again. Story, in the way it was understood by the culture, eluded me. Story and literature was something else than what I saw around me. What too often passes for literature in the dominant culture, its insistence on violence, tension, conflict at the core, its immersion in the language and images of material culture, put a wedge between me and books. This was difficult for a young woman who wanted to devote her life to the written word.

Desperate, I turned to Anaïs Nin who, laughingly, gave me the following direction: "A novel is easy. You begin with a dream and you end with a dream and then you just fill in the middle." Obedient, I followed her advice. A dream came immediately for the beginning and a dream came for the end and then the middle was implicit.

In the first dream, a woman was flying in her hair. In the last dream, her soul was born when it emerged from her mouth, in the manner of Siberian shamanism, as a fly. Again, something more than the [unpublished] novel, *Flying With a Rock*, resulted. I learned to follow the dream, though the title refers to the moment of fear when one is poised between the worlds. In *The Teachings of Don Juan*, Carlos Castaneda hesitates before a moment of vision. His teacher is about to teach him to fly by turning him into a crow. He is, predictably, afraid. And so he asks, "What if I tie myself to a rock?" Don Juan responds wryly, "Well, if you want to fly with a rock, fly with a rock."

In the novel, I was also considering those moments at the threshold between worlds. Entering the dream world and taking it seriously was such a threshold. But once I crossed the threshold, I was someone else. I had become a woman who follows her dreams. I had stepped into another universe with its own laws, assumptions and agreements. And there was no going back.

*   *   *

In July 1976, I dreamed about the DINA – the Chilean secret police under Pinochet. They were proceeding to torture me so that I would not speak. In January 1977, I discovered I had cancer. The dream foreshadowed the disease and revealed some of the causes of it.

Cancer brought me, as it has brought so many of us, to my knees and finding myself on my knees, I began to pray. The prayer was not a call for help. Somehow being so broken and afraid, immortality shattered at age 40, I was able to see through the obstacles that had insulated me from all but the human realms. I had a glimpse of the existence of something beyond me that human beings everywhere on the planet have in the past recognized and called, in their many languages, God. I didn't want God to change my life in ways I thought it should be changed. I simply hoped to know something of God. And, if possible, to be a servant. To carry the holy in the world.

Disease is the messenger, it calls you to your real life. This was not only my own experience, it became the teaching I was to carry.

I was awed by the vision and devoted myself accordingly. Had I known him then, Augustine would have said, "The spirits are heavy upon you," and he would have guided me through initiation. I would have asked him, had I known him when he was suffering from the heaviness of the spirits: What is the story that you are being asked to enter? But, I had no such companion except for the lonely intuition that something was being asked of me and disease had made it apparent.

It was just after the cancer diagnosis that the dream of *The Woman Who...* occurred. So within a short period of time, I was called under two different circumstances to the reality of other realms that can influence and coexist with ours. These were not realms designed to answer our prayers for what we think we want and need in this life. These are realms that when we enter them, when we accept the invitation to align ourselves, incorporate us into them increasingly. If we are faithful to the laws of these realms as they are revealed and as we perceive them, we walk, as it were, in two worlds at once. But our primary allegiance from then on is always to this other realm and the essential goodness it extends to all beings. How do I know this? A little bird told me.

The dream then. The book was written. It surprised me. I could say that the text was given the way the title was given. It emerged as a kind of miracle, an in-breaking of Spirit into the realm of the human for which I had and had not been prepared. At each moment, we stand before the mystery of the rational and irrational, we gather courage and if we choose, we can step across.

Something else came from the title. It was the implications of the first three words: The woman who... I wanted to know how we can know ourselves, how we can tell the story of our lives. The phrase "the woman who ..." which I began to use without referring to the book, established a woman's identity at a time when a woman's identity or right to it was still in question. Later I came across the healing songs of Maria Sabina, the legendary Mexican curandera who invoked the healing spirits through the incantation of the phrases:

> I'm a birth woman, *says*
> I'm a victorious woman, *says*
> I'm a law woman, *says*
> I'm a thought woman, *says*
> I'm a life woman, *says*...
> I am a spirit woman, *says*
> I am a crying woman, *says*...

And later still, the work of the poet Ann Waldman whose own magical chants gain their power from the assertion of the same and similar phrases. In a time when the woman is trivialized there is a great power in the repeated assertion: I am...

I am the woman who.... I am the man who.... I am the woman who is a mother. Tell that story. I am the woman who healed from cancer. Tell that story. I am the woman who follows dreams. Tell that story. I am the woman who is confronting her death. Tell that story. I am the woman who is meeting her death.

*   *   *

I hold my hand up and look at my palm. Here is my death. Here is our death. This close. How must I/we meet it? There is no abstract answer. No formula. The answer lies in the life that was given. In the life that was given to me, to you. Each of us is given a different path, a different story. I meet my death by scrutinizing this life, the life to which I was led in order to see what must be said, done, lived now.

How everything comes together. How one circles back to the beginning to step forward. I remember this now: When I discovered that I had cancer, I was writing a book that became the KPFK radio drama, *The Book of Hags*.[34] In that book, I was asking these questions: Why do so many women have cancer? Why now? And why so young? A month after I finished writing the book, a lump in my breast was diagnosed as cancer. One of the protagonists in that book, a novelist, had already set down the following: "This is the book I would write if I were to die in a year."

I believe there is a question or a grouping of questions at the core of every work of art. The artist or writer doesn't answer the question, she addresses it. Sometimes the artist spends a lifetime addressing the same question or set of questions. Perhaps we can say that serious artists have been given or have developed core questions to which they devote their lives. There is the apocryphal story told about Gertrude Stein. When she was dying, those at her bedside asked, "Gertrude, what is the answer?"

"What is the question?" she is said to have replied.

Every disease or difficulty raises questions. Addressing these questions rigorously and forthrightly is central to healing and peacemaking. Interrogating our souls in the manner that we might imagine the 42 Assessors of ancient Egypt interrogated the souls of those who had died as they were passing through the Duat, is the life work of consciousness, of healing and creativity.

Shesmu 42, The 42 Assessors.

When the deceased has been admitted into the Hall of Judgment, he is confronted with the 42 Assessors, or Judges, of Maat. They are under her jurisdiction, for Maat is Cosmic Law and the heart of the deceased is weighed against a feather.[35]

10

Questions. Here are some questions that must be asked now. These are the questions that I learned to ask when I had cancer. These are the questions that arise when working with people with life-threatening illness. These are questions that can be as easily applied to the wounding that occurred to the United States on September 11th. These are some questions that will help us interrogate our lives.

What story is encoded in the wound or disease? What messages do the disease and wound bring to us? How does the encoded story reveal not so much what happened but what might be the particular path toward healing? In what ways, in particular, does the particular disease (event), occurring at this time, in particular, to this individual (nation) in particular, reveal the ways one is (we are) being called to change one's (our) life in order to benefit ourselves and the community? What healing does this lead us toward?

I am being too careful here. Sparing us in a way that violates the conversation between us. In what ways are we, knowingly or unknowingly, also responsible for what occurred on September 11th? We have acted brutally toward other people. How must we scrutinize our souls?

The path to healing and the path to the well-being of the community are the same. We follow the story as best as we can. We change our lives as best as we can. When our lives change, the lives of those around us change. Healing is contagious. The different lives we live are not as prone to cause disease as they once were. We step out of toxic and noxious circumstances as best as we can. We revise our priorities. We say health or goodness is of primary importance for ourselves because they will be offered simultaneously to others. We can make a primary commitment to the earth because in that way we make a primary commitment to all people and all beings.

We heal ourselves by healing others, by the gestures we make. A cure may be effective for us but may not favor the well-being of others.

We have invented strange ways to cure cancer. Surgery, radiation, chemotherapy. The sword, the nuclear bomb, chemical warfare. These are strangely like our immediate response to retaliate. We are attacked. We attack. Our psyches are organized in terms of enemies. We created more pain and anguish. No good comes of it. This is not the way of the healer.

To heal ourselves we begin to work at the root, to do the radical labor. We find the imbalances and the inharmonious circumstances in our lives and the lives around us. We root out what undermines us and we affiliate with what sustains us. We find the circumstances under which disease incubates and what prohibits disease from entering.

When she returned from Africa with a cough that she could not cure, Valerie Wolf asked for a dream. In it, she asked the old ones for the medicine for her cough. "There is no medicine," they said, "except that you must make the environment inhospitable to the disease."

Make the environment inhospitable to the disease. This is another way, altogether, of understanding the path of healing, whether on the physical or emotional level, or whether we committed to discovering the way to heal the body politic. The difference between attacking cancer and healing the body. The entire body. The body politic. The world. The entire globe.

*   *   *

Michael and I are in the car on the way to the theatre but we will never get there because of traffic. If we continue at this pace on the freeway, we will arrive when the play is over and the audience dispersed. Locked into the small space of the car, the tensions between us increase. Michael has been saying the first *surras* of the Koran, the essential prayer of Muslim people, as his doorway to the Divine. It is an act of alliance with the innocent people we are killing. He learned it from several Muslim men he met in the chapel at the hospital where he works. They take down the prayer rugs, he takes down a prayer rug, they/he raise their hands to the sides of their heads as a gesture of being willing to hear and submit to the words of God, and then they all bow down, forehead to the floor. My heart breaks open when I hear that he is doing this and he recites the words for me in Arabic and English with great reverence. But as I listen, I cannot forget the women in burkhas, the women who are not permitted to go outdoors alone, who are not permitted to earn money, or study, or see doctors, to do anything on their own. I cannot forget the women who have been stoned. I cannot forgive this. I watch the gestures that he and I are both making now toward the Muslim world and I cannot forgive myself that I didn't make these gestures, didn't step forward, when the war was essentially against the women. I praise and denounce my husband at the same time. I admire what he is doing and I hate what he is doing. He praises the prayers without commenting on the passages that are aggressive. Just at the moment when I am cutting the aggression and violence of my/our traditions out of my heart, he is stepping toward the traditions. The anger that is generated between us fills the small space. I think the car must be red hot. It must be glowing on the outside. It will explode in a moment and then we will remain on this freeway forever. When it is impossible for the two of us to be in the car at the same time and equally impossible for either of us to exit, I understand what is happening. I put my hand on his arm. He jumps defensively and then calms. "I know what is happening," I say. "The war is in our house."

The war is right here. I have spent months scrutinizing my own religion and then Christianity, wrestling with the aggression and violence inherent in the two traditions. I claim that which speaks of beauty and ethics. I disclaim every word that does not bring peace to everyone. But I am unable to criticize the Koran in the same way as the Old and New Testamaents because the President has declared war against the Muslim world in my name, and so I must stand alongside these people who are being tormented now.

Some say the teachings and the religions that have come from these Books are sufficient to justify calling them sacred. I disagree now. The times are too precarious. Wars come from these books. This war. This untenable war.

I make war against my husband for his kindness. It is a shameful act on my part. But I feel I must defend the women who are being used for propaganda purposes by our government, who are undefended. They are not part of the coalition government so I must do this. I must fight for them. Still, war is not the answer. I know this. I read it on the bumper sticker on my car: WAR IS NOT THE ANSWER. I try to return to my heart. To be conscious. To find kindness in me.

*   *   *

I think of the practice of my friend Peter's daughter, Sheba and her husband, Mike. He has recovered from a stem cell transplant. The treatment took him down to the bottom, his immune system was destroyed entirely, and then he was brought back to life. When he was hovering between life and death because of the treatment he was undergoing, his buddies surrounded him. Peter said that the appearance of the firefighters at his bed was like the entrance of health itself into the dreary world of the hospital. Every community that was connected to him in any way prayed for him. One night we had a music Daré on his behalf. He was quarantined in his hospital room but Peter came and sang the Kanzeon Sutra:

Kan ze on	Praise to Buddha,
na mu butsu	All are one with Buddha,
yo butsu u in	All awake to Buddha.
yo butsu u en	Buddha, Dharma, Sangha,
bup po so en	Freedom, joy and purity.
jo raku ga jo	Through the day, Kanzeon.
cho nen Kan ze on	Through the night, Kanzeon.
bo nen Kan ze on	This moment arises from Mind,
nen nen ju shin ki	This moment itself is Mind.
nen fu ri shin	

He sings in his sonorous voice, full of grief and hope. The father fighting for his son. The poet acting on behalf of life. Gazing, without looking away, at the terrible reality. And so calling compassion, so calling generosity, so calling life into the world. Kwan Yin. That afternoon, Mike had had no T cells. The next day his count improved drastically. Health is returning.

Mike returns home. He recovers. He returns to work. He loves life. When he and Sheba come home each night, they do a small ritual so that the war that is outside does not enter their house. "Let us do a ritual," I beg Michael, "so that the war does not enter our house. We must declare our house a war-free zone." I design a bumper sticker: MAY YOUR HEART AND MIND BE WAR-FREE ZONES. The message is for me before it is for anyone else.

We go down to the core, we scrutinize ourselves and our loyalties and we root out that which does not serve the life force of all beings. We know now that our lives depend on it. And the lives of every one and everything around us. To work toward healing oneself has become a sacred labor. Disease may fell us but we cannot lie down; it is calling us out of ourselves to do whatever we can on behalf of the community and all beings. That is what it means to meet our death.

I did not know all of what it meant when I wrote that the path of healing and the path toward a good death were the same. I do not know all of what it means that the path of healing oneself and the path of healing the community are the same. I do know that we are in this work together.

How does healing occur? Heal the life and the life will heal you. This is our work now: We must heal the life around us and we will heal accordingly.

11

*O*mphalos. Uroboros. The continuity of the present and the mythic past. A world that is not divided between past, present and future. Everything there. Simultaneous and coherent.

This is not being written in a straight line. I do not go from here to there. I begin a text and then it circles back on itself. Sometimes I say writing is like an accordion, you must keep expanding and filling in the middle, but that is not the only way. You can circle back and fill in what completes the thought, you can add the musical associations of meaning and then spiral up again. You spiral around a point. You find the center and circle around the perimeter. This is what we did before the *omphalos* at the Great Enclosure of the Queen.

*   *   *

In the early 70's, I was challenged by the questions posed by Sheila de Bretteville, one of the founders of the Woman's Building, a designer and feminist with a most original and penetrating mind who was investigating the forms of woman's culture. For myself, I reframed the questions she was asking this way: Is there a woman's culture? Is there a woman's literature? If so what might its forms be? How is it related to woman's culture as a whole? Is it shaped or is it indigenous? Do the forms develop from our nature or from the roles we have been playing for centuries? Or is woman's literature being invented now in response to the circumstances of our awakening? And finally, shall we try to invent literary forms? Are there ways in which the essential nature of the culture of women as lived over centuries might be made visible and viable by being translated into literary forms?

Teaching *To the Lighthouse* by Virginia Woolf was a form of awakening for me because I saw the coexistence of the form and the image. The lighthouse. The light at the center. That eternal intelligence that passed now here and now there, illuminating equally whatever was in its path. A literary form as well as a literary trope. A way of knowing and of perception independent of chronology for meaning. It freed the text from the tyranny of development and progress. It was liberated from the theology of chance and will, accident and willfulness. It freed the form from the drama of climax. It was not reliant upon the hegemony of the human resolve and determination or its failures. A narrative in alignment with the way of the contemplative mind, its ruminations and reflections, its movement and return. Or a narrative alignment coherent with the cycles of life, birth, growth and death, the seasons, the round of a day. A slow and steady way, reliable and well-suited to the dark from which the creative act was evoked.

Speaking of woman's culture in the early seventies, we found ourselves focusing upon certain ideas, trying to fathom their implications. Woman's culture, we said, was complex, multi-faceted, multi-dimensional, inclusive, non-hierarchical. It was not authoritarian nor absolutist. It was not totalitarian. It was not pompous. It was like bricolage, made of scraps and remnants, gathering what was torn and broken. It was organic and dynamic. It was personal and subjective. It was vital; it was not abstract. It was bloody from birth and from the deaths that nature imposed. It was not eternal, it was not monumental, it was not institutional. Woman's culture was circular rather than linear. Women think, we said, with the heart not dispassionately with the head. Or as I wrote during that time: I believe in metaphor – in what brings us together not what sets us apart.

No longer can we assign these qualities to women and the qualities of the dominant culture to men – such attributions created even more divisions. But, we can recognize many of these qualities as central to indigenous mind.

I am surprised at where this exercise of reflection has taken me. I am circling back to what was important when I first began teaching. In order to go forward I have to go back. I did not expect to come upon this. I have come to a time in my life when I am trying to find a way out of "us and them," out of good and evil, out of the delusion of duality. There is a pattern. It is more consistent than I could have possibly imagined and it reveals itself now in this manner and now in this way. I have circled back again and again without knowing that I was in the spiral of a story to which I had given my entire life.

So we go forward and then we will circle back to all the questions raised here that cannot be answered in a linear sequence or one that implies separation. Discrete and distinct events may follow one another with no inherent correlation but that of sequence, but that is not the way of meaning. Or events may be related causally, but even these connections have more complexity to them. We are in a field of knowing and relationship and I am trying to find a form that honors those connections. This is an aesthetic choice but that is not it entirely. A culture that has developed from focusing upon distinction and separation from the natural world has brought us to this hell moment of history. The way back may be through inter-connection but we cannot achieve it with the old forms. How do you write a field of relationships? How do you right them?

*   *   *

Augustine took the second group of people who had come to Africa for initiation out for a game ride at the Chobe Wild Animal Preserve in Botswana. We had taken the first group to Hwange in Zimbabwe several weeks before but had found that landscape almost destitute of life. I was ill and could not go out and Michael stayed with me. "Look for the Ambassador," I called out to them, reminding them of the elephant that had approached us in such a remarkable manner several years before and of which we will speak later. They went to the place where we had met the Ambassador but neither he nor other animals were there by the river. But when they turned inward on a road Augustine had not driven before, a female elephant stopped them. She ambled to the open back of the truck where Chuck, Wilderness and Robin were seated and paused before them. For a long time, ten, twenty minutes she stood there, occasionally catching one or another of their eyes, making circles in the dust with her trunk in the manner of those elephants who have become painters.

"What was she saying? What was the message?" they asked when they returned. "What's a circle?" I asked in return. We have been thinking in circles recently. We sit council in circles. We join women's and men's circles. But what is the circle? What are its implications for culture? How does it reshape our minds? How might it heal?

I am a woman who has been brought to circles again and again in the last thirty years. I had not thought that such a moment in history as we are living in would cause me to circle back to a class I taught in 1971.

The Circle. Daré. Council. We sit in a circle and pass a talking stick. We address a question by telling the deep and true stories of our lives: How do I walk in two worlds at once? What do I know about healing? When was I able to bring healing to someone or a situation? What grief am I carrying? What experiences revealed the presence of Spirit? What was the moment that called me forth?

The stories become one story. We carry them and contemplate them all month. The stories become our stories. Our wisdom develops from these stories. "No ideas but in things." No wisdom but in stories. Circles of stories and stories in circles. ֍ Samech. This is how a community is invoked.

There is no beginning and no end to this story, unlike my life, our lives. The snake with its tail in its mouth, continuity with the mythic past, encircles and protects the world egg. The stories are not only of our own making. Some stories are inscribed upon us by the Divine in an alphabet difficult to discern. ֍ Samech. The circle. The endless cycle. The wedding ring. Support. The continuity of endings and beginnings.

These are the stories that call us to Spirit. Flashes and moments interspersed here and there as if outside of sequence and without a recognizable pattern. Stumbling in the dark. Hither and thither. And yet seemingly inspired. And then they are revealed. A constellation forms out of the incoherent scatter of stars. We recognize a pattern and choose to follow its intelligence, we try to fathom its meaning or influence. We understand that it affects us by the strange and symbolic arrangement of its parts. It is a figure of light and it is a story. This dynamic affects us in ways we cannot fathom. This configuration calls to us. Each direction toward or away can be called our fate. To yield to the Divine, though it calls one away from the collective, its ego priorities and certainties, is to enter a story seemingly directed at us in particular but that resonates with the life and intelligence of this planet. It circles toward something else, a mystery that is beautiful beyond telling.

*   *   *

1990. Michael, theatre director Steven Kent, and I stood among a group of *mystes* that we had brought to Greece to enact the Eleusinian Mysteries, the great rites of transformation dedicated to Demeter that we had enacted ten years earlier for, as far as we knew, the first time in 1500 years. We spent a year reconstructing, recovering, re-imagining the Mysteries. Now we stand together before the *omphalos* of Delphi. This is the center of the world. What does this mean? It means we were attached to the earth here. It means we come out of this place. It means that we were carried here in the womb of the earth. It means the earth is our mother and so this is the place of ritual power and possibility.

People were called to the Mysteries for the sake of their own souls but they were not separate from the fate of the community. The final words of the Mysteries are: Hye Kye, Rain, Be Fertile! That day we prayed for rain to end a drought so severe that water had to be delivered by boat to Santorini Island. As we were returning to the hotel on the very last day, after we had completed all the rites, rains came. We were in a story, an ancient story that we were living alongside our own individual contemporary stories. Continuity between the present and the mythic past. The convergence of personal healing and the healing of the land.

Five years later, during the third enactment, at Eleusis itself, two women, ceramicist Colleen Wimmer, and the archeologist Constance Pieseinger, reached into a crevice to plant sacred corn. This site, we had been assured by an initially most skeptical resident archeologist, had been thoroughly scoured for ancient objects. In the Telesterion, the very sacred place where it was said the Great Goddess Persephone would appear in a vision to the pilgrims who were enacting the Mysteries, the two women found a votive figure, the Goddess herself, most probably dating from 500 BCE or earlier. The sacred circle. The past and present integrated into a common story that flowers into an ongoing future.

*   *   *

Here is another beginning. I met Barbara Myerhoff on my 21st birthday, September 17th, 1957, the day after I arrived in California. She was studying then to be an anthropologist. The Huichol Indians of the area around Tepic, Mexico were the subjects of her dissertation and I quickly became the recipient of her stories and experiences when she would return from her fieldwork. We were a strange duo, the two of us, for she went out and did the work and I incorporated her findings and discoveries into my imagination. It was always the case that I didn't find the courage or means to go out then and be among the people who called to me so powerfully. And, Barbara didn't find the means to begin to live according to the understandings that moved her so powerfully on an intellectual and spiritual basis. It was Barbara's work that resulted in the novel, *Flying with a Rock*, that I discussed earlier. And it was Barbara who informed me that the ending of the novel, the soul flying out of the woman's mouth in the shape of a fly, was an ancient image from Siberian shamanism. I did not know this when the image came to me and I was compelled to write it down.

Barbara's connection with the Huichol was the means through which the assumptions of western mind were first broken down in both of us. We were alarmed and we were engaged by the recognition that these world-views, so foreign to us, were assaulting the citadel of western rationalism in ourselves. When Barbara died of cancer in 1985, many of us thought that her death was due in part to her inability to fully step across the line to Spirit, whether in the form of indigenous mind or the orthodox Jews that she had studied at the end of her life. The rigor of her training as an anthropologist and her commitment to academic life and procedures con-strained the other impulse to enter into a native or tribal mind and world-view. Anthropologists are always cautioned about "going native." Barbara was torn apart by the irreconcilable tension between one way of knowing and another. One of her informants who became an honored friend and associate, a renowned very orthodox Rabbi who was willing to officiate Barbara's funeral alongside a reformed woman Rabbi who was also a friend and colleague of Barbara's, had spent years underground in the dark, in a basement or cave, studying Torah. When I learned about the Kogi, I was intrigued that their spiritual education also took place in the dark.

Here is one of the conflicts that is tearing us all apart: the light of edu-cation and enlightenment pitted against the dark of the mysteries and spir-itual awareness; the tension between Apollo and Dionysus whose temples, nevertheless, were situated alongside each other in Pergamum and Delphi, between Europe and Africa, between European and native, between the Church and the natives of North and South America, between religion and spirit, between order and chaos, the sky gods and the earth mother, white against black, day against night. Dualistic thinking sets one part of oneself or the universe against the other. But there is another way that is based upon the ecological model, the way of Gaia, the order of the universe. A model that truly honors and is dependent upon diversity and so is inclusive and respectful of all ways and all beings. An order that recognizes the interdependence and autonomy of the animals and the spirits existing within and alongside the human realm. An order that sees the holy every-where and so is not predicated on the existence of the enemy in order to establish its own identity.

*   *   *

After Michael and I became lovers, a year after Barbara died, I gave him a T-shirt with an image of the shaman of Trois Frères. He looked at me as if I had penetrated a deep secret. Our marriage was sealed then through this meeting in the territory of the old ones. I hadn't known what that image might mean to him, but I was gratified that he understood the gift. Memory changes the course of events. Now I know that the story that I am in is fed, like a river, by other stories, tributaries, including one that began in 1986. As one story seems to begin there, whatever follows is on its trajectory. We are going somewhere I never expected to go. We can draw a straight line between the shaman of Trois Frères and Siloswane, the Bushman cave in Matopos, Zimbabwe where shamans painted on the walls thousands of years ago still leap into the air while the women dance beside a giraffe. Past and future meet in a seamless present moment that is the story of the way the dreamers and the dancers found the ecstatic pace which allowed them to dissolve the wall of difference between human and animal, to enter the spirit world where they can co-exist in a common life.

After the fall of the Towers, I was called back, with great urgency, to that Bushman cave, Siloswane. After the giving of gifts, we went off separately to pray. I prayed that the ancestors and animals enter into me with their insight and wisdom. Now as I watch my mind, I recognize that this has occurred. A prayer answered. A fearful moment. A strange mind. Indigenous thought. It is not shaped by religions, their Books, distortions, enmities and wars. This mind is an entirely different mind altogether. The Bushmen reached to the animals and the spirits simultaneously. They hunted and performed rituals. They danced in the secret caves. They drummed and called the gods. They were not separated from the natural world and so they were not separated from the dharma. My heart is with them.

*   *   *

Driving along Pacific Coast Highway in mid-afternoon. Sun bright on the green blue waters of the Pacific. I am wretched with concern about the world. I hear a voice in my mind that I know is not my voice or my mind.

"All you have to do is put the forms in place."

I laugh. All I have to do… the forms. What are they? And afterwards, don't I have to see how they are used? Whether they are recognized? Respected? Be sure they aren't co-opted?

"All you have to do is put the forms in place."

"Who are you?"

"We are the Sanhedrin."

I had never, in my conscious memory, said the name "Sanhedrin" or thought of these seventy sages who descended upon Moses to help him in judgment or leadership and who remain as the council of wise ancestors to guide the living.

Teach the pattern. Put the forms in place.

12

Events occur in chronological order but their meaning is not in their chronology. In our memories they organize themselves into various interconnecting webs. Past, present and future are variously colored co-existing threads. We weave a life out of such coincidences that have become stories.

One day I journeyed in the ways shamans journey and met an elephant. Elephant was not the animal I imagined meeting. But elephant is the animal who came. I looked hard and deep into her large, wise, grieving elephant eye. Or she looked equally hard into mine. She was in one world and I was in another and we are each real in our worlds. Later I traveled to South Africa to meet her. She evaded me. The last day I was there a breeding herd was finally sighted and we set out to meet them. The veldt was redolent with the smell of elephant. There were the trees freshly overturned, there the grasses trampled, there her footprints in the mud by the water hole, but the elephants had crossed the river and we were not permitted to follow.

Instead of meeting these elephants, I was told a story of an elephant captive in a zoo in Toronto where Patricia Langer was living. Gillian van Houten, a writer and photographer who was hosting Patricia and myself at Londolozi was concerned about Angus. She and her husband wanted to repatriate Angus to South Africa in order to make a film that tells the story of the African elephant. They wanted to take Angus from village to village so that Angus could be an ambassador to the children. Nelson Mandela had agreed to welcome Angus home. But, Gillian said that aside from the prohibitive cost of transporting Angus from Canada to South Africa, Angus is afraid to return; he is afraid of his memories of the cull.

Conscience required that Gillian witness a cull in Kruger Park and write about it. *The Elephant Cull* was published by Femina in 1993.

154

The cull is done from a helicopter hollowly nicknamed the angel of death by the crew. The elephant is shot with a dart containing an immobilizing drug called scholine and then a bullet is fired into its brain. If one could use the word humane in this context the cull is done this way to prevent an inaccurate shot wounding the animal. Much has been done to improve the drugs used. Once immobile, the elephant remains fully conscious – the skeletal muscles are the first to collapse, the heart and respiratory muscles follow soon after. It is critical that the bullet follows swiftly, otherwise the elephant will suffocate. The calves destined for relocation are then darted with M99, a drug that renders them unconscious until they are revived with an antidote and loaded into crates....

Hugo identified a group of 14 and the chopper swooped in low. We continued working the herd to see if it would fracture further but this was a cohesive group, a family. With the chopper in pursuit, the matriarch ran this way and that seeking escape. The others followed closely behind her, mothers circling their babies and creating a wall of protection with their bodies.

...Hugo announced that we were going in and the chopper swooped. The matriarch, accepting the finality of the situation, pushed her baby into a bush in an attempt to conceal it and turned in defiant anger to face the chopper. Stripped of her majesty and her power, defenseless, she was going to defend her baby to the end. The dart gun fired, an anticlimactic thunk. She staggered under the impact and began to lurch as the drug took effect. She fell to her knees, struggled desperately to rise to her feet and then collapsed kicking.

The family, now leaderless, milled around in panic and confusion. The chopper circled holding them up as one dart after the other was fired until all the adults had been struck. By now the matriarch was completely immobile, but through the lens of my camera, I could see her eyes and I knew she was fully aware of the mayhem around her. Her baby stood next to her, pressing close to her inert body, pathetically trying to push her up with his little body and tugging at her with his tiny trunk. He regurgitated water on her in a last desperate attempt to revive her and then huddled closer to her body, his head hung low.

...By now all the adult females were down, struggling and kicking. ...The calves were milling aimlessly around the dead cows, secretions pouring from their temporal glands indicating their terror.... A young bull, his family lying dead or unconscious around him, was the last left standing, fighting a full 10 minutes before he too staggered and fell.

It was all over. For a moment frozen in time nothing moved beneath us and an eerie stillness settled over the scene, the only sound the flip-flip-flip as the helicopter hovered over the scene of the carnage.[36]

It broke her but she could not look away. She had to report it. So she knew what Angus feared as I know what Angus feared because I made a pilgrimage to the death camps of Central Europe. I wanted to speak to Angus about remembering. I thought I might understand something of the torture of memory and also about what is being asked of all of us in these times. Something asked particularly of those who are willing or able to remember. Of course, the death camps are not my memories; they are the memories of my people. I came there after the fact and I was only there a month. Still, I spent ten years writing about it in *The Other Hand* and in those ten years the memories entered into my soul and flesh.[37] Not my memories but as if they are my memories. Because of this, I thought there might be understanding between us, between this woman who is claiming a memory and this elephant who is tortured by it.

But when I went to see Angus, his trainer and keeper took Angus elsewhere. And no matter how I tried to come to see Angus another time, it could, apparently, not be arranged. What I did see was a bull elephant in mutsch, legs akimbo, chained to the wall within a small cell. Such is the fate of male elephants in captivity whose bodies demand that they seek out a female in order to mate. Chains. Restraints. They are forced to live like this. "A male elephant in mutsch," a keeper said, "is mean. They are not trustworthy. They have to be restrained." It can go on for months. This was the fate from which I wanted to save Angus. I wanted to warn to him about the prison that was coming and to ask him to consider the alternatives. To consider what his return might mean for the elephant people.

When I was in Africa, Augustine's mother was afflicted with continuous pain in her leg and hip. The pain was always there as was her memory of an exploding land mine. Augustine had had a dream warning him of an impending disaster. He had tried to detain his mother who had been visiting him in Harare, but she had set out determinedly. Of the group she had been traveling among, she was the only one who survived. As we did not speak a common language, she would stop us as we passed and carefully point to the mystery of the places of pain. Her gestures were haunting, she traced the path of injury from hip to calf again and again. We followed her, our fingers poised upon the breaks hoping that the balm of prayer might bring at least temporary relief. Land mines seeded by one war after another like alien vegetation gone wild and noxious are now part of the flora of Africa. Of all the animals, including human animals, tormented by these land mines, elephants suffer the most, thanks to Great Britain and its colonial policies.

On the way from the zoo where Angus is confined, Patricia and I stopped in a small town in search of an unlikely caffe latte and came upon a curio shop where there was a photograph of an elephant's eye; a photograph of my dream.

Later that night, in a lovely cabin on a lake in Canada, I saw possibilities. The matriarch elephant is the one who teaches the young bull elephants the land. Without her presence and wisdom, the young bulls are disoriented. During the culls, all the matriarchs are killed. Sometimes a few young bulls are relocated to foreign areas, other countries. (Because elephants remember what has happened and communicate it, it is now the policy to kill all the elephants, all the witnesses to the cull.) Angus was such a bull, taken to Canada, to snow and servitude. I became an advocate for Angus. Might he be met in Africa by a matriarch who could teach him the geography upon which his life and sanity would depend? If so, it seemed to me, he would not be so afraid of his memories; ground under our feet sustains us even in the worst of times. Then, perhaps, Angus could do the work being asked of him on behalf of his people.

Afterwards walking in the woods in Arizona, I found myself looking for signs. I came across a gray weathered trunk of a tree foreshortened by wind and lightning. A remaining branch extends as if the face of elephant. Hyper-imagination. No matter. Individually each event is coincidental but story draws them together into a little nexus which has its own power and intelligence. What begins willy-nilly becomes the web of fate.

The next year I met the Ambassador and then a few months later I finally met Angus.

13

JOURNAL ENTRIES:

February 20, 2001. I am teaching at WOW, a woman's conference in Seattle:

Air strikes against Iraq. War maneuvers with Israel. A stolen election. The President... the Pretender. Is this our equivalent of the fall of the Weimar Republic? What is coming? How will we meet it? Last year, I asked my students to read *Hope Against Hope*, by Nadezhda Mandelstam, the wife of the poet, Osip, who was killed by Stalin in 1938. It chronicled the years between 1932 and 1938. The worst of Stalinism. How people were coerced to go along with Stalin and millions suffered and died. A story of state terror that paralleled the rise of Hitler.

* * *

I meet with three women, one of whom, Shawna Carroll, has been my student since California Institute for the Arts, in the 1970's. The three women have been friends for years and clearly love each other. Their minds dance together and sometimes it is as if they are of a single mind that unites the three of them without anyone being lost or diminished.

* * *

The pattern: The dynamic simultaneity of minds attuned through common purpose and intent. An openness of heart, a love of the Divine and so acting as if one mind. One mind without leadership or assertion, aligned in the wave. A single piece of music composed for and of different instruments, each playing or singing his/her own distinct line. The genius of jazz. Coherence intuited. The precise communication of a flock of birds. The herd of elephants I walk among or behind in my mind. The intelligence of the herd that incorporates the breeding herd, matriarchs and calves with the more remote intelligence of the isolated bulls but still, all of them, acting in concert. *Mandlovu.* The female elephant. The Great Mother. *Mambokadze.* The Queen. The Virgin Mary. *Mandlovu* mind.

*   *   *

MANDLOVU MIND

Suddenly, I am of a single mind extended
Across an unknown geography,
And imprinted, as if by a river, on the moment.
A mind held in unison by a large gray tribe
Meandering in reverent concert
among trees, feasting on leaves.
One great eye reflecting blue
From the turn inward
Toward the hidden sky that, again,
Like an underground stream
Continuously nourishes
What will appear after the dawn
Bleaches away the mystery in which we rock
Through the endless green dark.

I am drawn forward by the lattice,
By a concordance of light and intelligence
Constituted from the unceasing and consonant
Hum of cows and the inaudible bellow of bulls,
A web thrumming and gliding
Along the pathways we remember
Miles later or ages past.

I am, we are,
Who can distinguish us?
A gathering of souls, hulking and muddied,
Large enough – if there is a purpose –
To carry the accumulated joy of centuries
Walking thus within each other's
Particular knowing and delight.

This is our grace: To be a note
In the exact chord that animates creation,
The dissolve of all the rivers
That are both place and moment,
An ocean of mind moving
Forward and back,
Outside of any motion
Contained within it.

This is particle and wave. How simple.
The merest conversation between us
Becoming the essential drone
Into which we gladly disappear.
A common music, a singular heavy tread,
Ceaselessly carving a path,
For the waters tumbling invisibly
Beneath.

I have always wanted to be with them, with you, so.

*   *   *

Friday, December 14, 2001. 4:44 p.m. I must interrupt. I am in Pine Mountain working on this manuscript. It has been written forward more than a hundred pages, but I have gone back to the beginning to edit it, and have just reached the beginning of this chapter when the phone rings. Jami Sieber is calling from Oakland. She and Agu are leaving on Tuesday for Thailand where she will be living among and playing her cello with the elephants who have been part of the Thai Elephant Orchestra.

During the spring of 1999 in New York, I [David Soldier] met Richard Lair, known as "Professor Elephant" in southeast Asia, the author of the primary reference on the Asian domesticated elephant. Richard, an American expatriate and advisor at the Thai Elephant Conservation Center (TECC) near Lampang Center in northern Thailand. One evening… we naturally wondered whether elephants could learn to play music.

Elephants are highly social animals and we thought they might enjoy making music together…. On arriving in Thailand on January 6, our crew teamed up with Nipakorn, director of the TECC and Richard. We constructed giant slit drums, three large marimba-type instruments much like Thai renats, and a string instrument that sounded like an electric bass (the diddley bow). We made a gong from a circular saw blade confiscated from an illegal logging operation. We bought harmonicas, finger cymbals, a mouth organ (kaen) from Issan in Northeast Thailand and appropriated a bass drum from the TECC show. Altogether, we experimented with twenty instruments.

The mahouts said the elephants especially enjoyed playing the renats. The elephants took easily to the harmonica, which sparked the first elephant music fad: one morning I arrive to hear the sound of harmonicas from all around – from the hills and from the river. The elephants were walking in from the forest playing harmonicas, which they hold easily in the tip of their trunks.[38]

We were speaking about *Mandlovu* mind. The ways the elephants have been reaching out to us. The ways in which we have made an alliance with them, answering their call. I came back to the computer and began reading. Within a few lines, I came to the words about the elephants.

Tuesday, February 5, 2002:
Some lines from Jami Sieber in Thailand, dated Jan. 28, 2002:
All I hear are prayers. All I hear are simple melodies and thoughts. It is like life here. A rainstorm... the crickets and frogs at night... an elephant walking... getting up in the morning to greet the day... the monks singing in unison the chants that are ritually sung all over the country... no harmony... nothing too complex.

Every note that I play has images tied to the elephant. ... I am starting to envision an endless musical stream that flows from one piece to another.

I played a simple melody today and the working title is "Anybody out there?" It was inspired by the book I am reading *The White Bone* by Barbara Gawdy as well as my experience here. The elephants are in search of their tribe after a slaughter where most were killed and the rest scattered in different directions. There is this constant longing for one another and for the place they call the Safe Place that is mythical and comes to them in visions and dream. It is a heart-wrenching story. Even as I write this, I am crying thinking of the elephants, who I have come to love so much, feeling at such a loss. That searching found its way into a simple melody where as I played it, I listened to the space in between the notes. That is where the response would be to the calling. That is where the answer is held. I can feel it all so deeply. . . .

*   *   *

May 4, 2001. Journal, Toronto:

Patricia Langer and I are at the bedside of R.B., a Cree elder, to whom Patricia and her students have been bringing healing for several years. R.B. is dying of cancer and attributes her illness to a curse. She asks me to journey for her to lift the curse so she can be restored to health. The Cree believe that disease is caused by failures within oneself or by another. In the journey, I meet Torn Shirt who, R.B. believes, cursed her. It becomes clear in the journey that Torn Shirt is to heal R.B. We wrestle about this. If Torn Shirt agrees, it will accomplish two deeds. R.B. will be healed and Torn Shirt will be acknowledged as a great healer. But in order for this to be effective, R.B. has to agree to receive healing from the woman she believes is responsible for her dying. Nothing can occur here without forgiveness on both sides. To believe in the essential goodness and substance of the other. To accept that they, when confronted, would choose the path of healing rather than carry the blight of having cursed on their soul.

*   *   *

May 7, 2001:

Healer Training: Deliberately and meticulously undoing the mind so one will, at the end, walk around consistently in healer's mind. Each accomplishes this in her own way, in her own time. There is no program through which one can attain the necessary quality of mind, way of thinking. Determining the nature of one's story, of the ways in which Spirit has revealed itself to each individual. The story determines the path.

*   *   *

June 20, 2001:

I am in a story. The story of a village healer. I said the words and they came to pass. This is called alchemy or kabbalah. A village and healers were brought forth in Malkut. It is strange this passage between the four worlds.

I looked for the right story to begin the book. A story, I have said again and again, is a magnetic force, the pull of a dense star on light and matter, pulling it toward, into itself. A story shapes the material by its pull of what matters toward its light. A story is not a line; it is a cluster of stars. Each time I think of the book, the first story changes.

*   *   *

In this moment, this is the first story. Today. The solstice. Five years ago, I was in Norway at the Arctic Circle. I had returned for the summer solstice. That afternoon, I had seen a great bonfire with a small boat at the core of it feeding the flames. I returned to my small room and entered deeply into ritual work and prayer in order to be aligned with Spirit, in order to offer myself as one of those who carries Spirit in the world. Walking out on the jetty at 3 a.m., the exact moment when the solstice occurred, I aligned myself exactly with the break between two mountain peaks where the midnight sun that never sets would soon emerge and shower us with golden light. Absolutely still, I meditated upon the cease-less blue. Then a sudden storm materialized out of the emptiness and the entire sky instantly turned black casting cobalt shadows over the land as a great shaft of light broke through the sudden clouds and the sun was born. A small speedboat had been making its way toward the marina. When the sky closed and then the light exploded, the driver of the boat stood up, cried out exultantly, and spiraled out to sea in ecstatic rills.

> Have I seen the Midnight Sun?
> Sky turns black
> as the light is born
> Comes the blue
> that lies between
> dark and light
> and day and night.

> Have I seen the Northern Lights?
> Letters of flame
> sign the Holy Name
> Comes the blue
> that lies between
> what is seen
> and what's unseen.

I have seen the midnight sun
birds ecstatic in the dawn
Comes the light
from paradise
sky of fire, sky of ice

Comes the green
that's in-between
what is living
and a dream.

I have seen the midnight sun
rain falling on Platinum
Rainbow as a covenant
God Exists
And Beauty's won
Rainbow as a covenant
God Exists
And Beauty has won.

*   *   *

God appears in many forms. I perceive God's presence in light, another sees God in the appearance of Owl or Crow or water. Different manifestations for each of us who pray for such a vision in order to know how to walk in the world, and different manifestations for different cultures, therefore the different names. The gods of the crossroads have different names for the same mystery of the reconciliation of the different worlds. Hekate, Eshu Elegba, Hermes or Tehuti, profoundly distinct and essentially the same. Jesus and Adonis and Tammuz, different and the same. Our task is to recognize that the name we choose only approaches the Awesome Presence and we must be careful to prevent the Presence from being reduced in our minds by the narrow parameters of the name we use.

*   *   *

November 23, 2001. Journal:

I was at Sinai on my birthday as I had been when I was 60, five years ago. I was there on the equinox, my 65th birthday, Rosh Hashanah, with Augustine Kandemwa. This is the life of a village healer and this is the story of it, that it could be re-imagined, that it could come to be. But also, this is the mind of a village healer, a mind changed down to the core, to the cellular level, this unimaginable life that has come to pass.

A village. A village when villages no longer exist. They can't be legislated or willed. They appear. They can be invoked. We didn't know this until we were benevolently enchanted. When the village appeared, we were within it and of it simultaneously and it, of us and within ourselves. Our circumstances co-arising and co-creating.

Village. Healing. The fact cohering out of the imagination. No geographic location but, instead, container of mind, spontaneous and original, relationships that continue beyond and independent of the healer. The village becomes a reality though it is constantly forming and reforming itself. A dynamic pattern that is real but is not fixed. And any and all of the members of village may also be constituted as village healers. Nexus of interrelationships. How to find the beautiful words for this?

*   *   *

October 11, 2001. Dream:
I dream of a woman who is trying to commit suicide. She wants to turn the gas on in the oven and when the room is saturated, she is going to strike a match. I do not know if I can prevent her from committing suicide, but I have to prevent her from inflicting her death on everyone else in the house. Running back and forth between those who cannot leave the house and the woman who cannot be dissuaded from blowing everything up, I am overwhelmed with fatigue and anxiety. If I linger here too long, if I make a single mistake, if I am not fully attentive, if I do not follow the inaudible directions... exactly. It is only a matter of time.

*   *   *

Wednesday, February 13, 2002:
I am copyediting the second draft of this manuscript. It is 1 a.m. Michael calls from the hospital. The FBI has announced an imminent terrorist attack by a group from Yemen. It is hard not to be cynical and wonder what the government will devise to draw attention away from the Enron scandal. The Enron scandal should rightly bring this Presidency down. We all pray that a war isn't instigated to prevent this. It would not be first time in American history that hostilities were provoked for political gain.

*   *   *

Many years ago in a dream, a red racing car delivered me to an old mansion. I went in, as I had been taught by the spirits, with my hands outstretched before me and my palms vertical so that I could move easily through the mahogany doors carved with the stories of the agonies of the saints. A man was standing in the middle of the room of power that had the work of the old masters on the wall framed in gold. The furniture was hand carved and hand polished and the velvet drapes and embroidered cushions had been sewn carefully by women with delicate hands. There was a man wearing a superbly tailored gray flannel suit standing in the middle of the room. Heartbreak overtook me. I reached up to stroke the outline of a bullet hole. "You have been wounded in your right temple," I said. The man was God. I turned helplessly and walked through the closed doors again so I could meander through the formal gardens on my way to the street which wound round and round down from this circular height, as from a breast, to the blue waters below.

*   *   *

July 17, 2001. Dream:

A dry, sandstone ravine as one finds in the southwest. I am apprehensive as we climb, if not to the top, to a high point, not unlike the road to a medicine wheel with prayer flags at the Ojai Foundation, which has become a center for training in the way of council. I am assured it is safe to go this far and, indeed, there are others at the top, tourists perhaps. The dangerous ones are the radicals, the activists, who are not practitioners of the old ways but use the rhetoric for nationalistic purposes. Despite the old ways, despite trying to return to them, the people have fallen into violence. Violence everywhere.

I am taken down to a gorge where the people come for healing and counsel and am given a place to sit on what is without question a stone of honor. I protest that I have not been born into the Way. But it is clear that I must take my place as a medicine woman.

July 28, 2001. Dream:

Invaders. War. We are wondering whether we can escape. We look to the hills behind the house. It seems impossible, but if we can cross them, we may have a start. Going up the coast through brush and undergrowth, I come upon a Native American tribe [in the dream there are no signs of identification] and become one of them. I don't know if this is to protect me or to create an alliance. Behind us everything is burning. Again, our hope is to escape to Canada, staying ahead of the flames. We assume, or hope, that the invaders will be preoccupied with the fire and we will escape.

Valerie tells me that setting fires behind one to assist one's escape was a common practice among certain Native American tribes.

14

Dream at the threshold of going to Africa:

Spain. An aerial view of the street as if filming or about to film from the second story of a building. A film is being made of street flamenco dancers. A poor girl. She will never have the money to become a dancer but she is wildly gifted. Somehow, the film crew has found her and she dances as if she is a professional though she is a mere child. It seems she has all the accoutrements and qualities. The dream is like a movie – a documentary and yes, this is her life!

I watch this from a distance above. She cannot fully be seen. We are before a marquee in a European city, crowded and poor, colors of khaki and dirty reds, dark browns. Poverty colors. Desperation. She dances on the street under the marquee and then goes off into the building or theatre, looking back, a thrust to her head, her body exquisitely poised. Her partner is there, invisible, unnoticed, but present. A crowd has gathered; she always dances here.

Later, a throng. The streets filled as if at a street festival. Something is about to begin or is occurring concurrently. A man staggers through the streets. His belly is large but his legs and buttocks are alarmingly thin. His jeans are pulled down and his penis is displayed. Antherium. I lurch toward him to try to offer assistance. What has afflicted him? What has caused this derangement? He hurries to the man who is seated prominently, as if on the throne of the poor, on the sidewalk with stadium seating rising behind him. A ragged and demented but powerful king among the throng. This king anoints the man's penis with firewater. The man, drunk, desperate, staggering, muddied, exposed, is desperate for this extreme ritual, risking everything for the intensity of what he imagines will relieve or restore him.

Now there is new danger. The filming or dance, or street festival has led to danger. The ones they call the Ascensionists have appeared. They will kill anyone with their swords. It is not known what they want. I see an old man on the street also looking for a place to hide from the bloodbath. I pull my dog into a kitchen that is open to the street. Perhaps it is a restaurant kitchen. We huddle holding the door closed so we will not be killed either. The kitchen is, I think, a good place to hide. They will not look here. It has no attraction for them. Polished sedans from the 1930's pass us. They are driven by grim or sober young men in formal dress. In the back seat are young girls in dark red, strapless formal dresses, hair in upsweeps, all looking around as if on parade. There is danger but it is not as dangerous as I first feared. The dog that was compliant on its back now wriggles free.

Then I see them. Brown shirts. They are marching down the street, filling the roadway, ten abreast. I am climbing a steep wide flight of stairs, as steep and broad and narrow as the stairs to the top of the Mexican pyramids… but these are European stairs. There is nothing at the top. No structure. The Brown Shirts. There are not that many yet. They are not the majority yet, but they are very dangerous. We must leave Europe today. If we stay longer, it will be too late. I recognize this energy of men who have been dehumanized and have become soulless and violent. We have twenty-four hours to leave Europe.

I take the dream to Daré. We reflect on the last lines. Twenty-four hours to leave Europe. The Ascensionists. I don't know who they are, but we can just imagine. They are the forerunners of the Brown Shirts. Spain. Franco. Mussolini. Hitler.

Twenty-four hours, we say, to leave European mind. The trajectory that was launched from European mind has brought us here. I begin to think about the Weimar Republic. World War I was followed by unprecedented freedom of mind and spirit in Germany. And then it fell and what followed was the unimaginable. What is happening now in our own country and in the world?

*   *   *

It is only a short time after the beginning of a new millennium that has not brought new hope. We are standing in the ashes. In 1989 I made a pilgrimage to the Death Camps of World War II and literally stood in the ashes that had not disappeared in 44 years. You could stoop down and run your fingers through them. Sometimes there were little pieces of bone; they were my ancestors. One didn't know whether to leave them where they were or bring them home for a proper burial. One didn't know which piece of earth would accept them, where these souls might finally rest. Sixty years later, we are still standing in the ashes. The children of the ashes are in the center of a global conflict that may come to total annihilation. These are my people. I do not question that these are my people. I do not walk away from my people because of this. That is, I do not pretend I do not come from them. I do not deny the wisdom of the tradition. I do not renege on my being Jewish; should I want to, history teaches the impossibility of escaping one's origins. Nevertheless, I mourn where we have been taken and what we have become. And I must scrutinize the tradition that birthed me and sustained me until this time – ethics and Torah on the one hand and the violence of the Old Testament on the other – even as I scrutinize the ways in which my people have been driven mad. Crazed people in a crazed time.

*　　*　　*

Friday, December 14, 2001. Ariel Sharon, Prime Minister of Israel is bombing the Palestinian Authority. This is the man who was implicated in the massacre at Sabra and Shattilah in Lebanon. How is it possible that we have come to this?

Or, let us look at it this way: This is how we came to this. This is the consequence of the holocaust. We hoped and imagined that a people might come through it and somehow remain sane. But they are not sane. Their souls have been eaten.

If this is true, what can we say of the future? So many peoples have suffered the unimaginable and the unendurable. What will become of them? How will their souls be preserved? What will they know or remember about ethics, kindness, compassion? Will they be able to encompass the idea of healing that requires them to consider that the "other" is essential to their survival?

*　　*　　*

Three weeks after terrorists flew into the World Trade Center Towers, my friend, Marc Kaminsky, in Brooklyn, "a neighborhood away" tells me he is still suffering from bronchitis from smoke inhalation. Two buildings were hit and several more came down. In what condition might New York City be if it had been bombed the way we are bombing Afghanistan now or the way we bombed Iraq, Lebanon, Viet Nam? In 1989, before the Wall came down, there were still piles of rubble from World War II near Unter den Linden Platz. I look at the trajectory of history, trying to learn from it. What are the assumptions of the religious traditions that have informed my people and my country? I am compelled to say this: If these traditions have brought us here, then we must not continue on these paths. I cannot say if I am being called into or out of exile.

*　　*　　*

Parallel universes. Planes had headed into the glass, steel and concrete structures that represent world trade and militarism, or as Michael puts it, the movement of resources and money from the south to the north. Laura Bellmay and I were praying for her life, after a recurrence of breast cancer, at the Great Enclosure, the place of the Queen at Masvingo, Great Zimbabwe.

Laura is not a broker or scion of power, but she is a student and teacher of forgiveness.

Masvingo is the 15th century remains of a medieval Shona city, the greatest sub-Saharan center of spiritual and regal authority on the African continent. Nearby, a group of workmen were slowly and carefully rebuilding the wall. It is true, their labor did not look efficient, but this is a sacred site they were restoring, and they met the work, it seemed to us, with quiet reverence. But let us say they met the work casually, they took their time, they did not make a great effort. Then even their ease, the clear and apparent friendliness between them, the playfulness that also characterized each careful gesture, these qualities also become part of the Enclosure, and are as much determinants as are the physical specifications. Perhaps they didn't clearly divide their work lives from their non-work lives. Perhaps they cannot make such a distinction.

When one builds a sacred site, one is not simply aligning stones so that they fit exactly without mortar. The work requires expertise and precision, as it also requires that one knows deeply that one is building a sacred wall. To one who cannot see such distinctions, a structure built with exacting fidelity to the architectural demands but with indifference to its spiritual function may look like what was intended, may look like a temple, though that is not what it has become. The slightest shift in attitude can cause a temple to become a tourist site. The bricks are there but the spirits have fled. Poof! The hands must collaborate with the heart to achieve a sacred intent. Even the most tedious and routine labor done with a sense of the final intent adds significantly to the ultimate achievement.

We noticed that the laborers treated us with a measure of diffidence and respect that we would not have found in our country where the sacred is a fugitive. Though we said prayers, made prostrations, wailed even in pain and grief, not knowing then the true nature of the grief we were experiencing, thinking it was personal, they made no comment, no whistles, no catcalls, no commentary. We found privacy in their presence, and when their workday was over, without saying a word, they, including the guard, left us alone in the Enclosure as if trusting us, and so entrusting us, to honor and protect what is so precious.

We are in the realm here of the relationship between the sacred, invisible world and the secular visible world. They have been so far separated that the secular world can no longer see the handprints of the sacred and so does not believe it exists. We cannot read the handwriting on the wall. One story was being enacted in one part of the world, and another story entirely was being enacted at the other side of the world. We were walking out of an ancient door into freedom and health while a plane was flying into a modern window that would ever afterward open onto hell.

Trouble was not born on September 11th. The Taliban had been torturing the women of Afghanistan since the United States brought them to power. Osama bin Laden, feeling betrayed by the United States, had allegedly masterminded attacks on the United States years before. French newspapers indicate that he and the Taliban were negotiating oil pipelines across Afghanistan with emissaries of the Bush government as late as July 2001 though, theoretically, he was on the most wanted terrorist list. The same pipelines that now, after the war against Afghanistan, are becoming a reality. The so-called underdeveloped or developing world has long felt the painful necessity of progress, the price paid for it, and, its ultimate unfeasibility. The Israeli-Palestinian impasse has been endangering the entire world since the "Allies" established the "troublesome" Jewish survivors there despite the fact that it was inhabited by the Palestinians. These same "Allies" who wouldn't admit the Jews into their countries wouldn't take any responsibility for their part in the holocaust, though history shows how deeply they were all implicated, if only, but not entirely, through indifference. Countries in the Middle East were long suffering from tyrannical governments, oppression, poverty, fundamentalism as were many other countries on the globe and various populations in the United States itself. The results of the year 2000 Presidential election are still obscured. It is not clear whether we have a legitimate government or a coup. Even Congressmen like Dennis Kucinich speak of the "unelected" president. [See Appendix II.] Or if the coup is a corporate coup or a military coup. The environment is devastated and all life is threatened even without any further action on our part.

Before I went to Africa, I was called to journey. The spirits said: Make alliances with those who honor and know how to speak with the spirits, with those who can still speak with the animals and the elementals, who know the holy. Make alliances with those who do not separate themselves from the natural world, from the world of creation. Make alliances with those who live within creation, not outside of it. The spirits said: Make alliances with those at the edges of the world, far from the centers of power. Make alliances with whale and elephant, with wolf and snake, with wind and fire, with water and earth. These and those who have befriended them will be your companions. This is the way of the indigenous mind. This is a mind that can help save creation.

*   *   *

As a young girl, I could travel the subways from Coney Island to 42nd Street and not come to harm. I was no more than ten when I first walked in Manhattan by myself and looked up at the Empire State Building marveling at my good fortune that I had been born in such a city. I thanked the Deity for this great gift. It was 1946. The war was over. I had been born, everyone said so, into unprecedented possibility.

The Bomb and McCarthyism did not diminish most people's enthusiasm for the future. Nor did the Viet Nam war, nor all the other wars, pogroms, genocides that are becoming habitual. What had been unthinkable in the two World Wars is now precedent. We became what we had not been able to imagine. We did it in the dark. We did not know it was ourselves. We thought it was someone else, this shadow of ours that we cast.

...Donald Rumsfeld, the Defense Secretary, says he has told the Pentagon to "think the unthinkable."

15

I have always lived in the world as a stranger. I have always lived in exile. These co-existing contradictions. From the beginning, I had allegiance to elsewhere. A luminous woman appeared at my crib one night; her simple and undeniable presence oriented me to what life is, to what my life could become.

* * *

August 17, 2001. We have returned home to Daré, to Augustine and Simakuhle, their children and Bulawayo. Tomorrow seven women, most of them my students, will arrive for initiation: Valerie Wolf, Hawk, aka Beverly Antaeus, Moseka N'Daya, Moriyah Colaine, Juliette Hanauer, Elenna Rubin Goodman and Barbara Borden. Tonight we must prepare to receive them. Augustine is going to call the spirits to ask for their assistance in the work that opens before us for the next four weeks. He has dreamed some herbs and gathered them from bush and we will take them before we journey. There is, in Zimbabwe, an organization of indigenous healers but Augustine would never join it. They are creating an inventory of native herbs and plants for American and European pharmaceutical companies so that they can isolate the active ingredients and extract or manufacture them for commercial use. Augustine has objected to this. He does not standardize his medicines. He does not use the same herb for the same disease. He treats the patient not the condition. When medicine is required, either he or Simakuhle will dream the herb, and then he will go out and gather it. It is upon this exact relationship with the spirits and ancestors who send the dreams and teach him the healing ways, that his exceptional reputation as a healer is based.

Michael and Simakuhle, who is nursing little Michael, join us in the Daré room where Augustine sits on leopard skins among pots of herbs and bowls of water. He makes the offerings and says the prayers. We pray for the well-being of the people who are coming, that they may be aligned with the spirits and that peace and healing may emerge for the sake of all members of the community and the world.

The room is dark. We begin to journey. After a while, though we have agreed to silence, I can hear Augustine singing and praying. He is trance-possessed by an old grandfather and I can hear him speaking in Shona. But I cannot return. I am elsewhere. I am in a room where the old ones are seated cross-legged around a fire, chanting and praying. They have done this for centuries. They have perfected the ways of calling the healing spir-its into the world. This is not the way of my people. But this is a Way. And I feel the honor of being incorporated into it. I am journeying the way they have journeyed to other realms for millennia. These other realms exist. It is possible to go through the gate. To go there and return. To bring back vision and insight. To invoke the healing spirits to return with us for the sake of the community. I forget where I am because prayer takes me over as if prayer, itself, is a spirit. I give myself to it. There is a black woman to whom I am particularly drawn. I recognize her by her thin legs and bony knees, by the movement of her hands as she seems to be calling the uni-verse into a circle, by the angularity of her face and the smooth seriousness of her countenance. She is an old woman and she is utterly beautiful. It is as if I lower myself into her arms but I am simply lowering myself into her consciousness, into her aspect and her kindness. I realize that I have met her before in visions. Once she was sitting by a riverbank playing the earth as if it were a theremin. It was a time when I was preparing myself to become a crone and an elder. Some days later, after the women arrive, we will be in Masvingo. Sitting in ceremony with *Ambuya* MaGumbo in her painted rondavel at Masvingo, I will recognize the woman who has come to me now and who came to me in a journey so many years ago.

*   *   *

Zou, the young partner of *Ambuya* MaGumbo, like many Zimbabweans carries the name of his animal totem. The first time we met, he was suffering from fatigue with pains through his body. He hoped for a cure and Augustine and Michael attempted to bring lion spirit into his body so that he might become strong. But the strategy failed. Zou cannot carry lion spirits and despite his name he cannot carry elephant spirits. I looked at Zou and saw a small bird with a fluttering heart and took the bird in my hands and gave it the freedom to fly into the bush and hide among the leaves. We cannot become who we are not. The spirits enter us if they wish but we cannot place them where they do not wish to be. We could see that Zou's spirit was lifted.

The second time we met Zou, I saw that his heart was breaking and so master drummer, Barbara Borden, brought her djembe into the rondavel. The heartbeat of the drum entered his body and he came back to life. When we looked up from our labor of restoration, we were being photographed by a group of Catholic nuns who were gathered at the door marveling happily at so many white people working on the black man who is himself a healer.

The healing spirits swirl through the room, sometimes they land here and sometimes they land elsewhere. The great healer is the one who has made his body and life so hospitable to the spirits that they always have a home.

The third time we saw Zou, he said he was healed, but he had only one regret. His dreams had disappeared and he was lonely for them. I gave him a night name; we called him Joseph. I told him the story of Joseph the dreamer and how he had saved the Egyptians from famine. We poured water into a bowl of herbs and anointed him and we prayed as Augustine poured the river Jordan around him. Sometimes the African spirits come forth and sometimes the spirits are from elsewhere. This time Joseph came with his coat of many colors and brought Zou his lost dreams.

This is how I know that I am being welcomed into a tradition. We are making alliances. We are entering into reciprocity.

16

Dreams before meeting the Ambassador:

I was on a roof garden atop a skyscraper. Elephants appeared. They came out in a rush, wanting the children. Reluctant to indulge fear, I felt it nevertheless. An elephant ran by me so close and so fast I assumed he didn't see me between him and the stone walls of the roof garden. Unaware of my presence, he could have easily crushed me. But he didn't. I noted this and calmed myself.

Meanwhile, I heard the silent elephant demand. They wanted the children. I decided not to be afraid and reminded myself that I had been waiting for the elephants and it was necessary to trust them. It was essential; this much I knew. I held my granddaughter Sarah, who is a tiny one, up to them. Others were offering their children to the bull elephants who were growing breasts to nurse the human children. One came by me and stood up on two legs. A voice whispered "Hermit." I gave Sarah to this one who took her gently and happily with his trunk and she snuggled into his chest with great delight. I didn't need to be told the hermit's name. He was Chiron, king of the centaurs, hierophant, great teacher of all the mythic heroes, most renowned as the wounded healer. The elephants disappeared with our children. The roof garden was empty. I dimly perceived that I had offered up my granddaughter to the sacred.

Then a blonde, carefully coiffed woman entered dressed in a Broadway showgirl version of Annie Oakley with short skirt and petticoats, fringed red and white leather vest, cowboy boots and pistols, a lariat, making nervous figure-eights. She was panicked about the safety of her child but pretending that she was trusting. Her anxiety and determination were apparent, they exuded from her like a strong and noxious odor. It was certain that the elephants would smell her fear and also her determination to exercise her will. Now I could smell will; it had an caustic metallic odor. However she approached them, she was certain to provoke the elephants. They would stampede. The children would be killed. The elephants would all be shot. And the woman would never know that it was her action which had caused the tragedy.

I took her aside, insisting that she give me the lariat and the pistols and that she leave the area to allow me to get the child. I was, myself, apprehensive because of the stink of her anxiety and anger. Finally, she relinquished the lariat and guns and departed. It was my task to get all the children back before all the humans panicked. I couldn't accomplish this unless I had full trust *in* and *of* the elephants. How it occurred, I do not know, but the task was accomplished and everything was saved.

*   *   *

We are walking in the bush in a sacred circle. We walk around twice. Perhaps we see the elephants. A man is telling me about walking this circle. The second time, he walked it with the group, someone died and was offered to the animals. But this is not the important focus. What is important is the circle that was walked and the presence of the animals, the elephants, in particular.

Each world has its own laws. When you travel in the western world, it is advisable to buy insurance. When you travel among the spirits, it is best to make an offering.

*   *   *

An offering.

Twelve years after we parted with great enmity, Rose advised her acupuncturist, Diane, that our land is the only place for her hybrid wolf. Diane called and we arranged a meeting to discuss the possibilities though I was skeptical. This was not the right time. But when she brought the wolf, she informed me that she had to leave him with us as she had divorced, had lost her house and had no place for him. There was no time to work with him so that he would feel at home. He was a puppy and needed care, attention and training. The advantage and difficulty of our land is that he is able to run free, to be outside a fenced yard. But, in order to be able to live here without wandering away or becoming aggressive to other animals, he required some training and a great deal of love. We were leaving for Africa in less than two weeks.

Akasha, the wolf who had been with us for several years took to the puppy immediately. Until this moment, I was anguished about leaving her for six weeks. Pami was working long hours and had little time to be with Akasha. Isis, the white, arctic wolf was very old, probably dying. She and Akasha had tolerated each other but they did not provide comfort or companionship for each other. Isis died just after September 11th, having burrowed into the bushes at the outside of my bedroom, in the very spot where Owl, also a wolf hybrid, lay the night before he died. Akasha and I had bonded deeply and I was concerned about how she would fare alone. I had organized the community to come to visit her regularly, but I was afraid this would not be sufficient.

The wolf remained with us. I believe that taking him into the family was the offering I was to make before setting out to see if I could connect once again with the Ambassador, a sincere genuflection to the animal world, recognizing the parity of needs and trying to accommodate them as best as I could. The wolf puppy is black and white, like Owl was, and sleeps in the foliage exactly where Owl used to sleep. He has a brown eye and a blue eye. I couldn't resist this. We call him Blue. When we returned, Akasha had, as requested, trained him. He stays on our land. He doesn't transgress the property line. He does not go out the gate. He is not aggressive, although he and Rusty the neighbor dog go after each other from time to time. Akasha was urged to be sure that Blue does not become the alpha wolf. Rusty, who is entirely benevolent, assisted us here. Blue was quieted. When we returned, we saw that he has come to prefer to sleep outdoors against one or another of the glass paned doors of our house. He has become the guardian.

17

It is time to tell the story of the Ambassador.

For a period of time before I first went to Zimbabwe and South Africa, I met elephants in my journeys and then in my dreams. This was entirely unexpected and at first I thought there had been a mistake, for surely the animal that would come to me would be a North American wolf since I had lived with them for twenty years. Timber Wolf became my companion after my son, Greg, left for college. A year before Timber died, Isis came to live with us. First she was the impossible puppy who disturbed his tranquility, but she quickly matured and became his beloved. Before she was a year old, she went into heat and he tried to mount her with his arthritic legs. Ultimately, the litter wasn't his. But he lay alongside the little compound where she lay with her pups as if they were his. As if she and he had, indeed, become lovers. Then he died. We called him the Buddha of the beasts. He was my familiar and I believed that he or another wolf would always be my totem animal.

Nevertheless it was Elephant that came.

Many months before I first went to Africa, I asked a friend, Amanda Foulger, a shamanic practitioner, to teach me the basics. She taught me to journey and led me in an introductory exercise to meet an animal spirit guide.

I dreamed of an elephant, the sensuousness of her stride, her lustiness and passion, the glory of her sense of her own beauty, the weight of her age, her subtle and intricate relationships with her daughters, sons, grandchildren, members of her tribe, her fears for the savanna, and her humiliation and rage for her kin who had been hunted, killed (culled) during her lifetime and for those of her beloveds who have been kidnapped, enslaved, and bred in public captivity. When I awakened inside my relatively puny body, remembering the knowledge I had briefly held, I felt bereft but strangely comforted by the final image of the dream. As I separated from her, I was confronted by a great unblinking elephant eye, which transmitted everything I had experienced in a wink. And now I return to that memory. See the eye. It flickers. I receive. Now, it's gone ....[39]

Enough dreams followed that I longed to meet the elephants eye to eye and it was my great hope that this would occur when I visited Gillian van Houten at Londolozi in South Africa for the first time. We came upon a bull when we went out on a game drive but he was off in the bush and when we pulled up close it was obvious that we were irritating him and we quickly retreated. All the game drivers on the preserve were alerted to my hope, and they would call us whenever they spotted elephants but the reputed breeding herd remained out of reach. The last evening I was there we picnicked at the site where they had crossed the river and disappeared.

When I returned the next year, I had had yet more dreams and expressed the prayer that I might be able sit in council with Augustine's people and with the elephants. I had put it this way in a council of Elders letter that I sent out before I left on the trip:

We must find ways to sit in council with the animals and the natural world, with those other intelligences who are so deeply threatened by imprisonment, slavery, consumption and extinction.

When I arrived in Africa, I made my hope known to Augustine so that this possibility, mysterious as it was, was part of our consciousness when we went to Chobe, Botswana.

"How does one sit in council with elephants?" Michael had asked.

"I don't know," I had answered. "I do not even know how to imagine it." But, nevertheless, it was my intent.

Michael, Augustine and I were joined by two friends from California, Dr. Michele Sang O'Brien and Amanda Foulger. We had agreed that each person would have a day to devote to her own spiritual pursuits and I chose the day that we were to spend entirely in the park. I prepared for this moment by reviewing my dreams and entering deeply into meditation and prayer.

Then it was time to enter the park.

There were three bull elephants alongside the road and a mother and her calf down below us across the river. I could not find oranges in the store to make an offering, as I was told that elephants love oranges, but I did find grapefruits and so I climb out of the back of the truck and leave them on the ground. Then driving most slowly, greeting the birds and the impala, we followed a turn in the road that opened to a vista with a large bull elephant around three-fourths of a mile away, eating grasses alongside the river. There were two land rovers next to him and I asked Augustine to drive toward him, but not too close, as I would like to avoid the humans. There was something compelling about him. Perhaps it was only that he was so close to the road and there was no brush obscuring him. It was as if, even at this distance, there was nothing between us.

Augustine began driving toward him, but just then a fisher eagle flew over the car and landed on a branch of a neighboring tree. This is Augustine's sacred bird. He calls it a peacemaker. It had happened before that this sacred eagle, Chapungu, had come during a ceremony, and the barrier between this world and the spirit world thinned enough to be virtually transparent. Of course Augustine parked beside what we would afterwards always call the "Chapungu tree" and though the eagle flew away immediately, we stayed there. I began chanting aloud, an ancient kabbalistic chant. I knew the elephant was hearing it.

Slowly the elephant lifted his head from the grasses and began walking along the river. He did not stop to graze nor did he look around but walked with clear determination and intention. I say the words again because they carry what must be communicated here: focused, deliberate, determined, conscious, aware intention.

He stopped directly in front of the truck and raised his trunk toward us. It was over itself and under itself and up and over again. That is, he tied his trunk into an impossible knot. I had never seen photographs of such a movement, of such a mudra. I was on my knees in the flat bed of the pickup. Michael was alongside me. My hands were open on the edge of the truck so that the elephant knew that I was empty-handed, that I had no weapons.

Then the elephant bowed his head. There is no other way of describing it. He bowed his head and unfurled his trunk.

In my mind, I spoke to him:

I know who you are and what kind of beings your people are. I have some sense of the extent and depth of your intelligence and development. And I know that you are a holocausted people. I know something of what this means because I also come from a holocausted people and I have studied other holocausts on the planet in this century. I apologize to you for my species and what we are doing to you. I cannot tell you the extent of my shame and grief. If there is any way for you to imprint me with your wisdom so that we can form an alliance, so that we can, together, accomplish something on behalf of the earth, I am here and I am not afraid.

Then, I silenced my mind. I had said enough. Humans have said enough. I wanted to be empty and to listen. The elephant moved toward me with the same grace and determination as he had moved down the river until he was less than a trunk's distance from me. He could, if he wished, wrap his trunk about me without moving closer. Later Augustine told me that his hand moved twice to start the truck but each time he stopped. He decided even if it came to it to allow me my chosen death.

The two trucks that followed behind the elephant to this point started up their engines and left. Perhaps they were afraid as the elephant was so very close to us. Now we were alone with *Ndlovu*.

The elephant stopped at this distance and looked me in the eye. We stayed this way a long time. Ten minutes perhaps. At least ten minutes. He was a great bull. He was one of the old ones.

Then he turned and moved to the back of the truck and faced it. I turned to him and put my hands out again. We looked at each other eye to eye. There is a meditation practice called *trespasso* where people look into each other's eyes. The task is to be as naked as possible, to allow oneself to be seen as well as to try to see the other. We were doing *trespasso*.

Another ten minutes or so passed. Just before the elephant turned again, I realized that I was in the first dream encounter. This was the moment in the dream when the old matriarch looked into my eye and I was altered forever. And this was the moment in a later dream when a bull elephant wrapped his trunk about me and I was not afraid. I recognized, again, that I was not afraid.

I heard words in my mind and I let them be spoken silently. *I promise you…* is what I heard myself say.

He turned and went behind the truck as if to disappear up the hill into the brush, but turned again and faced the truck and so I turned also and on my knees again acknowledged him. I placed my hands together before my heart, the way one does to bow and honor a holy person. It occurred to me that I was in the presence of one of the faces of God.

Another ten minutes passed. You cannot imagine the silence that descended. The elephant departed, climbing slowly up the hill, and disappeared into the trees. We all leaped out of the car and threw ourselves on the ground in full prostration. Augustine made an offering of snuff and prayed.

When I had words, I asked what must be asked. "Did you see this? Did this happen?"

We did not explain or understand anything except that Amanda said: "You are an ambassador and they sent their ambassador and you have made a covenant with each other."

It was getting late and one must be out of the park by 7 o'clock. We made our way slowly, stopping to watch the sunset and the different creatures. The secretive hippos and their little ones were coming out of the water, small birds were landing on their heads and backs to eat the parasites. We watched them but time tugged at us.

But then we couldn't believe our eyes. Elephants were coming down the hill and crossing the road to the river. At first only a few females and their babies, but then more of them. Waves of elephants. Waves upon waves. Augustine stopped the car and we jumped out and kneeled again. I could hear Amanda sobbing behind me. Even now as I write these words, I am crying again. The elephants continued to come. Dozens of them lined up alongside the river and still more were coming. Bulls and cows, old ones and young ones, babies and adolescents. It was like… I do not know… I think… it was like the world ended and then it was saved and the animals were coming forth into the new dawn. That is what it was like. There are no other words for it.

Someone suggested that we find another road back so that we wouldn't have to cross between the elephants descending the hill and those on the river; we did not want to come between a mother and her calf. But I knew that we must go along the road. They knew we were there. We had to show up for whatever it was they were calling us to do. And so Augustine drove very slowly and very carefully along the river. The elephants were lined up for at least a quarter of a mile, as if for a parade. Now it was Amanda and Michele and myself in the back of the truck as we passed by them. They were bowing their heads and flapping their ears at us. And we were bowing and waving and saying, "Thank you. And bless you. And thank you. And bless you."

*   *   *

I promise you, I will do what I can for your people. I promise you that your people are my people. I promise you.

18

When the animals come to us in dreams or visions, they are not, as the common jargon would have it, our power animals. They do not bring us power. They come to us so we can serve them. So we can carry their intelligence and vision in the world. They come to bring us back through service into the net of all beings.

Elephant came without warning. First, Elephant came in dreams and visions and then Elephant came in reality. It was unexpected. Incomprehensible. Elephant came and spoke of family, kin, cooperation, relationship.

K. Lauren de Boer, editor of *Earthlight Magazine*, Joanne Lauck, author of the *Voice of the Infinite in the Small*, and I, issued a call to readers for stories of their experiences with animals.

People are beginning to tell stories of encounters with animals that reveal intent and agency, and not only on behalf of their own lives but in relationship to human and other sentient beings. It is possible that animals are acting on behalf of each other and the planet in ways that western people have not dared to recognize or imagine. If this is true, then it represents a shift as challenging as that which occurred when Europeans recognized the earth was not the center of the solar system. For humans to live among other sentient beings respecting their intelligence and spiritual development as distinct from but equal to our own might change the ways we live in the natural world and walk among these others.[40]

We do not choose. The animals choose us. We have to learn to yield to what comes. The world is at stake, after all. Our own preferences are irrelevant.

*   *   *

I learned about the foolishness of my own preferences when I was teaching at California Institute for the Arts in 1971. I had devised a Guide meditation for my students and decided to attempt it myself. When I entered into the semi-trance state, I expected Ariadne because I had been writing about her, Theseus and Dionysus, about Apollo and Dionysus, the tension between law and ecstasy, the kind of dichotomy that interests a thirty-five year old divorced woman who was teaching at a new and sometimes wildly innovative institute for the arts. But it was Athena who came, clanking down the corridors of my imagination, fierce, exacting and armored. I had never thought of her consciously. What she said was so unexpected, I had to acknowledge her reality. She said, "You have never been mothered. You have been born out of your father's head as I was." She said, "You are living in a time when men cannot imagine that a beautiful woman may be intelligent or that an intelligent woman might be beautiful. Paris chose Helen over me." She said, "It is foolish to go out in the world and do battle without donning a suit of armor first. Pay attention; I am a warrior."

As I write these words, I pause to ponder them. What armor is appropriate to this moment? What protects one who must say what must be said? What protects one in a time when it is clear that we must have no more martyrs? This is not the time to indulge the stories of the crucified ones. We cannot make another sacred holocaust.

Can one write a book that is itself an esoteric act of healing? Can one say what must be said in a time when silence is being imposed? When a Homeland Security office has been established that breeds all the diseases that come out of silencing?

Today is June 7, 2002:

When a besieged administration demands more security and greater power to spy upon its citizens in response to the questions about what it knew in advance about September 11th, what do we do? This is not a time for silence. It is the time for what the I Ching refers to as "sweet articulating and wise words." This is the time to ask Spirit for the songs that will protect us and will sustain us. That is, the time for music Daré in its most essential form.

*   *   *

What did I learn when I wrote the *Book of Hags*? I learned that cancer is silence. That it grows out of what is suppressed, forbidden, prohibited. That it is the raging growth that demands its own life. That the forbidden and repressed goes underground and then it explodes. An imperialistic force that devours the body that is its host.

How did I learn this? Through that dream about cancer that I spoke of earlier where I was arrested by the DINA, the Chilean secret police, but a Nazi matron was going to torture me. I recognized her from Alain Renais' film, *Night and Fog*. One is tortured, supposedly so one will reveal urgent information, give names. Our government is considering torture and is citing the Israeli "ticking bomb" hypothesis. But really one is tortured so everyone will remain silent. In the dream, the Nazi woman said, "*Sveig.*" She said "Silence!"

I tell this story again and again. Finally, I tell it in *Tree*, the journal I kept when I had cancer. I tell it there so I can offer what I have learned. Cancer is silence, I repeat, urging all of us to our real lives.

*   *   *

I would like to find the straight line that would make this story coherent, in which one event, story or idea would follow inevitably from the other without the confusion of that which is peripheral and associative. But there is no direct line. There is this little cosmos, this world of inter-related parts and events, people and associations, stories and grief. Just then, and now, and the time long before, must be together on the page because they are the continuum and the context of an ongoing event. A dynamic. There is that tiny moment glimpsed out of the corner of one's eye and here is the historic moment, momentous and overwhelming. A child lights a cigar rolled with the healing herbs of the bush. A cruise missile blows up a village.

Today is October 15, 2001. Senator Tom Daschle received an envelope with white powder in it. Anthrax. Two days from now they will shut down Congress. We cannot separate the madness of the sender from the madness that we have enacted in this century. We have all been driven mad.

Steven Kent was in New Orleans to direct John O'Neal in his show *Junebug Jabo Jones.* Walking down the street, they passed a poor black man who was wildly gesticulating to himself, his arms flailing in argument with an invisible crowd. "There is one crazy man," Steve said. "No," John responded, "there is a man who's been crazed."

*   *   *

These are some of the questions I am contemplating: How does one heal someone who does not know he is mad? How does one heal someone who is mad but cannot be incarcerated? How does one address the madness of someone who is not only at large but in power? A terrorist leader, for example. Or a president. Someone who thinks he is president and has convinced everyone that it is true or that he is too powerful to be challenged. How do we heal a general? Or a munitions manufacturer? A scientist who makes weapons – cluster bombs, nuclear bombs, anthrax…? The government is hinting that these anthrax envelopes are not coming from people connected with Al Qaeda or the terrorist network.

When the spirits come to one to ask her to be a healer, they do not only mean healing the physical body, they mean that she should learn what heals the heart and what heals the mind and the soul. They mean she is to learn how to heal the community and the country where she lives and the earth. But if the patient does not come to her for healing, does she have the right to try to bring healing anyway? The basic ethic of healing is that you must have permission from the afflicted one before you can do any work on his or her behalf.

*　　*　　*

Michael and I had left the path alongside the Chobe river and were going inland when we paused to let a herd of impala sprint across the road in great haste. It was after the last one, the sentinel, had passed over from the brush to his lookout at the edge of the herd that we watched the crippled impala with the broken leg make her painful way into the bush. This one will be taken next, we knew, according to the agreement between the predator and the prey. But not this one, I prayed. Not this one. Protect this one. Having seen her plight, I couldn't relinquish her to the inevitable fate.

Do we have the right to pray for a being that has not requested it?

"What you didn't see," Michael said, "were the three hunger-driven wild dogs behind us, their tongues slathering, their lips curled, their eyes intent."

As I prayed, the impala disappeared into the bush and then we didn't see her again though we could not imagine how she could be hidden from us in the scant shrubbery. One moment she was moving so slowly in her crooked way, her leg bent out before her and then she was gone.

We cannot do what we want. We cannot impose our will. We ask, but ultimately the action is of the spirits. A story coheres out of the bits and pieces that Spirit offers us. It is never only its own story. The story is related to other stories. The story is formed of pieces that are not itself. The story is a nodule of a net that contains many stories and one is understood because the other is understood. The story is not merely a telling, it is not merely a remembering, the story is an action. The story is a bringing something forth. The story, followed, enacted and living, is a world coming into being.

*   *   *

Some years ago, a dreamer in Harare, Zimbabwe dreamed that President Mugabe came to her to ask for healing. She said, "Perhaps I can heal your body but it will be temporary because I cannot heal your soul of the crimes you have been driven to commit."

*   *   *

Patricia Langer and I were in South Africa for the first time, the guest of Gillian van Houten at Londolozi. We had gone out for a game drive in the late afternoon, tracing the territory where Gillian used to stroll with Shingalana, the female lion she had hand-raised from a cub and then brought to Zambia for a year so Shingi might find a pride or a rogue lioness with whom she might ally. Towards the end of Gillian's pregnancy, when she could no longer climb into her Zambian tree home, she reluctantly returned home to South Africa. It was then when Gillian was away, that the local lionesses turned on Shingi and wounded her so fiercely that Shingi died some hours later in the arms of JV, Gillian's partner. The leopard, the old grandmother, the Mother whom JV had photographed for years, allowed JV to sit beside her in the bush as she faced her death even though the leopard had never been domesticated, had never lived, as Shingi had, with people. Who do we have to become for a lion or leopard in the wild to die in our arms?

We were driving across a meadow when we came across three lionesses. They lay under a small bush and we stopped and turned off the engine. Their silence invoked our silence. We stared in each other's eyes for a long time. *This is Gillian,* I spoke to them in my mind, *Shinghi's companion. Can you relieve her loneliness?* One can be lonely for an animal the way one can be lonely for a child. When the animal we have raised dies, a hole forms in our heart no less a hole than the hole that a human death makes. The three lions roused themselves and began walking away through the yellow grass toward a stand of trees. The stride of the lion as certain as the stroke of creation. First the one and then the other, slow and majestic. And then the third, but she was severely injured and I could see the crippling pain shoot up when she stepped on her back foot.

"Do something, Patricia," I implored.

"Do you want me to get out of the truck and hold her?" Patricia was bewildered.

"No, but you/we must do something." We began to pray or we began to visualize healing. I don't know what we did. We did whatever healers do when they are anguished for the wounded one who has been given into their hands.

You do know what is coming. Life can be as fearsome as death. I am afraid of what I am going to say; I am afraid to remember it. The lioness limped in pain across most of the meadow and then she walked more jauntily and then she ran with each paw hitting the ground powerfully. The third lion was healed. "This is a gift from Shingalana," I called after her.

* * *

Not to know the proper relationship to Spirit and power is dangerous to the individual and the world. I didn't know about this when I was young. When I was in my thirties, I had a dream in which two Native Americans taught me a rain dance. Upon awakening, I wanted to experiment with what I had learned. I did the dance for no reason but that I wanted to see results. Drops of rain circled in the swimming pool. This was not sufficient for me. Like any young woman or man, I was hungry, greedy, fascinated by my ability.

I didn't ask the right questions: Why did I have this dream? When does one use such power? With whom does one consult about using such power? Who might appropriately temper and advise someone? On whose behalf does one use such power? When does one resist such power? When does one refrain from indulging such power? What kind of spiritual practice does one need to develop in order to hold such power? Is it right to interfere with the weather? On whose behalf? And will other people elsewhere benefit or suffer?

I didn't ask these questions. I had no one to consult. My culture does not consider the reality of such a connection to the natural world or to ancient traditions. I played with the dance. I was a young woman. I had never been warned. There was a terrible flood. Chastened, I put the dream away. I didn't forget the consequences, but I forgot that I had been called through water.

Dreams and portents from this watery world. Events choreographed by another unseen and unfathomable intelligence altogether. To know the difference between following our own will and yielding to the will of the spirit world. To know the difference between spiritual intent and willfulness. To be aligned with all the beings in the world or to set ourselves adamantly apart. To be with creation or against it. Whether we believe in our own spiritual power or not. These are the dilemmas we are facing.

A story. Another healing story. Another mystery.

A few weeks before my second trip to Africa in 1999 when I would meet the Ambassador, a doctor found a large mass in my uterus, the size of a grapefruit, he said. "It may be ovarian cancer," he said, "you will want to check it out when you return from Africa." I only had a few days before leaving and he knew he wouldn't be able to get insurance authorization before I left. But, I was not willing to go to Africa carrying the fear that I might have a grave illness. It was a Friday and I managed to get an appointment for an ultrasound scan the next Monday, grateful that I was privileged with the ability to pay for the procedure on my own and aware of the number of people who would not have been able to act this way on behalf of their own lives.

Following my theory, that it is often best to do the healing work before the diagnosis than afterwards, I entered into ritual on Sunday night. Michael accompanied me. We had just read some texts on sound and healing and Michael went to search for music by Mozart. I created an altar. Uncharacteristically, I placed a photograph of my father there, intending to pray to him as an ancestor to bring healing to me.

I meditated and prayed for a long time. Michael was not able to find the CD that had been there just a few days before but he had an audiotape in his hand that had no label on it. "I don't know what this is, but I want to play it," he said.

He put the tape on and I heard voices speaking in Yiddish. Slowly, I began to understand what was being said in the first language of my childhood. It was a recording of an event that had taken place in 1981 honoring my father. The occasion was the publication of the very first book he had ever written. It was to be the very last book of his to be published. Various people spoke of my father and his work. As I listened, I was astonished. I remembered very little of this. I had certainly forgotten that it had been recorded. Then Barbara Myerhoff spoke. And then I was called to the podium. I could not remember what I was going to say. I said I had a gift to offer my parents. This was also the day that a book of mine had been published. The book was *Tree*. It was the journal I had kept when I had cancer.

It was the book I had written that had brought me to healing. It was a journal about cancer as a physical disease but it was also a journal about political cancers. It was about me and it was about Chile. It was the text that taught me that community offers healing and that personal healing can be an offering to community.

In the book I quoted a phone message from Ariel Dorfman whom I had met in Chile the year before the *golpé* and the year before he had had to go into exile. I had taken it down verbatim from the phone machine when he had called from Holland.

"Oh gosh, Deena, we really do love you very, very much. *Le queremos much mucho.* . . . I was writing some stories which have to do with what we live, with the experience, with the fact that when you are against the wall, you use the wall to fight the enemy and not only to fight the enemy but to find out what you yourself are, to discover your own body, to discover your own soul and your own love and to find a hand which is next to you when you are against the wall, when they are shooting against you against the wall. And what is most important is that I discovered there, you, very, very deep inside me, you were among the people, perhaps the people who most in the world saw the joy and also the difficulties of life in Chile. And do you know what I remember now? I remember now the trees, the first day we met, the light coming through the trees when we talked of the revolution. So that is what I can give you. I mean I can give you that and the stories and all our love and we can give you our love and we can just say that – nothing can happen to you at all. Nothing really can happen to you because you are so deep inside us and we love you so much and we need you so much and you are a witness to so much that we did and you helped us to do it just by existing and now that you have trouble, we have trouble, and we can destroy that trouble together, just by living, just by being the way we are, by being better people and loving more and loving each other more. *Nada mas*, Deena . . . .

This was the book I had written, after *The Book of Hags*, when I had discovered that I had cancer. It was the book of coming out of silence. The book that had been a response to the dream of the Nazi matron who had wanted to silence me. This was the book I had written to heal myself. This was the record of the beginning of the healing of cancer through speaking of the relationship between cancer and silence, between the holocaust and Nazi Germany and the overthrow of the democratic government in Chile. It all came together in that moment, cancer and fascism, healing and community.

I was speaking of this book and of healing and of tradition in order to honor my father. At that event, I apologized for speaking in English but I promised that I would carry the values that were in that language whether I could speak it or not. And there was my father speaking in a dying language of lineage and continuity. My father whose picture I had put on my altar. And this was the music we found instead of Mozart. And there was the direction of healing and the teaching regarding healing that I had myself learned in the ordeal and crucible of cancer sixteen years earlier.

The ultrasound was negative. I had a large fibroid the size of a grapefruit but it was benign. And so I went to Africa with a clear mind and there I met the Ambassador.

When Michael and I returned to Africa in August 2001, we went to Chobe first. That means we started in Paradise. We were to have a few days together with the animals before we joined Augustine and Simakuhle in Bulawayo.

Michael and I had been packing late into the night. Around midnight, we discovered my passport was missing. I had used it last to leave Canada several months previous. It was not where I usually keep it. We went through every file drawer and safe box but it was gone. I could not find it myself; this I knew. I picked up the elephant rattle, because the elephant remembers. Next to it was a segment of elephant brain with what looks like a Bushman figure on it that had been given to the writer and artist, Katherine Metcalf Nelson, by a native healer in Kenya and she had given it to me. It had been my intent to take it back to Africa. At first, I had thought it was to go to the Bushmen, but then I realized that it was to be returned to the elephants. Bones belong to them. But I had wanted the skull. I had wanted its beauty, its story and its power. I was clutching something that belonged to others. Now I set it next to the suitcase knowing I must take it with me as is right. Within minutes, I found my passport in a suitcase I had packed and unpacked several times since I had been in Canada without ever seeing the passport there.

Janet Mayhall had read our astrological charts for us before we went to Africa predicting minor mishaps and discomforts, though assuring us there would be no grave difficulties. But when we got to Big Falls, the suitcase with the skull in it had disappeared. This meant that we would not be able to offer the skull to the elephants at this time. We called the airline offices repeatedly, but no one could find the valise. Then we could not rent a car in Victoria Falls and drive it to Botswana as we had arranged. Still, we got to the border within twenty minutes of its closing. Again, there was no four-wheel drive to rent in Chobe. Then there was a car for a day only. Then there was a car for the entire time. There were rooms for us only for three days. Then there was a room in another hotel for the last day. What was not possible, became possible. We were able to be among the animals.

The giraffes came forth with their yoga alphabet. One bent toward the east, her head and neck extended while the other aligned herself, extending her head and neck to the west. On this river plain, their collaborative labor of breath and reach was devoted entirely to beauty. They moved with slow dignity. They bent into a great arch in order to drink. Every motion honored beauty. Bow down. They collaborated to write the holy letters in the air in the ways that flocks of small birds engrave a sacred spiral script on the sky. Despite all the time I have spent in game parks, I had never seen this dance. We felt as if the sacred had invited us into its presence.

Each day, we returned to the place where we had first met the Ambassador. I recognized the tree immediately and there was the white fisher eagle who had led us to this spot twenty months before. I thought it was absurd to think that the Ambassador might appear. The first connection had been a great miracle. It was wrong to expect another. Still, I believed that I had to make the gesture, but cleanly, without hope. When I questioned myself regarding this, I answered that I felt it necessary to be the woman who was willing to keep an appointment with an elephant.

When we returned with the second group, four weeks later, Robin Wilds found an eagle feather at the foot of the tree which she would give to Augustine at Siloswane. Chapungu is, with lion, Augustine's totem. And now, since the meeting with the Ambassador, *Ndlovu,* Augustine is often trance-possessed by elephants.

We had four days with the elephants. The first day a large elephant family stopped before us on the other side of the water hole while the rest of the herd went on. I rattled with the Bushmen rattle I had found in the Joberg airport and chanted to the elephants. They stayed with us, making circles in the dust for over two hours. When they went on, several elephants that had preceded them but had stopped at the river to the east, returned and stayed with us, it seemed, for an immeasurable period of time. Over the four days, we saw and meditated among dozens of elephants, perhaps hundreds. We were never very far from the company of elephants and they, it seemed, remained near us for exceptionally long periods of time. I wanted nothing but to be among them, to watch the little ones, to listen to the occasional trumpeting or long rumbles. When they sounded, I opened my body so that the sound might penetrate me and I might be tuned accordingly.

*   *   *

When I came home from Africa, I pondered the passion with which I pursued the Ambassador. In my fervor to keep the appointment, I was privileging the Ambassador over the members of the breeding herds who stayed with us for hours. In retrospect, I recognize that they affected me as profoundly as the Ambassador had. I know my mind has been altered by their presence. I know that I carry a degree of kinship with human beings and other species I never had before. I see that I have the ability to enter *Mandlovu* mind, to take part in the dynamic river of combined intelligence with others, human and non-human, without needing to assert my own particular identity or will. This has been the gift of the elephants. I forgive myself for my insensitivity, understanding the political value of bringing home a good story. Nevertheless, my desire, my will, obscured the subtlety of what was transpiring. And who knows how much I missed altogether through focusing on what I thought I wanted. We spent the sundown hours by the river near the Chapungu tree on the last day. We were joyous with all the animals we had seen but I was also saddened that I hadn't come upon the Ambassador. The last day, toward sunset, we returned to the Chapungu tree, waited there and then began to drive toward the exit. There was a small family of elephants near the water hole where we would have to turn inland and away from them.

The sun was going down. A young male lion was making his way alongside the elephants who paid no attention to him. He walked with slow dignity, seeming to thread his way through a herd of impala who faced him without running. Later, a game warden would tell us that an impala made too small a meal for a lion. The elephants watched with some casual interest but did not move, and the lion slowly sauntered away from them into the fading copper expanse of sunset silhouetting the ecstatic arcs of the giraffes. It was time to leave the park; the gate would close in half an hour. I had been watching a lone elephant in the far distance. As we watched, he began to make his slow way toward the herd we were watching, and, by extension, toward us. We were afraid to dally but his deliberate approach mesmerized us.

In the last minutes that we could remain, he approached these elephants, roughly shouldered his way through them, elbowing a young elephant aside. Then he splashed through the shallow pond and came up the slope, having taken a very indirect route in order pass directly in front of our truck. Pausing? Not pausing? Looking? Not looking at us? And disappeared into the brush. Then he trumpeted. And again.

We had fifteen minutes to reach the entrance of the park; it was scarcely sufficient. If the gatekeeper had not been waiting for us to drive her to her house as we had the two nights previous, we would have been locked within.

Dare we think this was the Ambassador? Dare we not recognize this was the Ambassador?

19

Saturday, September 29th, 2001. The sky is burning. How else describe this heat? The grasses are dry yellow. The slightest spark will bring the entire mountain down in a great conflagration. The two Towers came down because the heat of the jet fuel fire melted their internal structures, not because of the impact of the plane that had become a bomb.

Valerie Wolf dreamed of a bee that turned into a lion. They are the same in the world of yellow fire and they are the same in the world of sting, and they are the same in the universe of yellow grasses, the savannah, the fires that have been burning the forest down ahead of the men coming with their axes and chain saws. Phaeton drove the chariot of the sun too close to the earth and the earth burned. Condor in one legend, and Spider in another, were the ones who pushed or pulled the sun back into its orbit when it wheeled too close to the earth and everything burst into flame, fire to fire. Until 1945, it was, perhaps, wise to fear the dark, but after we dropped the atom bomb, it became wise to fear the light. That is why Patricia Langer went to Santorini, the living volcano in Greece, to make offerings to the god of fire and why everyone in Hawaii knows that Pele is one to be feared, deeply respected and honored. Our mothers teach us, "Don't play with fire," but neither they nor we understand what these cautionary words really mean.

What is there to do but consider the waters that will sustain and redeem us, but only if we enter them. Hwange was dry and hot and the only solace we had there was watching the elephants stand in the waters of the pan and cover themselves and their little ones with water and mud.

August 23, 2001. Hwange.

Seven women, Moseka N'Daya, Hawk, Moriyah Colaine, Elenna Rubin Goodman, Barbara Bordon, Juliette Hanauer, and Valerie Wolf. It is impossible to relate the stories that manifested, the events that occurred in order to initiate each woman. Each woman's story so different, though we were all in the same place at the same time for two weeks. Each woman's story a book in its own right. Before one enters into initiatory circumstances, especially those as radical as making a journey to Africa and entering into mythic time, one can possibly imagine the events but can hardly imagine the impact. We had an itinerary. We had a ceremonial map. But initiation rarely occurs through the enactment of the ritual event. The ritual event prepares one for the unknown. It brings one to the door but it cannot open the door. In its way, it is the offering. By participating sincerely in the ritual event, we signal the spirits that we are ready and willing. But once we step across or are taken through the door, we are beyond, beyond even the realm of our intent. We are in the hands of the gods. That is how initiation happens.

*   *   *

The first trip we took was to Hwange, a game park near Big Falls. When we returned, little Michael was in the hospital with severe bronchitis and Simakuhle was staying there with him. When they returned home, she was exhausted from caring for him but also because a man in the next bed had died in the night and Simakuhle had taken on his anguished spirit. She could not feel her own body, she could only feel his suffering. Augustine is expert in removing a foreign spirit from someone's body, but in this case, because it was Simakuhle, he was helpless. He had done his best on behalf of the spirit, sending it to its home, but Simakuhle remained listless. He called us together, as he does, under such circumstances, and pleaded with us to heal her. I could see that Simakuhle was becoming rapidly dispirited. Even Michael's little cries barely roused her.

What ritual we designed does not matter. Barbara drummed, of course, kept the heart beat and carried us across to another state of mind and heart. Elenna danced to call the spirits and raise the life force. Moriyah, Hawk, Juliette brought all their energetic and shamanic skills to the circle. Simakuhle's sister sang the sacred songs. Shelter and Girlie sustained their mother with their heart. The men took up the spears of the Ndebele warriors and danced the protection of the perimeter. None of these advance rituals and preparations matter ultimately. They created the context within which the healing we could not have anticipated or programmed occurred. What does matter is exactly what we could not have designed.

Moseka N'Daya entered after everyone was seated. As there was no place for her to sit comfortably in the very crowded room, we brought in a stool and placed her in the center of the room next to Simakuhle who could barely hold herself up. And so when the ritual work began, Simakuhle leaned into Moseka N'Daya who embraced her. In that moment Moseka became the mother that Simakuhle had never had. The invisible exchange between them was almost visible as Moseka was able, by her generous presence, to rouse the mother in Simakuhle herself. Simakuhle's energy returned and soon she was able to rise to her feet to dance, stamping her feet hard as the Ndebele people do, Elenna alongside her.

What we didn't know was that Moseka was carrying a great and unspoken pain about her own mothering. An unbearable pain that she had deeply suppressed but that had distorted her entire life. She had not come to Africa to heal this. She had come to Africa because her daughter had been enchanted with Shona sculpture. She had come because she had, by chance, been Michael's patient at UCLA. She had come because dreams and circumstances had insisted that she find her ancestral roots in Zimbabwe among the Shona people. She had come because she had dreamed of Augustine but hadn't known this until she met him in the flesh. But now, as she embraced this anguished woman, she was able to redeem her own life. The spirit of The Mother came through her and then she embodied it. It left its mark. She became the mother. Moseka and Simakuhle bonded then as mother and daughter. And the bond holds even now that Moseka has returned to the United States.

Some days later, Moseka and I spoke long into the night about the circumstances of her own life that were healed in that moment. So much that she had forgotten was remembered. She spoke the details of the secret story and then other stories that she had not thought might be related. So many stories were woven together into one story. She began to understand that she had been living her entire life in response to the secret story that had occurred when she was a young girl. As a young woman, she had had one understanding of the story and this understanding had shaped her. But now as an adult woman, with adult children, she was able to understand the story differently. It became another story and so it had other implications. Revisioning changed everything. In both instances of ritual and story-telling, healing occurred through unanticipated circumstances.

In the practice of psychology, the telling of the story, the act of remembering, the weaving the details together, are the way of healing. Psychology would say that the moment of bonding facilitated the telling of the stories so that healing would occur. Ritual understanding assumes the silent moment of bonding was the healing and the telling of the stories was the way that the healing was understood. At the end of her time in Africa, Moseka went to the sacred pools in Matopos with Simakuhle. They did ritual work together as a way of reifying what had occurred between them. They brought the same awareness, skill and intention to the ritual that a psychotherapist and her analysand might bring to a therapeutic session. But here again, the spirits interposed themselves and took charge. Simakuhle was trance-possessed by an old grandfather spirit, a *sekiru* who completed the work in ways neither woman could have anticipated.

In healing work, we use the ways we know, the skills we have and the forms that have been given to us. Preparation, exactitude, skill, training, craft, insight; these are all essential. But they are not the entire healing event. They unlock the door. It does not matter if we are skilled psychologists, physicians or ritual practitioners; there is always an opportunity to open to the moment so that the spirits can step in and heal through us. We recognize their presence when we allow circumstances to develop in ways that we could not have designed. I believe that the spirits were as present with Moseka and myself in our little hotel room when her story (and so she) was reconfigured in ways we could not have imagined, as the spirits were present with us in the Daré room when we were engaged in ritual, chanting and drumming. One way of understanding accords the power to the individuals alone and the other way accords the ultimate power to the spirits.

The ritual we had designed for Simakuhle's healing had been exquisite and appropriate. It had a narrative that was consistent with the ways and traditions of Simakuhle and the Ndebele people but that also allowed each of us to offer our own gifts to the situation. But the ritual was not what healed her. Our ritual set an intent and prepared the way. Then the spirits entered and did the work in their own way for their own purposes. Spirit used the occasion to extend the realm of healing from Simakuhle and the soul of the dead man to Moseka as well and perhaps beyond. We cannot know the full implications of what occurred. When Spirit heals, a world is healed. Again, our task is to bring ourselves fully to the moment and then allow a wisdom and power greater than ours to move through us on behalf of all beings.

Ultimately, the true moments of initiation occur spontaneously. They take us by surprise. We are initiated in part by how we meet the unpredictable. We are initiated when we give ourselves over entirely in the extreme moment to what is calling us from the other side. Then we are in the unknown.

*   *   *

Many years ago, I went to see Bryan Jamieson because I was interested in Story. He claimed to take people through what he called "past life regressions." Several of the people I was working with as a counselor and as a writing teacher had experienced his magic. Without being storytellers themselves, they had returned with astonishing stories that informed their work profoundly. They were beyond anything my clients and students had ever imagined, rich in mythic and psychological detail and sometimes carrying historical accuracy in areas which they were not themselves informed. I was not interested in the psychological aspect, but I can never refuse a good story. For this reason, I found myself in his small apartment in San Diego. "I am going to guide you in a meditation," he said. "Don't be reactive. The meditation is ridiculous. But, it has worked for me for many years." He had to warn me about the absurdity of the exercise – and it was absurd – without undermining my confidence in his work. He implied that it didn't matter what words he used in this instance. What would transpire, where I would be taken, what I would see, did not depend on the meditation, but on something else. On what? It is difficult to know. Something would transpire between him, myself and the spirits or the imagination or …? How or why that came about was a mystery. So, in order not to be distracted by trying to understand the ineffable, he used this meditation as if it was important, but admitting up front that it was not the thing in itself. I could say the meditation worked, but that would be silly. Still, I can imagine someone trying to duplicate the meditation in order to duplicate the process and reach the same results. Something did happen. Perhaps it lay in the series of questions he asked me, or the way he guided me once I had entered the realm of story. Who can say? His success cannot be attributed to the meditation or the chair he had designed, the blindfolds, any of the accoutrements of this experience. Were I wishing to do similar work with others, I would not spend much time examining his technique or trying to learn the meditation. Recognizing that his extraordinary effectiveness had no relationship to technology, I would try to understand the place where his particular gifts, passion and intent, coincided with the hopes and passions of my students or of myself.

In that particular instance, I was not so much interested in how he elicited a story from us, but in the story itself. I wanted the experience. I did enter into other universes as deeply as I ever have except when I am in the process of writing a novel. Three other worlds, complete in character and plot, totally unexpected, totally unfamiliar, totally intriguing, outside of any of my imaginings, manifested. One of them has remained as a memory so vivid, I return to it the way I return to contemplate personal experiences that have affected my life profoundly.

Egypt. I am a man. My name is Anu. I am beloved and respected by the Pharaoh. It is my task to create the irrigation system that will flood the fields well into the dry season. I relate this to the waxing and waning of the moon. Pharaoh is Ra, the sun god, and I am devoted to the moon. I am a priest of Tehuti. There are rumors of belligerent tribes approaching Egypt. The Pharaoh wishes to stop the water project so that he can divert all the money and manpower to war. I know this is foolish. If we have water in times of drought, we will have resources he cannot imagine and militarily we will have a great advantage. The Pharaoh is the sun god. One cannot question his authority. But I must. I approach him. I make the mistake of confronting him in public. I have challenged his authority. I have challenged the authority of Ra. I am a heretic.

Because he loves me, the Pharaoh only sends me into exile. I retire to a cave in the dry mountains. Each night the moonlight enters the back of the cave and I mark the place on the wall tracing its movements from month to month. The mountains rise from the flat land like the mane of a lion down his back. The very flat yellow land and the dry mountains rising straight up from it.

This night I am watching three men make their way up the great stones toward my cave. They are trying to surprise me but I watch each step they take as the moon rises and reveals them to anyone who would look this way. There is no one in this vast desert but these three men and myself. They are coming closer to me. In a moment they will bring me my death.

When we are driving from Cairo to Suez in order to enter the Sinai peninsula, I saw the mountains that contained the cave from which Anu followed the moon.

*   *   *

Bryan Jamieson is not a writer and his work does not have to do with writing. Because I am a writer, it matters very much what words I use under any circumstances, but, particularly, in a ritual event. Some of what I can do is related to the power and exactness of language. When I lead people in a journey or a guided meditation, I consider the language very carefully. That is because language is my *mojo*. I have to use it well. But this is not true for everyone.

For a dancer, like Elenna Rubin Goodman, the exactness of her gesture is what is essential. In order to be effective ritually, she must find the precise movements to accord with the specificity of prayer. Moriyah Colaine is in a constant dialogue with the land. She seeks a precision of communication with the plants and animals on her newly acquired Ruach Ranch that is as exact as the interchange between a writer and the word.

*   *   *

Elenna's initiation began when, on meeting her, Augustine remarked casually that she saw the colors of humans in the ways that one might see the colors of flowers in the field. This opened the door. He did not know that she had devoted her life to racial issues and he also didn't know that she had been wounded many times in doing this work. It was a chance remark, if anything that a profound healer says directly to someone can be considered chance. Understanding in an instant that he had said something that moved her deeply, Augustine looked directly in her eyes. He was assessing whether he had been correct. Or he was emphasizing his intuition. However she interpreted his gaze, she understood that he truly saw her; she was who she hoped she was. He had seen and verified that. Naturally, it meant more to her that he had seen this than that I might see it. He didn't know her or her story. He is a black man. He was born into and suffered apartheid. No one could confirm the truth of her soul better than he. She stepped through this door from hope to reality. This was the beginning.

We meditate, we bring gifts, make sacrifices, we invoke helpers, angels, spirits, gods, we engage in purification rites, fast or eat ritual foods, we light candles or sit in the dark, we drink wine or abstain, we examine our conscience, confess our misdeeds, make pledges, adorn ourselves or tear our clothes, we travel to far places, make pilgrimages or sit in a cave. Every religion on the planet has its versions of these activities, but these are not the means through which initiation occurs or spiritual capacity is achieved. These are necessary rites. They are what we do to prepare ourselves, to demonstrate our intent, to create a vessel; these are the equivalent of knocking at the door.

For this reason, the accounting of the details of ritual and ceremony obfuscate the events and reveal far less than is implied. They are interesting but they are not the thing-in-itself. The initiation will not happen without them and also they are not central to it. One face of our obsession with material events is our desire to be able to do everything ourselves. This is one shadow of our desire *to know* and to control. We value what is reproducible because it empowers us. And because we crave power, we want to be able to reproduce anything and everything. Technology reassures us that there is no power greater than ours. If we understand the technology we will be able to reproduce the event ourselves. For the materialist, there is no "magic" in an event, there is only the difficulty of discovering and refining the formula. When mechanical thinking such as this is brought to the spiritual, one misses entirely the field that one is trying to enter.

This is the dilemma of the visible and the invisible. The materialist does not know how to negotiate the field of the invisible and so presumes it will be revealed at another time or that it does not exist. He or she may then use the technology that is available as if it were sufficient, without understanding the consequences of his or her incomplete activity. Such a one cannot see or isn't concerned with what is missing, but the healer will recognize that what is missing is *everything*. This is one difference between a dark sorcerer and a true healer. A dark sorcerer will work for effect without an alliance with Spirit, while the healer knows that there is nothing but the alliance with Spirit. The healer uses the ritual events in order to prepare the vessel so that Spirit can pour itself into the world. Or we can put it this way, if someone cannot recognize the soul, he or she cannot recognize soullessness. And because the soul cannot be had through technique, purchase or resolve, it lies outside the will to power.

*   *   *

Valerie Wolf asked me to be her teacher, understanding, ironically, that certain things can't be taught or learned, not in the usual ways. The next step was to request apprenticeship. Neither of us knew what this would look like in our lives, but we had some images from native cultures. We knew it would take a long time and that the deepest teaching would occur through our relationship to each other, that the process of apprenticeship would make us kin. We knew that there were no teachings or instructions for every situation. I myself felt affinity with Augustine who refuses to take on students who would like the pharmaceutical formulae or an inventory of herbs for each situation. In any moment, the healer or dreamer or prophet carries what Spirit insists on conveying in the moment. When one dreams the herb, it doesn't mean, necessarily, that this herb by its nature is the exact remedy for this condition. Nor even that it is the exact remedy for this person with this condition. Another healer may dream another herb under such circumstances. Or another person administering the herb to the patient that Augustine dreamed might not have the same results unless Augustine was engaged in the treatment. The healing lies somewhere in who Augustine is or has become over the years, in the dream, the fact of it, the way the patient comes to Augustine, whatever happens when Augustine gathers the herb, administers it, and prays for the patient. What is it that happens? We don't know. Can we find out? I don't think so. What do we do, then? We watch the devotion and sincerity with which Augustine proceeds and we try to develop ourselves with equal integrity in relationship to the spirits and in our concern with those who are ill and the context of their lives. We pray to the spirits to teach us how to pray. We learn how to listen and hear what the spirits are saying and what they want. We learn to live and work accordingly. It is from this that our healing powers derive. The way of the apprentice is to be alongside the medicine person so that the teacher's spirits can also act upon the apprentice to bring her or him into consciousness.

This is another reason that healing is an ongoing activity. Once one is committed to such a path, one can never step away, not even for an hour. If you are in relationship with the spirits, you cannot close the door the way you may close the door of your office. You go to sleep, you attend to other things, but you are always available. This does not mean that one is always physically available to patients or members of the community. We can and must, occasionally, say "Not now," or we will not survive. But we are always available to the spirits. With the spirits, we cannot create office hours. Initiation is the means through which we learn the constant dialogue, through which we invite the spirits to move through us, to live within us, to use us well.

Prayer: May I be well used.

The medicine person uses the traditional ways in order to ready the participant, but, again, he or she is only giving the initiate over to the gods. As carefully as a practitioner may work, the healing moment is entirely original and unpredictable. The Navajo Singer must perform the ceremony without making a single mistake, for the slightest error destroys the spiritual intent of restoring the sacred perfect universe that has been rent. Disease is not a microbe to be attacked; it is a tear in the fabric of existence that has to be mended. Disease does not come from contagion with the living so much as from acting in ways that violate the sacred order. So the work of the healer is to restore the sacred order. This cannot be done by rote. A great Singer must remember every word, song, gesture of the ceremony perfectly, but accomplishing this does not make a Singer. To be a Singer one must be gifted and then one must study, train and develop. Eventually, one is ready but it is not because one has memorized one's lines. You can't be a Singer without an exceptional memory, but that is the least of it.

Initiation. Let us return. Initiation is the passageway through which one becomes a healer or gathers healing abilities. It is the beginning and it is completion. Whenever Augustine meets someone gifted in an area, he asks the person to initiate him. He is asking to be taken to another door and assisted across. "When will I come to the end of initiation?" he once asked plaintively. We were sitting across from each other on tree stumps before a smoky fire in his yard next to the ritual pool. Augustine was tired after a day of doing healing work and he was aware that we were going to enter into ritual circumstances and he already felt the weariness of the preparation and the exhaustion of the inevitable process of being broken down. Perhaps he also felt the burden of carrying yet one more gift. Longing, necessity and weariness coinciding. Before I could answer, he answered in the words I would have said. "There is never an end to initiation." "Rather the opposite," I said, "the more accomplished and devoted one is, the more one offers oneself up again and again to the spirits." Perhaps going to Sinai was one of the great initiatory moments in Augustine's life, but as much as it was the culmination of an extraordinary period in his life, we also know it was a beginning.

The moment described above between Elenna and Augustine was not the end of her initiation in Africa. It was the beginning. The event at the threshold that would influence everything else that came. It came at the end of years of work and devotion. And it augured that the work would continue, that it was her work, and she must do it despite its difficulties and the pain it often brought with it.

At the moment Augustine recognized her, we were outside at Serafina Farm. Elenna and Barbara Borden had arrived in Bulawayo a day early and we had time to show them the farm. Along one wall of the living room fifty-pound sacks of *sadza* or corn meal were stacked. Enough to feed the family and Daré community for over a year. This coming year, Augustine assured us, they would have two growing seasons and that would mean the meal could be sold to offset some of the farm's expenses in the effort to become sustainable and it would mean that there would be food for the community. Michael had waited a long time for this moment. It represented fulfillment of several years of hard work on his part and on Augustine's part. They had done it. Together. A white man from California and a black man from Zimbabwe. Remarkable, really.

It was then that we knew that we needed to acknowledge this moment in ritual. Barbara Borden did not have to reach for her djembe. It was attached to a woven strap that was around her neck. But something passed between Elenna and Barbara and then between Elenna and myself. We were going to go out into the fields and Elenna would dance for the earth as Barbara drummed and the rest of us prayed in gratitude. This was another initiatory moment for Elenna. She had been motivated to come to Africa, a journey that represented great expense and sacrifice, in order to gather all of herself. An accomplished professional woman, she wanted to know how to use all of her gifts in the service of the community and the spirits. The most beloved of her gifts is the dance and this is also what she wanted to offer.

In this moment, she could perhaps make the offering free from the terrible constraint imposed by the constant question that American culture poses: How will this training prepare you to make a living? How can you charge for this? What profit will you gain? What is it worth? She was to offer the dance on its own terms.

After forty years of teaching, it is apparent to me that the greatest obstacle between North American people and their creative gifts is their obsessive concern with commercial value. Rather than creating a society in which we welcome the creative gift and look for ways to support it as a contribution to the culture at large, we value it primarily as a commodity. Thus the culture drowns in commercial artifacts that are essentially destructive to our lives and spirits and we are deprived of those that would deeply sustain us.

You can be the most accomplished dancer, but this does not mean that your dance has spiritual or ritual power. It was not the beauty of the dance that mattered, though it was certainly there. It was the sincerity of Elenna's spiritual intent. She wanted to bless the land. She wanted to bless the corn. That is, she wanted the land and the corn to be blessed. She wanted to reenter the ancient traditions of blessing. And so she had to give herself so completely to the dance that the motion of it would call down the beneficence of the spirits on behalf of Augustine and his people at the same time that the power of it took her across from one universe to another. In the universe into which she had been born, the dance had become a commercial enterprise, an entertainment, a performance. In the universe toward which she was propelled, the dance was a sacred act with spiritual power. It was a tradition thousands and thousands of years old. By the force of its beauty and passion, it was effective; it did call abundance and fertility into the world. It was a blessing. At the core of the healing event is the purity and sincerity of the healer's intent.

And so she danced. And so Barbara drummed. And so we chanted and danced with them. And so the spirits descended. And so the land was blessed. And so Elenna and Barbara were transformed. And so the women who had arrived only a few hours earlier became other people than they had been. Or rather became no one. Dissolved. In the fervor of her dance, and in the fervor of Barbara's drumming, they disappeared themselves. Two weeks later, they would appear again, or someone would. Other women altogether. Practitioners of the art of blessing. This is something of what initiation looks like.

Sometime after we returned from Africa, Elenna called from Oakland to ask if she could attend my Wednesday morning healer-training circle that would meet only once a month for this one year while I am on sabbatical. This meant that she would drive to Topanga for Daré on Sunday and would stay through the following Wednesday or Thursday. On the between days, she would come to dream group, we would meet privately and she would be involved in the life of the community. It gave her a chance to study shamanic practices with Valerie Wolf and to pursue other facets of the education and development of a healer. Two years earlier, she had asked me to be her teacher and now she had designed the form for such an interaction. One night she dreamed that she came to my house when I was working with a client. Rather than be disappointed that she couldn't see me, she busied herself in the kitchen and made a soup. This hasn't been enacted exactly yet, except that one of the Wednesdays that we met was just before Thanksgiving and so she stayed for the holiday and her partner joined her. Just as her dreamed presaged, I was working and couldn't complete the shopping and so she and her friend Illana Berger, who also joins her/us once a month, took on that task. Interacting with the teacher in a familial or intimate setting reveals what cannot be learned formally. Such interactions are the places through which one can evaluate the meaning and veracity of what is being taught. Are the words being lived? Does the healer take her own medicine? We cannot measure what happens when we are learning through relationship and we do not want to try, but it is certain that the effects are substantial and that the student and the teacher are both deeply transformed by it.

The first time I visited Augustine, I had been trying to assess the healing profession's obsession with boundaries and professional distance. Recognizing that I would be living in the same house with Augustine, I wanted to see what effect that closeness would have on what I learned from Augustine, on the effectiveness of his work with me, on the respect I carried for him. What would happen to our relationship when I saw him up close, very close? For several weeks we would be living as they say on top of one another. Michael and I would be sharing sleeping spaces with other members of the family and Daré, twenty or more of us would be sharing one bathroom, and we would have no time or space for privacy. This would remove and also enhance all possible projections. Would I still recognize and receive the fullness of his power as a healer?

One morning, I came upon Augustine seated on a square of cardboard on the front patio. One of his patients, a woman suffering great mental anguish, had been living at the Daré for some time. She was standing over him carefully washing his hair. When one wears one's hair in dreads, washing the hair is a complex operation. I have rarely seen such sweetness between a "patient" and a healer. Some hours later, Augustine was working with the woman. The act of caring and kindness that she had extended to him did not in any way diminish the work he was now doing with her. Perhaps it was the opposite. Perhaps healing came to her exactly because she could extend herself to Augustine. Perhaps the healing that Augustine offers to the community comes in part from the ways he is able to be with them as a full person.

Why do I speak of this here? Just as healing is a profoundly intimate event that includes the entire life in its concerns, so is teaching. Just as healing cannot take place in fifteen minutes in an anonymous examining room, teaching cannot take place in 50 minutes in an anonymous class-room, let alone through a video screen. When we come to the depth of teaching, or healing or initiation, we must do it face-to-face and life-to-life. The difference between gathering data and being educated is vast. Education not only gives us information and, hopefully, teaches us how to think and evaluate it, but it provides the means for us to incorporate what we have learned into our lives so that we can act from it. Such training requires personal contact and exchange. Increasingly championing profes-sional distance, efficiency, objectivity, information, all the tropes of alien-ation, we do not understand what we are losing – true kinship, human warmth and love, the village, the tribe, intimacy, trust, depth, wisdom and the healing presence of the spirits.

You wouldn't write a protocol for teaching that includes washing hair or making soup, but it is necessary to see that the initiatory process comes out of relationship and through the enactment of unpredictable events. Ultimately, initiation, like healing, is an entirely original moment. One pre-pares and then without warning the spirits come forth and take us in what appears to be an exactly right and inevitable but also unanticipated way. And so we become someone else through how we respond. And so we become, we can say, ourselves.

*   *   *

Valerie had dreamed that she was bitten on the hand by a lion. Elenna also had a dream of a lion and afterwards we could see the ways in which lion spirit moves through someone. First, we saw it in Augustine, who is, *Shumba*, lion totem, as Simakuhle is *Mashuma*, female sheep or goat, and as I have been honored by being called *Mandlovu*.

We had stopped at the bank to exchange dollars on the way to Hwange. Moseka, Juliette and I were in the back of the car waiting for the others. A man approached the car. I assumed he might be coming to chat with us. It is not usual for black people and white people to be together so affably as we were in Zimbabwe and our obvious friendliness to each other may have intrigued him Or perhaps he wanted to ask us for money. But when he started speaking, there was belligerence in him and he seemed dangerous. We didn't know what to do. Augustine was on the other side of the car and we didn't know if he was aware of the man's presence. Then we saw him look at the man and begin to walk around the front of the car toward him. In the few seconds between one side of the car and the other, Augustine was completely transformed. His chest barreled, his shoulders became large, the expression on his face changed drastically. We were in the presence of a male lion. There was no doubt about it. We each saw it and were awed. When he reached the man, he was Augustine again and put out his hand, laughing, as he does, with warmth and concern. They had an exchange. It was pleasant. But the man had seen the lion and had retreated.

*   *   *

Because of all the dreams, we assumed that Elenna and Valerie would be initiated into lion totem and so we looked forward to meeting the lions at the park.

*   *   *

A short time after we came to the raised platform in the park where we would spend the night, we were gifted by the presence of several elephants who came to the nearby water hole. When Michael and I had returned to Big Falls for our plane to Bulawayo, the suitcase that no one had been able to locate was there. It was still locked though several items had been taken from it. Dispensable items like binoculars and film. But the skull was there. I unwrapped the delicate skull from the yellow silk scarf, printed with tiny ivory elephants that protected it and went down the stairs. Augustine followed after me. He did not want me to return the skull. He was convinced that it belonged me. That Elephant wanted me to have it. That the spirits wanted me to have it. That I would use it well as a healer and that Elephant, *Mandlovu*, would benefit from what I might be able to do on behalf of the animals and the world. Perhaps this is the first instance when I couldn't accede to Augustine's understanding. We were not to leave the platform, but I went down anyway and approached the water hole with prayer in my heart. This time I really wanted them to have it. It would seem like a miracle if they would take it. I placed the skull on the ground as close to the water and the elephants as I dared go. Then I stepped back and Augustine took my hand and we prayed. Then we dropped to our knees and prayed again. A full prostration. The elephants, the bull, in particular, watched us with what might be called mild interest. He did not approach us and he did not move away.

These are your bones, I said in my heart. *They belong to one of your people. The Native Americans of my country believe that the bones of their people must not reside in museums but must be returned to them for proper burial. It is not right, they teach us, to make an artifact, even a holy one, from the bones. My people also have suffered from desecrated graves. I was greatly honored to be given this skull as a gift. It was passed to me from an African medicine man, by a friend, but I must pass it on to you.* Then we stepped back and waited.

The two elephants, one on each side of the water hole, came, then, to the side closest to the platform and each walked back and forth along the length of the pond in close proximity to the skull, but without stepping on it and without picking it up. Then they went off. Augustine said that the elephants had given the skull to me. "It is certain," he said. They had spoken to him, he insisted, and I was to keep this as a sacred object and use it when the situation called for such medicine. The sun was setting and the elephants were walking off to the west. Barbara Borden took her drum and I took my elephant rattle and we went further toward them. She drummed the heartbeat and I rattled in gratitude and awe. Augustine went to do ritual work with some of the other women who seemed, according to their dreams, to have been taken by lion spirits.

But the lions did not come. And we saw no tracks. When we went out for a dawn ride, we came upon no animals. When we drove through the preserve in the afternoon, again, we sighted no animals. The drivers were quiet on the subject of what appeared to be devastation. It was clear to all of us that Zimbabwe was in dire straits economically, and certainly this would affect the various parks. The drivers wouldn't comment on this either but they did say that there had been a census and the lions had been tagged. In order for this to be done, they had to be shot with tranquilizer guns and this, the drivers said, had disoriented them and fragmented the prides.

When Michael and I were waiting for our plane from Harare to Bulawayo we had spent several hours in the company of an environmentalist who raises money for an Oxford University environmental fund. Speaking of Hwange, he told us that poachers had begun the practice of luring lions just beyond the perimeter of the preserve by hanging fresh kill in the trees. When they attacked the prey, rich hunters stepped forth from their comfortable perches to shoot them as trophies. We were heartbroken when we heard the story, but we were not sufficiently alarmed. It didn't occur to us that we wouldn't see lions, that we wouldn't really see many animals at all.

We were subdued and disappointed driving back to Bulawayo. There was justice. We had come to see the animals in the wild, that is, to see how they lived. In their own habitat, according to their own ways and conditions. And we had seen the absence of the animals. Sometimes healers need to be sustained and sometimes they need to bear witness. To understand reality. To come out of innocence. To see what you are being called to, what you are being called to do, and why.

*   *   *

WHEN PARADISE IS NOT

I thought it was the morning of the birds. The first constellations of water fowl landing before the dawn and then the lone hippo silhouetted in the yellow field before he entered the pan and submerged himself.

We set out and came, at the end of our foray, to the pan where the hippo was heading, where his small family waits under water. Between this moment and the first moment there was emptiness.

You could see where the elephants had been in the night, their huge feet pressing mud into the shape of their bodies so they would remember. Two crowned cranes rose black and white, magnificent, and flew to the other side of the water. One could think or hope we were witnessing creation but this was not the vision we had been awakened for.

This is not the ark. This is not preservation or salvation. Emptiness and desolation. No wild. No animals. No brothers or sisters. No companionable wisdom or intelligence. No movement or beauty between one pan and the other except for the hardy yellow horny bird and an occasional invisible peeper. Otherwise the palate is dry and the symphony silent.

This is the end. We crossed the world to see it although we hoped to be graced with visions teeming with life and color so that our own small pains might be relieved.

Dear sweet God. *Tatenda*, for this vision of the endless suffering we have wrought.

I had spent days in Chobe in Botswana watching large herds

of elephants roll in the mud, submerging themselves and emerging with the dark wet earth covering their bodies with the source of beginnings.

Between the waters of Chobe and the dry heat of Hwange are barriers of concrete and obstacles of cities and barbed wire, obstructions of farms, the borders of nation states. The work of creation has come to an end.

We saw this. We saw the dark shapes disappear in the white dawn. We saw that there had been many and now there are few. An eagle circled the pan unraveling a spiral of DNA over the trees at the edge of the white termite mound. No one came to stir the waters.

We pray that the animals will return this afternoon to gift us with their small numbers so we can forget this terrible vision of the future with which the Divine has graced us so. We will think we were simply unlucky. We will blame something or someone outside ourselves.

But we have seen it all... life teeming and life exterminated. So I pray. It is all beyond me. Not death, that is so easy, but life. We seem incapable of serving it.

I pray that we will each be given the means, real and ample, to enact restoration. The image, the idea, the eidolon, the symbol, the sign – they are totally insufficient. What remains only in my mind or what I can learn to live without serves nothing.

We want to live apart. We do not want to work with our hands. We do not love mud. We do not praise it. How then do we imagine creation?

20

Halfway House between Bulawayo and Victoria Falls. A bite to eat and a Stony for everyone, that remarkable ginger beer that one finds in Zimbabwe and Botswana. Michael and Valerie are seated at an adjacent table discussing a dream, when I call them over to join us. Valerie picks up her glass of ice and the soda can and sits down, forgetting in that moment to focus on the movement of the bee she has been watching carefully as she was stung on her forearm shortly after she arrived in Bulawayo. She lifts up her glass to drink and a bee that she does not notice has been drowning in the liquid as she poured it from the can onto the ice, stings her on the tongue. If I had not called them then….

When one is stung or bitten in a dream, we assume it means initiation and we look toward the animal to teach us something after it breaks us down sufficiently for its wisdom, the quality of its knowledge and character, to enter our consciousness. Second sting. Valerie has always had a slight allergic reaction to bee stings. Within seconds her throat is swelling and her heart is pounding. We gather around her. We find Benadryl in the first-aid kit and there are stronger antihistamines in my toiletry-medication case in Bulawayo and so we rush to return home. There is a hospital along the way; we begin to speed toward it but when we are there, Valerie, who is feeling better, refuses to go to the hospital. She is more afraid of the response of conventional medicine, particularly for an American citizen, whom she fears they will treat aggressively, and so she opts to wait until she can take the antihistamine. Juliette, who has been working alongside and filming healers for many years, has perfected the art of working with subtle energies and so she takes Valerie into her arms in the back seat and sustains Valerie's life force. Their friendship has been strained the last few days and Spirit seems to be providing a way for them to be together. By the time we come home, Valerie is exhausted but she is no longer critical. The allergic reaction is subsiding.

Juliette slept with her in the same bed, or rather stayed awake all night praying and checking on her friend's breathing. Earlier in the year, as Juliette was setting out for Utah to film the work of a healer/colleague of hers, I had reminded her to look for beauty. Beauty is indigenous to healing work, I had said. My comment and its urgency had seemed mysterious to Juliette and she hadn't seen, she thought, what I insisted must be there. Now, I felt compelled to tell her that the great beauty of healing was upon her.

*   *   *

In 1987, Michael took me to Canyon de Chelly on the Navajo reservation where the Anasazi lived. It became our holy place and so it was at the rim of the canyon that Michael and I decided to marry. We return to it year after year because it was the place where I first understood that such Beauty comes from a great Heart. We had been seated under a small tree meditating in the sand that we had managed to clear of goat droppings:

> Crazy old woman,
> Screaming at her flock
> Chased us across the dry river
> To Paradise.

And there it was: Light on the cliffs. The stones luminous in the sun. Slender trails of green trees like the hair of the beloved. Blue copper markings from thousands of years of rain dripping down, engraving a gleaming sacred script. Beauty. The Great Heart.

*   *   *

Just as with a Navajo sand painting, the task of the healer is to re-establish the sacred universe and render the signature of the Divine visible – beauty. In each ritual, the healer attempts to make offerings to the Divine that are in keeping with the generosity of creation. Again, we cannot determine in advance how to proceed, the individual circumstances of the moment and the people involved, the disease and the way it is manifesting, all of these are to be considered and met.

When we offer a music Daré to someone who is very ill and improvise music by jamming with the spirits, the nature of the disease and the way it manifests in the patient, his or her spiritual and ethnic history, as well as with each other, the other musicians – all of it – we are trying to create a harmonic recognizable to the soul that will allow the body/mind to rest and be restored by the evidence of the cosmic order and his or her place in it.

In the Navajo healing ceremony, the patient is placed directly in the center of the painting and the Singers are enjoined to perform the Way that is appropriate with exactitude. Every word, every gesture must be perfect. I looked at Valerie and Juliette sharing the same queen-size bed in a humble and crowded bedroom in Bulawayo in Zimbabwe. Juliette was leaning toward Valerie to listen to her breathing carefully, noting the congestion in her lungs, and her exhaustion. Sometimes she held Valerie tenderly, running needed energy into her. Beauty. The tableau, not unlike a pieta, was utterly beautiful. In the morning, Valerie seemed weak, but stable. We all agreed she had recovered from the bee sting. I brought my attention to other things.

Gilbert and I were seated in the grass speaking about his future. He was speaking of starting his own Daré as a *nganga* at the same time that he was revealing his vision of the armies who protect the good from the evil spirits, who have fought wild battles against great enemies on his behalf. It has been Augustine's work to confront disruptive spirits to decipher what agitates them so he can help return them to a place that will give them sanctuary and ease their disturbance. I do not think that a vision of armies can exist within the generous consciousness of a *nganga*. "It is your job to learn how to transform enemies in the spirit world to allies," I counseled Gilbert who was daunted by such a task but also intrigued. It is a spiritual task, he told me, that he never imagined would be offered to him. He had not been so ambitious. But, he admitted, if it is right for him to do such work, he would be honored. He must ask his spirits. He would rather do battle as he has in the past. But....

Suddenly, women come running to me. Valerie, they say, is dying. Just then I hear a moan from Valerie whose system seems to be coming to a halt again; her breathing shallow and her pulse extremely faint. We thought she had fully recovered from the bee sting. From her stupor she calls to me. "The Ndebele grandmother has come. She says, 'The Lion spirit is all that's keeping you alive. Get your shaman. Your spirit already walks with Death.'"

"I am dying," she says when I come to her side and, indeed, I cannot find the life force in her. I do not know what to do. She will not go to a hospital. Something else is required. "Go get your shaman and tell her to bring you back," the grandmother told Valerie. I am her "shaman." We are in Africa. We came under extreme political conditions. Her husband and children were afraid to let her go. They were afraid she would die in Africa. I cannot let this happen. She cannot die. But I do not know how to save her life. "Take her to the Daré hut, and get the drum and call all the women together."

This was a new territory. Confronted by this crisis, I didn't believe I could do anything. I didn't know if I believed anyone could do anything. I just knew I didn't know what to do or how to do it. But I had to act. I had only had one experience that has somewhat prepared me for this moment. But it was not a moment of crisis such as this one.

Mike de Ponce, the young son-in-law of my dear friend Peter Levitt, had had a form of bone cancer. This is the firefighter we spoke of earlier. He underwent surgery and chemotherapy and was well for a time. Sheba and Mike married. Then the cancer reappeared in his back on their first anniversary. Everyone in the family was distraught. Mike is an extraordinary man, much beloved in his community. His colleagues say he is the kind of firefighter that volunteers to be dropped into the inferno when his friends are trapped there to help get them out. When he had chemotherapy, and lost his hair, firefighters from Santa Barbara to Los Angeles, and their sons and a woman firefighter, shaved their heads in an act of solidarity.

Now he was ill again. Peter was driving down to Santa Barbara from British Columbia where he now lives. Before he left, he heard about a young Shona woman whose father in Africa had been a *nganga*. She had never learned the medicine from him, but in recent years, the spirits had started initiating her. It was not her idea but she had yielded to them. Rumors that she had become a profound healer reached Peter in Canada. When Peter came closer to Santa Cruz where she lives, he realized that Michael and I had been trained in the tradition by Augustine and he came directly to us.

I did not know what I would say to Peter until I heard myself volunteering to journey on Mike's behalf, though I had never done it before. Michael and Peter and I collaborated on what might be done and how. Finally, I was ready. We had decided to call the grandfathers together, living and dead, on Mike's behalf. This particular cancer usually attacks juveniles and so it seemed important to call the grandfather spirits to him. Having decided this, we called Mike so that he might be available spiritually for whatever might take place. We were astonished to hear that his mother had just come to his house with a firefighting pin that had belonged to his grandfather upon which she had just engraved Mike's name.

And so I set out with Michael and Peter praying alongside me. Somewhere in that place that is no place, that is in the mind and is not in the mind, that is in the imagination and is not in the imagination, some- where in the void of the dark and the light, I called out desperately the extent of my fear and ignorance. "I do not know how to do this," I called, "but there is a young man who is very ill and we must save his life. Please help me." Then I called to Jesse, Peter's father, who had died within the last few months. An angry and frustrated man. A man who had been violent when he was young but who had had astonishing visions when he died that had bonded him with his son, Peter, more deeply than ever before. Calling for him, I had no doubt that having dropped the skin of human life, he would assist us if he could, if such a thing were possible for him, for anyone. If Spirit existed and if he were an ancestor, all of these ifs, then he would assist us.

There was a man beside me in this sea of nowhere. He was wearing a coarse, woven yellow linen shirt with the sleeves carefully rolled up. The fabric reminded me of the fabric of my father's shirts when I was a young girl. But my father had not had a yellow shirt. I didn't know what Jesse had looked like, but I was struck by the angles of his face. He wore a wide tie that he had pulled down below the top button of the shirt. His collar was open.

We began to speak. I pleaded on Mike's behalf. At the end, I was reas- sured in my heart that he would be alongside Mike. I felt his deep concern and the sweetness of his heart. It was not how Peter had spoken of him in the past. "Don't your sons know who you are? How is it that they haven't seen this part of you?"

He raised his hand and tossed it back dismissing my question. He flicked it away. It didn't matter. They didn't know and it didn't matter. That is what the gesture said. The way a father living in the Bronx might exclaim, "Boys! What do they know?"

"The yellow shirt, Peter?"

"My father always wore a shirt, tie and jacket to the office. Though he only sold maintenance supplies, he always dressed formally. Sometimes he took me to work and I watched him take off his jacket and hang it on the back of his chair. Then he rolled up his sleeves, opened his collar and loosened his tie."

"He made this gesture...."

Peter stopped me. "It was like this, wasn't it? Then Peter tossed his hand back by the side of head. And his voice, 'aaah', right?"

"Yes. His voice. Exactly, Peter."

*   *   *

We are together in a circle, Valerie is lying among us.

Barbara Borden has the hand-carved four foot high drum she had called us to purchase for Augustine and his community at the Ndebele village when all the shopkeepers and their families came out of their rondavels to dance and drum with us to celebrate and bless this gift. When the U.S. government first started bombing Iraq, Barbara began drumming for peace once a week in the village square in Mill Valley. When Fran Peavey organized women artists to visit women in the refugee camps in the former Yugoslavia, Barbara went. I have an eight-person drum made from a wine keg that we call Eve, in my house; it is a gift to our Daré from Barbara and the community. In the last year, she has acquired what she calls the Heart Drum. It was especially made for her to carry the heart and pulse of the community. When it was ready, she spent seven days in a cave (a most beautiful and well-appointed cave, but a cave nevertheless) in New Mexico, drumming and offering herself to the spirit of the drum. So it is not only the tone of the drum, but the circumstances of how it got here that makes it an ally.

I know what I must do. I have read accounts of such enterprises but I don't know how to do what is required. I must go to the other world, traveling the drum, and bring back Valerie's soul.

Healing requires intent. The heart and mind unite in a single focus. Healing is not dispassionate. That first time I was called to journey on behalf of someone ill, I felt as if I was being torn out of reality and I wondered, in that moment, why I would risk my life or mind on behalf of someone else. I barely knew Mike de Ponce. But he is Peter's son-in-law. My dear friend. On his behalf. For his life. For Mike. For Peter. The healer cannot be insulated from the fate of his or her patient. Such hierarchies of privilege do not serve the work. Each is jeopardized and the healer makes an equalizing gesture toward the afflicted one. I will go into the unknown, will risk whatever lies there, on your behalf. The reasons that bring a healer to face such danger are at the core of what makes a healer.

What does the patient offer? "You can't lie there passively," I warn Valerie. "You must also fight for your life." In my mind, I already saw her wandering by Lake Wallowa where she had first been initiated by the Nez Perce ancestors, where she had fallen in love with the old ways, and where her heart had been broken by the grief of these people's, her people's fate. She was walking by the edge of the lake, or she was already in the lake waters up to her knees, beloved Death alongside her, irresistible.

"You're a slut." I rebuked her silently for allowing Death to seduce her. But outwardly, I remind her of her promise to the spirits that she would serve them if her son was healed. The consequences of ignoring such a pledge are great; she would not be the only one to suffer them and death would not relieve her of the suffering.

Her daughter, Ursula, had dreamed that Valerie would die in Africa and in the dream insisted that her mother be strong: "I cannot live without you yet." This was the ground we prepared. A field of obligations and responsibilities, family concerns, oaths sworn to the dead. It was to this that Valerie would have to return. As I watched her dallying at the lake, I saw that she had become a moon-struck adolescent, overwhelmed by Death, the phantom lover. A romantic and shallow trope. A great rage rose up in me. Mother rage. The kind that can shake a child until it sees the danger she is courting. Against the enchantment of shadows and romance, I was positing the quotidian; it was a gamble and I would have to be skillful.

I don't know what possessed me then, to put three fingers of my right hand in her mouth, pressing her jaw with the left until she bit me. Insisting that she bite harder and harder, I felt her resistance but I wouldn't allow it. Short of interrupting the ritual, there was nothing she could do but accede to the demand. In her haze, she vaguely considered that I was calling lion spirits into her body, but it was nothing that exotic. I knew she loved me as much as she loved anyone but her children and her husband. She would not want to hurt me and I was insisting that she bite me even to the point of injury. I pushed her jaw up further against my fingers, tightened it, pressing hard so that she would draw blood, feel my bones. It surprised me, fleetingly, how much pain one can endure for the sake of a loved one. But I felt her yielding somewhat to me; she was waking up.

It is not possible to describe how one navigates from one world to another. There is a door, but it is hidden. There is a path, but it is obscured. The drum began. The women held Valerie. I lay down beside her. I prayed there in the dark, alone, for a long time. Then after what seemed like an eternity in the unknown, I called upon her dead father for help. Not for help, actually. I called upon him to right an old wrong. Her father had to make amends for trying to kill her mother.

"Your daughter is dying," I said. "And it is your fault. You have to answer to it." When Valerie had been a child, she had been the only witness to her father's attempted murder. Drunk and out of his mind with jealousy because his wife had left him, he had not been able to distinguish the mother who was at work from the babysitter lying on the couch and the young woman had been critically injured with the baseball bat he had been wielding. Afterwards, Valerie had to testify against her father and this sent him to prison. "We cannot ask our daughters to do such things," I reprimanded him. "She testified and afterwards she never wanted to live. You took her life force. Now bring it back." There in that other world, I understood what we had never understood, despite the many years she/we had worked to heal this moment. I understood that only her father could free her from her love of death.

He had to review his life. He had to find the sources and indulgences of drunkenness and rage. He had to look them/himself in the eye. He had to become conscious. He had to allow heartbreak. He had to feel unbearable grief and shame. He had to acquaint himself with remorse. And then he had to undo what he had done. He had to return to the house, look at the babysitter, lower the bat without using it, and finally step into the bedroom where Valerie was sobbing, the only one of her siblings to be awake. He had to apologize to her and then he had to comfort her and assure her that the world as a child should know it was restored. I let him rock her in his arms a long time, remembering what it means to be a father.

A long time undoing history. A long time, years perhaps, confronting his own rage and tearing it out of his body. Rage and oblivion; they could not remain. Somehow, I prevailed. He stopped the violence; bat raised above the young woman's head, he paused and lowered it to his side. He left the room, took Valerie in his arms. He comforted her and she slept. I could feel something shift in the room that was far away, light years, another galaxy and also the room where I lay still, wandering.

Something had changed in the room, but I couldn't explain what. I knew that I could return now after the proper offerings were made. But in my fear and anxiety, I had not thought of offerings. What do you offer for the life of someone you love?

Affiliation with the lions. Work on their behalf. A hive for Augustine's farm. Our joint commitment to try to send all of Augustine and Simakuhle's children to school. Then I prayed and gave thanks and began returning. Coming back I was possessed by rage again. Even before I had fully returned, I was pushing Valerie so that she would sit up. Finally, she understood and sat there quietly. Clearly, she had recovered, remarkably so; I knew this without our having said a word to each other. "Are you back?" I whispered without kindness.

"I am," she said.

"Where were you?" I asked in an unexpected and uncharacteristic fury.

"I was at Lake Wallowa and Death was there. I hadn't seen him so close since I almost drowned as a teenager. He took my hand. I loved him."

"But are you are back?"

"Yes." Her voice was remarkably strong.

"To stay?"

"Yes. Why are you so angry with me? Aren't you glad I'm back?"

Then I slapped her harder than I have ever slapped anyone in my life. Flat hand against her back. "Don't ever do that again." And hit her again, even harder than the first time, and sealed her soul back into her body as, I was to learn later from Michael, is the practice among the Yoruba in West Africa. "If you want to be a healer, you have to be one with the life force. If you want to be a healer, you can't flirt and dally with death. If you want to be a healer, you commit yourself to life, and you fight for it whenever the occasion arises. You fight for it, even unto your life." And then I suppose I collapsed. Simakuhle came and held me in her arms, singing prayers. Valerie was breathing normally, her pulse even, her fever gone. It was sunset and then it was dark.

*   *   *

There is a debate in the healing community, or rather, there is inevitably a debate in the heart of every healer: Do we have a right to pray for a particular circumstance knowing that we are interfering in the order of things? Can we pray that someone's life be saved? If we preface our prayer with: "May it be Your will; Your will be done; as You desire," is it then ethical to be asking for the life of a particular person?

Do we have the right to pray for the life of our patients when it might mean disturbing the cosmic order? What do we do if a portion of our gift is our ability to pray? Yaqui medicine man, pipe holder, doctor of oriental medicine, energy worker, *curandero*, Martin Castro:

"The family brought the old man to me. I could see that he was dying and the angel of death was right at his side. His sons lay him down on the examining table. 'Get out of here, Death,' I said, 'this is my office and it is a place of healing. It is not a mortuary.' We wrestled a long time. He was an old man and he was moribund but he didn't want to die and his sons wanted him to live. It was not easy to work on the old man and to fight Death at the same time but, finally, Death left the room and we were able to restore the old man who walked out of the office with some vigor. I don't know if/when Death found him again, but it is my responsibility to wrestle with that angel."

The next afternoon, I asked Valerie if she truly was able to commit herself to being a healer. It would mean that she would have to reenter the past and feel compassion for the little girl who had been thrust into the heart of violence by the father whose foremost task was supposedly to protect the daughter from such experiences. She would have to understand the extremity of that little girl's suffering in order to understand another's suffering. An essential teaching for the work of compassion. "I commit myself," she said.

"Then you will have to fight for life. You will have to be fierce. First, for yourself and then for others. You will often lose, but still you must be willing to struggle. Are you willing?" We were looking into each other's eyes.

"I am willing," she said. That is when I knew absolutely that she would live. She would live and so would others in the future as she had learned through her own ordeal how to reconnect with the life force. The ordeal. It seems one doesn't learn without it but it can't be programmed or entered on one's own. You have to go to the place where Death is and look it in the eye.

I learned through cancer; Valerie learned through a bee sting. In both instances, we were taken by the spirits and trained well for the work we would be given to do in the future. It has always been the spirits who train the healers. This becomes less and less feasible. The old ways are largely forbidden. What once was, has been eradicated over the last centuries by various religious imperial forces, Christianity in particular. Almost no one carries the full traditional knowledge of how to heal any longer. All of it has to be recovered and then reconstituted to accord with the circumstances of our times. Healing was never as certain as western medicine can sometimes be in limited ways. But, western medicine, based on the premises of enemies and invasions, offers no vision to the soul. Even while the practice of healing is not certain, it offers a way of life that establishes harmony between all the worlds. Doing so, it enhances the ability of the body and the community to resist illness and despair and to recover from the many assaults that come to it from the unfortunate modern circumstances that make our lives essentially unlivable.

21

When one is diagnosed with cancer, the world comes to a halt. It is not only that a life is threatened but that we suddenly understand that everything must be reexamined and reevaluated. Around 1977, a patient at the Center for the Healing Arts in Los Angeles, where ancillary treatment for cancer was first pioneered, wanted to create a bumper sticker that said: Cancer is the Answer. What he meant was that illness had awakened him and no matter how long he was to live, he would live awake; he meant he was alive for the first time in his life. For those who do not simply put themselves in a physician's hands for radiation treatment or to undergo chemotherapy, it becomes essential to plot two separate and arduous courses, the way of medical treatment, conventional and experimental, and the way of healing, with all the possibilities through which the body/mind, or the soul must now be attended.

When I first met Laura Bellmay, she had just recovered from surgery for breast cancer. Health conscious and soul conscious, she was trying to root out the dark places in her life as an activity that would ease her back to health. The aesthetic, ethical core of her personal work was forgiveness. She had written a letter to the editor of the *Hartford Courant* that had brought her to the public's attention and she received a commendation for the letter.

> I was drawn to the article, "Showing Mercy to Gay Son's Killer." Before I had finished the article, I was in tears… of gratitude…. I felt healed by reading of Judy and Dennis Shepard's strength to forgive…. As a victim of the violent crime of rape, I feel a kindred spirit with the Shepards. I have spent many years actively involved in the process of forgiveness as a way to break the cycle of violence and vengeance. I did not, and do not, want

to spend my finite lifetime in bondage to anger, bitterness and revenge. In forgiveness, I become free of this bondage regardless of what the perpetrator does... the wave of healing begun by the Shepards reached my doorstep. I am so grateful and know that I am not the only person heartened by their act of courage.[41]

Laura met cancer as she met everything else – with forthrightness. Freelancing as a fundraiser for socially conscious causes, she was drawn to the *Nganga* Project and took it on as a way of doing service in the world. The unprecedented opportunity for her to attend a donors' and fundraisers' conference in South Africa verified the rightness of this choice and she began raising money for that journey which she hoped would extend to a visit with Augustine and Simakuhle afterwards. This work and these concerns were somewhat a departure from her work in Connecticut, but her heart told her that this was something she had to pursue. Shortly before she was to leave for South Africa, she discovered another lump in her breast that was diagnosed as cancer. The trip was cancelled. I urged her to have a mastectomy, hoping that she might avoid chemotherapy and radiation. Just a few days after she returned from the hospital, deeply bruised from the surgery and inpatient nursing care, I was teaching on the east coast and was able to visit her. It was clear that she didn't want to live. Like so many people that I meet, she was finding life too difficult; she was unconvinced of its purpose and its joy. The physical abundance that she enjoys, even though she shares a relatively small income with her husband, in no way compensates for the spiritual emptiness and tedium of middle-class life. Each day she was obliged to cope, yet again, with the scars that are the consequence of the various forms of abuse that are endemic in our culture. Her daily life was lived according to strategies for overcoming demons, and the simple moments of joy and enthusiasm were notably infrequent. There were moments that were redeeming: her women's group, a full moon circle, and the presence of her therapist, a generous and magical woman who also followed her understanding of what healing requires and was unafraid of expressing either tenderness or unique intelligence on behalf of her clients. Still, Laura wanted to die, or rather felt defeated in her determination to live. I knew one reason that Laura should fight for life and I was praying that I might state it well enough to be convincing. "I want you to live," I said, "so you can go to Africa and see that the spirits exist. I do not want you to die before you know that it is possible to be with the spirits, here, in this world. I want you to know for yourself that one does not have to die in order to meet the Divine."

Despite our hopes that she could avoid it, Laura underwent chemotherapy all spring and summer. Her body was completely debilitated. She was depressed and greatly dispirited. Only one thing, it seemed, was sustaining her. Michael and I were taking a group to Africa, and she intended to join us. No one wanted her to go except for Michael and myself and her therapist, Nora Jamieson, who was also turning increasingly toward the healing aspect of her own work. Undermined by chemotherapy, her immune system devastated, fragile, weak, exhausted, Laura had to withstand the bombardment of concern that came from everyone. It was clear that her community believed that she would die if she interrupted chemotherapy, and she believed that she would die if she continued chemotherapy and missed out on Africa. And so, despite her husband's alarm, she came to Africa.

For Americans, Africa is an archetypal terrain. Primordial fears, irrational concerns arise. Exhausted to the point of tears from chemotherapy, from the treatment, not the disease, fatigued further by flying for hours, Laura met a South African farmer on the plane who was returning from a three-week vacation with his family to his home in Harare. He guided her through customs and then took her to his family's home, offered her a bath, a meal and a nap, and drove her back to the airport for the short flight to Bulawayo. Gatekeeper at the threshold.

*   *   *

Sunday night, September 9th, 2001. We had returned from Victoria Falls and we were preparing to perform a healing ceremony on Laura's behalf. Augustine and I had decided that we would journey, in tandem, to the ancestors to ask for her complete healing. It was understood, though Laura had never made the request, that she had come to Africa for such a healing and now Augustine and I had decided to do whatever we could, with no restraint, for her full recovery. Augustine, Michael, and I agreed that I would prepare Laura for the ritual work by asking her to clear the path of any obstacles within her.

"Disease is the result of an evil mouth." I had been studying the text of the sacred letters, preparing myself to go to Sinai, when I come across these lines. The letter that had come to me was פ Pei. The mouth. What is taken in. What is spoken. "Every created being possesses a 'mouth' which speaks and 'sings' an individual song...." I begin to ponder this and what it might mean. "Anyone's ability to hear the song of creation brings us into the present moment."[42] The evil mouth, then, undermines creation. Disease results from it. I went into the bedroom where Laura was readying for the evening ritual.

From the moment that Laura had announced that she was coming to Zimbabwe, we had assumed we would do such work on her behalf. But since her arrival, her condition had become more serious. Turning in the upper bunk of the train a few days before on the way home from Big Falls, she might have, we thought, broken a rib. As I remember it, through the extreme faultiness of memory, I heard the crack before she cried out. But most probably I only heard the sharpness as she gasped for breath after the lightning strike of pain. The probable break caused us to consider the possibility of metastasis. In addition, only days before she had boarded the plane for Zimbabwe, she had found a lump in the other breast but had not investigated further because any discovery would have prevented her from coming to Africa. A rib broken in a commonplace movement. A new lump. We feared other tumors. Laura was often extremely tired. She had given up all her work except the *Nganga* Project, in order to devote what little energy she had to her own recovery. Her situation was not good and despite surgery and chemotherapy, she was in great need of the miracle of healing. And if not Augustine, if not under these remarkable circumstances, then who and when?

The image that had been before all of us for days was the sight of a water buffalo we had come upon at the Chapungu tree, taken down by lions who lay sated a few feet from the kill that was surrounded now by a city of vultures and Maribou storks eating what they could amid the endless din of flies. Then a lioness, belly up, startled awake and ran down into their midst to protect her prey. Over several hours we watched the very large body of the buffalo disappear, the hide sag onto the ground, the curved horns tilt into the mud, as the lions and then the birds hungrily chewed at it. Hour after hour. Birds advancing. Vulture waddling up with wings spread. Lions asleep and then rushing forward. A flutter of wings, the sky black with them. And then quiet. The buffalo had become horns, hide and bones. Soon these would disappear too. This also repeated for eons. Africa is not sentimental about death or about the food chain. We, on the other hand, wanted Laura among us for a longer time.

"Disease is the result of an evil mouth," I read to her from the *Alef-Beit*. The sacred letters are not from her tradition, but we had been moving from each other's traditional ways of knowing in order to learn everything we could about healing and transformation. The idea that every good deed or word creates an angel is part of the teaching of the philosopher Martin Buber. Every cruel or evil deed or word creates an evil angel. "Silently speak good of all those of whom you have spoken badly," writes Yitzack Ginsburg.[43]

I began interpreting what these words might mean to her, but she cut me off. "I will get right on it," she said. "These words remind me that I have not fully forgiven the brother who abused my sister and me though I have attempted it. In speaking of what he did to my family, I spoke badly about him, with anger and without compassion. I will try to remedy what I can."

When we met in the Daré room for the ritual a few hours later, she was shining with joy. "There is nothing between us now," she said. "I know something of what drove my brother to act as he did. No one wishes to do harm. Understanding doesn't change what I have suffered but it prevents me from prolonging the tragedy. There are no obstacles within me that prevent me from being healed by this work we are about to do. Neither anger nor skepticism. I am ready."

*　　*　　*

When a physician performs surgery, she must know the exact nature and location of what is to be cut out, repaired, or inserted. The more known, the more successful the outcome. Sure-handed, the physician repeats what she has done before many times, attempting to increase her skill and confidence. She is doing what others have also done before her, again and again. Good medicine depends on such a tradition. But when healers journey on behalf of a client, they do not know necessarily where they are going or what they will find, who will accompany them, what will be asked of them. The X rays they rely on are the light of their own minds and the insights of those they are working upon and the revelations of the signs and stories they have carefully attempted to understand. That others have gone before them informs them somewhat of the nature of the path they seek, but ultimately, they are heading out into the unknown.

Laura lay down on a bed of blankets on the floor of the Daré room. Augustine was at one end of the room. Simakuhle lay alongside her and I was on the other. Robin Wilds agreed to keep the heartbeat on the drum, Chuck and Wilderness were to bear witness and Michael would track where we were and what we might need.

For weeks previous, Simakuhle had been burdened by a dream. She had dreamed that the ancestors came to her with the name of the plant that could cure cancer. In the dream she had refused them because she didn't want to be a healer. A few nights before, Simakuhle had confessed this to all of us. She had told the story quietly weeping but when she finished, a scream as from elsewhere tore from her throat and she collapsed in shame. "I could have healed you," she wailed. "And I refused. I didn't want to be a healer. I don't want to be a healer. I can't do the work. I have too many children. I hate listening to people's stories. It is my fault, Laura, that you are still ill."

Being healed and being a healer cannot be separated. The spirits call us forth through illness in order that we can ease others. How else will we learn the medicine? The night of Simakuhle's confession, Laura had crawled to where Simakuhle was sitting and rocked her in her arms. The next night she took Simakuhle into her arms again and cradled her for hours. "It is my life, Simakuhle," she whispered, "and it is my death. But, you must not refuse the spirits or you will never be well yourself; your heart will not heal. My cancer is not your fault."

"I have to go to Botswana and leave offerings at my father's grave." Simakuhle had answered. "My father never helped me." She was overcome with the memory of the father who had sold her, at age fifteen, to a cruel man for the bride price. After they had had many children, the man had died. Then she met Augustine and her dreams had indicated that he was to be her husband. This night, in Laura's arms, she spoke of feeling alone in the world. She did not feel the presence of the ancestors supporting her. For years, she had suffered much pain in her body and her heart. Doctors had recommended heart surgery, but there was never enough money for such an operation and also she did not trust the surgeons. She did not know if her illness was caused by her refusal to be a healer, since the call had come to her in many ways over the years. Or was it because she had never honored her father's grave? Desperate now, she was praying for the assistance of the father who had never stood beside her. But she did not believe that he would help her unless she had performed the proper traditional rituals. She had tried to go to Botswana so many times but one thing or another had prevented her, including inertia. The ways of the father had been fully undermined by colonialism. She understood that honoring his grave would restore the right relationship between them. The passport that would take Simakuhle to Sinai, which had been so hard to arrange, had been received. It would take her to her father's grave in Botswana to honor his spirits. But this did not solve her grief. She did know that her father could not save her from the demands of the spirits. If the spirits wanted her to be a healer, she could not escape them. It was more than sufficient for Simakuhle that she was married to a healer. Their life was difficult. They are very poor. She has nine children who are under 18 years of age. The household is always full of relatives. Still, the dreams come to her and she cannot refuse them even though she is too exhausted to accept the path they are insisting is hers.

Simakuhle's heart is injured. Is it a medical injury or a spiritual injury? This is not a question the doctors can address, one masquerades as the other. We can call it God Sickness. I have known this malady.

*   *   *

When I was suffering from ennui, I didn't know I had God Sickness. I thought I was merely exhausted and empty, unable to write or meditate, dismayed that no words came forth. I thought I was suffering once again from the affliction called publishing.

Thursday, December 27, 2001. Journal:

Last night, I was wondering why I was writing this manuscript. Will it ever see the light of day? The value of my entire life disintegrated in hopelessness. This morning, aimlessly looking through my journals and earlier writing, I came across a title I had given to an uncompleted manuscript that was based on notes from when I was in Zimbabwe the first time: *God Sickness.* I had worked on the manuscript for a few months and then I put it away without realizing that I was running away from a call. When you run away from a call, you can be afflicted with God Sickness. How do you recognize it? It has a variety of manifestations. Physical illness, depletion, discouragement, depression.

In titling the manuscript, *God Sickness,* I had assumed that I was ruminating on Augustine's experience and teachings. But then, as Michael was involved in his third book related to Augustine's work, I put my own work aside. I told myself that I was writing Michael's book. I hadn't accepted that I was writing about myself. Now I read the passages and understand that they refer both to my circumstances in July 1998 and also this moment. Unnerving to find them this morning. Depression dissolves through finding this text. It cannot be dismissed as accident. I must recognize the finger of God.

From *"God Sickness"*:

I know this place. It is the place of running away from God. I have been here before and will no doubt return. One is exiled to this place; one does not come of one's free will and one remains in the gulag until such time as one is fit to emerge, once again, into the world.

I come here exactly at the moment when I finished a piece of what I thought, what I think, might be God's work. At least, I pursued it as an offering. And then the work season came to an end and I made for the woods and some moments of beauty and a few weeks of resting in words.

For six years, I have come here to give myself to God. Among the trees where the bear, deer and mountain lion are padding quietly, almost invisibly, away from the telephone and the fax machine, preoccupations fall away and it is possible to ask: "What is Your will?"

Here is one of the places where I have given myself to God. And here is where I expected that I would be reunited with myself after a long stint in service. Here is where I expected to rest and refresh myself so that I could begin again. I did not expect, then, the extreme agitation that precedes rest and the absence of the Presence. Not now. Not at this time in my life. Not after the last few years.

I have come to a time in my life when there is nothing that I know. It has taken years of practice and study to arrive here. So even when I say, "I know this place," you must understand that it is just a figure of speech. Indeed, I do not know this place though I have confronted emptiness and I have been lost before. Each time it is different, because it is, each time, the perfect coda to a finished piece of music that was oneself. After awhile, one hopes, a new piece of music will begin, one will hear a bird song and try to strike a similar note in order to set out from there. If you hear anything at this moment, it is the aimless strumming of fingers upon strings. They say the universe emerged from such strumming and we always hope that we will strike the right chords and a new life will begin.

It has taken more courage to admit to myself that I am running away from God than I can express to you. I thought I had been running toward God open-armed for a long time. I had gone through the quiet and private ceremony of giving myself to God. I had given myself away. And now this. I discover I am running away by observing myself, by becoming a spy, noting my actions, trying to decipher my own covert thoughts. I cannot know what I am doing from within myself where there is only great silence and bafflement. But I can say this: Because I know nothing, I must begin to write things down exactly as they are or seem to be in the moment. Each word carefully weighed. It is not for you that I am trying to discover and record some truth. I have spent my life as a fiction writer and so I know that in order for you and I to speak with some level of understanding between us, I am going to have to lie, that is I am going to have to invent and hone a language of images and associations that you might possibly understand. But for myself, the language as it comes to me bare and halting, serves me, if I do not speak too quickly, if I do not jump to any conclusions.

In order to find the song from which one's life might be reconstructed, one makes an offering. In this case, I put out seeds for the birds. *Attracts Songbirds*, the plastic package asserts boldly. And, almost immediately, the jays have come squawking. So I see the direction where I am going.

Michael is not afraid of God or of the gods. In preparation for writing a book he has been thinking about for many years, he has done nothing these last few days but make offerings, sing praise songs and invoke the sacred in his own unique manner developed carefully over the years. I have not turned my back on such activities though I have been modest in my practice. I have meditated and I have chanted. But I have also capitulated to my urban and secular mind which wants to scrutinize all my intuitions, activities and, more particularly, all my conclusions. The mind that wants to work.

This is the difference between us: M. serves God first. Or does, first, what he imagines is serving God. But I believe my task is to serve God by serving the world and so I am always concerned about my credibility.

One day God appears outside of liturgy. Naked. How else to say it? Outside of the traditional paths already marked. Without priest or temple or text. It wasn't one day; it seemed to occur one day but the appearance was subtle, occurred over a period of time, a faint image slowly coming into form, slowly growing a body, compelling and startling. But also unreliable; that is, how could I rely on my own perceptions in such a profound matter? But also, how could I not accept the reality of the vision? Or more to the point, how could I refuse the call?

Those of us who have been drawn into a gnostic path are not always able to follow the conventional ways. These songs we sing, these offerings we make, the rituals and ceremonies we are asked to create, the signs we see, the dreams that come, these values we are enjoined to uphold, the original languages we are forced to create in order to describe our experience, the rag-bag of gestures we borrow from one disdained wisdom tradition or another, all lead to an intense and irrefutable sense that we are engaged in a direct conversation with Spirit. These ways override the ways and means of the world. All of this makes us appear odd, eccentric, even mad. To others, we fear. To ourselves. How then to walk this path and still accomplish the task of healing what is calling to be healed?

...M. and I take a walk along a stream bank resplendent with wild asters, small stars twinkling among the river grasses. My fear of God is the same as my fear of beauty. Each annihilates us in the service of vision. We must break out of ourselves and our lives in order to see what is to be seen. Or we will be broken. And after we are undone, then we must proceed to walk according to what we have seen in the invisible world. From then on, we speak other languages and are guided by intangible forces. We step out of the community of consensus and the known.

*   *   *

I was running from God then. I did not want to write the book. I had God Sickness. I recognize that I am being called to write. I capitulate. This is sufficient. This is the cure.

When we learn about illness, we are not learning about the other, we are learning about ourselves. That night it was Simakuhle, but it could as easily be myself. Earlier it was Valerie. Then Laura. Augustine knows these ways from his own experience. Now it is his wife who is suffering because the dreams are calling her where she does not have the strength or inclination to go.

I think again of Augustine's insistent teachings: Spirit wants to heal. He says we make ourselves a vessel for the Spirit and it enters us and works through us.

When one is ill or disoriented it is often because the spirits are sitting heavily upon us. What do the spirits want? They want us to come across to meet them. They want us to open ourselves to them. They want us to let them in. They want us to become healers.

One of the ways of healing is to assist the ill person in becoming a healer. So there is no hierarchy between the healer and the one who is ill; there is only a matter of time between them. The one who has submitted is now able to lead the other forward.

How do we assist someone in becoming a healer? One way is to help them remember the stories that arrange themselves to become the one story. Which story? The story of how you came to this place.

*   *   *

We are back in the Daré room. An unexpected connection had revealed itself between Simakuhle and Laura and this may mean that their healing is also tied to each other. This may not be rational, but there is a strange poetry to it. The two women recognize that they have been woven into each other's destiny. Is this not one of the teachings of Africa and indigenous mind? We are not separate from each other and our lives are strengthened when we recognize that we share a common jeopardy and a common fate. It looks as if we are burdened by each other, but, in fact, we are fortified. It takes a change of mind to recognize that the consequences of such interdependence are most often benevolent. Again, this is why we have come to Africa. To learn this. To take it into our consciousness. To change our lives accordingly. Simakuhle closes her eyes on the mat of blankets and reaches out her hand, just as Laura's hand inches toward hers. Their hands clasp. They are ready and they are together.

We are going to do ritual work for both of them at the same time. Augustine prays long and sweetly and then Michael prays to Eshu Elegba to open the way and to Spider Woman, *Ambuya Buwe Buwe*, to weave the world together for us all. There is a leopard skin on the wall. Alongside it, a notice regarding AIDS and the precautions that must be taken to protect oneself and one's family. A box containing condoms. Baskets of herbs, drums and rattles. We turn off the lights and close our eyes. Robin, eyes closed, begins to drum. We set out.

I come back to the same phrases: People have done this for thousands of years. Western civilization has not necessarily improved on everything that came before. We are more comfortable, those of us who are comparatively affluent, but we are not wiser. For thousands of years, healers have appealed to the spirits to move through them for the sake of the community. These are comfort statements that ease the heart when one enters into a world totally distinct from the world into which one was born and where one lives. I am trying to find my way through a world that I once believed had totally disappeared. I have gratitude that the spirits and ancestors might be among us. Hope.

I do not know where I am. Time and space are one. I have to swim through the dark ocean of the past. Away. Away. Moving far back into Laura's life, I cannot find helpers who will assist me. Her grandparents are unwilling to appear. Perhaps the barrier between this world and the other world is too great or, as Christians, they cannot cross the river even to save their granddaughter's life. Or as likely, I do not have the skill yet to move competently. Perhaps there are prayers that must be said, spirits to be invoked and healing cannot occur without this assistance, but I do not know them. I try to work on behalf of Simakuhle. I cannot cross the barrier of her need to accept the healer she is called to be. When I reach the place of the call, I feel only the taste of sweetness. Western people refer to this sensation as synaesthesia but this way of speaking is reductive. There is a place of knowing. I cannot go beyond it. At the perimeter is a wall. It cannot be penetrated. Within this place are the gifts that have been given to Simakuhle. They are palpable as mist and invisible. They look like baskets of sweet herbs for infants. They look like dreams. They look like shafts of light called understanding. They look like mothering. They look like a lap filled with fruits and watermelons. This place is sweet as honey. In this place, the father stands behind his daughter. Perhaps I understand something of the order of things. Simakuhle is to take on the call of the spirits and then bring offerings to her father's grave. First the healer and then the daughter. If the healer comes to the grave of her father, her father will be able to honor her offerings.

I leave Simakuhle and try to journey again on behalf of Laura but I cannot. I return and enter Laura's body. There is the cracked rib. Her bones are like ivories on a piano and I begin to play some music I have never heard before. As I play this strange instrument of her body, I watch the crack on the ivory diminish. Vaguely in the back of my mind are thoughts regarding the work we have been doing in Daré in Los Angeles regarding music and healing. We are learning to improvise music based upon the configuration of illness as enacted in the person, to play the psyche and its disruptions until it is captured, or perhaps better to say, captivated. Then we take it, musically, to the particular harmonic that that life is seeking. In this moment, I am also involved in music in a jazz and popular idiom. Only later will I learn that Laura sings in this vernacular. I do not know the music that is being played through me, but she does. I play the notes in my mind, or let the master piano player work through me. It is not possible to eliminate the break in her rib entirely or to smooth the ivory piano key so that the crack disappears entirely. But, it is better than before. A patch appears. Not the finest workmanship, but adequate to repair the damage. Her rib will heal and it will bear a scar. Piano music. Jazz.

It is then that I hear a plaintive whistle. A man walking in the back alleys of the city. New York. 4 a.m. Black man whistling slow and clear. Going home. Carrying his sax in a worn case. Slow drifting toward the East River. Light mist on his face. Halo around the street lamps. 1938. A sad and jaunty man in a gray fedora.

I open my eyes and see someone who looks like Augustine climbing over Simakuhle and running his hands over Laura's body. It must be Augustine but it is not his manner. It is not an African man, but a New Yorker, an African-American. The eerie whistle continues. He is singing the blues. This music is two hundred years away from Africa. Augustine does not whistle like this. Now the figure lets go into a long grief-stricken riff. He is sitting astride Laura's body and it appears that he is searching for something. His face is twisted as if he is suffering great pain. He cannot find what he is looking for. Then one hand touches her breast. He is still searching for something. I look over desperately to Michael, Wilderness, Chuck. Robin is lost in the drum; she sees nothing. My eyes meet Wilderness. Laura's eyes are closed. Her face is exceedingly calm. She is still holding Simakuhle's hand. Simakuhle is calm as well.

The first principle of healing: First, do no harm.

I do not know what is occurring. Everything I have ever believed is challenged. I want to stop this. I do not know what is happening. Augustine is clearly trance-possessed. How else explain this? But what is he doing? Who is this figure? What manner of Spirit is this? Can I trust Augustine? Can I trust this spirit? Is this a hoax? Have I brought Laura here only to be violated? Is it all a sham? Is western medicine right? Have I been bewitched and have I brought harm to those I love? Is this yet another instance of the healer or teacher violating the woman put into his care? Yet another instance of spiritual abuse? Am I causing more injury to someone who was already suffering from abuse? Or might I be witness to a miracle of healing? Can I trust the spirits? Can I trust Augustine? Can I trust myself?

I have known Augustine for four years. He is the elder I trust most in the world. I have scrutinized him and he has never come up lacking. I have not idealized him. I have seen him tired and confused, angry and hopeless. I have seen him weep. I have seen him despairing. I have seen him exhausted. I have seen him reactive. I have seen him under the most difficult conditions. But I have never seen him violate anyone. I have never seen him be cruel or act with unconsciousness. I have never seen him do harm.

Still, desperate, I follow each one of Augustine's motions – but is this Augustine? Who is this man? Is he himself or is he the spirit that is possessing him? For the first time, I find myself thinking in terms of good spirits and bad spirits, a dualism I have refused until now. In refusing to believe in dark forces, in evil spirits, in devils, have I been naïve? Crisis of faith. Who is Augustine? Are there spirits? Are we mad to have come to Africa? Does healing exist?

I examine Michael's expression. To whom is he loyal? To the woman or to the man? To the patient or to the healer? Would he allow everything he has worked for and believed in for so many years to be destroyed if

Augustine is acting badly? Or will he pretend that violation is not violation? With a look Michael assures me that he is watching Augustine. Michael has been with Augustine when he was trance-possessed many times. He has also scrutinized Augustine. They have argued, they have struggled together, they have gone to the bottom of racism together. Michael trusts Augustine but he is also telling me that he will protect Laura. Somehow I know that he will interrupt this ritual, that he will destroy everything he/we have built here, if he feels that Laura will be harmed. He will not sacrifice her. He assures me of this.

Looking once more into Wilderness' eyes, reassured by the fact that she has a daughter, that she is awake, that she is intelligent and kind, I begin to pray. Prayer reassures me. Augustine is no longer by Laura's chest. He was just there for a moment. He is moving toward her feet, his hands a few inches above her body. I pray that Augustine is the healer we have thought him to be. I pray that the healing spirits are moving through him. I relinquish any desire I might have had to be the healing presence for Laura and offer it all to Augustine. May he be a great healer. May healing enter the room and Laura's body through him.

Hearing Laura wince, I watch Augustine, lithe as a great cat looming over Laura's ankle, bite her left ankle, twisting, as if extracting something from her body. She screams. The great cat folds back into the forest in the way I have seen a leopard descend from a high branch and vanish into the underbrush. The whistle again. Haunting. As American as any sound might be. Call of the streets. Dark night city blues.

Transformation. Augustine has returned to his place and is sitting cross-legged again on a skin. And yet again, it is not Augustine. He turns his profile to me and I see a baboon in the man. The baboon overtakes the man. Baboon. Dog-headed Ape. Tehuti. Tehuti carries the face of the baboon in the way Christ is associated with the Lamb.

Tehuti is the name the ancient Egyptians ascribed to the energy of divine intelligence, to universal mind with all its powers of speech and creation. Lord of all knowledge and understanding, Tehuti was the inventor and god of all the arts and sciences. As "scribe of the gods," Tehuti formulates all the words of creation and records them in the Akasha, or universal memory. But his word only has power when he is together with Maat, who is the Cosmic Law, that is when the mind is centered in the heart. As a living *Neter* he established a common language, invented the alphabet and established the worship of the gods in the temples built by Ausar. He gave humans the first principles of astronomy, music and medicine and was the author of all books concerning human and divine knowledge. One of Tehuti's titles was "Thrice-Great," later becoming Hermes Trismegistus.

As messenger of the gods, Tehuti became Mercury, who holds the caduceus and who is the mind of the cosmos in its fluidic aspect. Here Tehuti is associated with the coiled power of the serpent and its healing knowledge, he taught the science of medicine, giving not only the appropriate remedy, but also the precise moment in which to take it. [44]

We are in the presence of a *Neter*, a great spirit. This time, it is a spirit I recognize and honor. I am awed and cannot move, but in my mind I kneel down and clap, as is the custom in Africa when a spirit enters a person. We do not applaud the person. The person has disappeared. We applaud and welcome the spirit. "Thank you for coming, great one. *Tatenda.*"

When it seems that the rite is over, I bolt up and run out of the Daré room. The large black dog jumps on me and I fall down. Three dogs are on me now. Later in our bedroom, Laura is very quiet, tired and also calm. There is an aspect of sublimity about her.

*   *   *

The first principle of healing: First, do no harm.

September 10th, we are driving north to visit the *Ambuya* and Zou at Great Zimbabwe. This is the first opportunity for us to try to understand what happened the night before. We are all still within the strangeness and the mystery of it. We decide that each person will tell their version of the story as we drive. Each of us, that is except Augustine, who is driving and mostly cannot hear what we are saying. I will ask him for his story later when we can all sit down together.

Wilderness contemplates what it means to bear witness. To carry the vision of what one is seeing without assuming one understands it. The difficulty and necessity to step out of judgment. She has been called to a large vision and she carries the overview. She knows the sorrow of violation and she knows the sorrow of distrust. She knows what it is to be injured and she knows the grief of interfering prematurely with healing. Because she is being called to be responsible, she must know what it is to trust when it is difficult to trust, and what it means to have faith in the invisibles.

I speak. Chuck speaks. Michael speaks. Finally, Laura speaks. When she was fourteen, she was walking down a city street when a black man approached her menacingly. She believed she was in grave danger as she ran and he pursued her. Finally, she got away, but the story had wormed its way into her soul alongside the violence of her brother and other assaults. Augustine's gentle hands, she said, had redeemed the story for her. She had not known such tenderness and caring from a man. When he placed his hands on the tumor in her breast, an old and painful story that had festered within her dissolved in his touch. Cancer and the sexual wound, braided together, and now, perhaps, one healed through the soothing of the other. "It was not possible," Michael said, "for the bitter sexual wound to remain unattended."

*   *   *

It is morning in Masvingo. Tuesday, September 11th. Augustine has asked us to fast before we go to the *Ambuya*. We are seated outside the lodge, drinking tea and listening to birdsong. I must speak to Augustine about what happened. I review the story very carefully and he listens respectfully. "I understand completely," he says and recounts several incidents where he thought that *ngangas* were using the mask of trance-possession to cover their sexual improprieties. "This is happening to us many times now," he says. He speaks, as always, with exquisite intelligence informed by great heart and sensitivity. He is sensitive to the reasons I was afraid, at the same time that he is aware of the plague of such abuse that is affecting people everywhere. He does not privilege healers, Africans or anyone. He is not hurt by my suspicions or fears. He is Augustine trying, as he always does, to heal whatever is brought to him.

"What is the story that happened to you the night of the gray fedora?" we ask, for each of us were in a story that was both our own and belonged to each other.

"For years," he said, "I was promised by the spirits that I would be given healing powers that would be very useful, but they never came. I prayed for them but they never appeared. Since you arrived, I felt as if the possibility was hovering very near. When I was trance-possessed, I could suddenly see into Laura's body. I knew then what to do for Laura and I pray that I will know better what to do for others. I saw the tumor and I was guided to heal it by dissolving it. But then I saw something in her ankle. I couldn't dissolve it. I had to take it out.

Augustine turned to Laura. "I hope I didn't hurt you too much."

"You did," she exclaims.

"Shame," Augustine concurs.

The conversation continued a long time as we explored together the responsibilities of the healer and the responsibilities of the community. We had not wanted to interrupt the ritual because we did not want to undermine any possibility that Laura might heal. But also we didn't want her to come to new harm. Would she protect herself? Were the women responsible to protect the daughter? Would the men protect the weaker one?

"I was fully able and willing to take care of myself," Laura said. "I would have been distraught if you had interrupted the ritual. I knew it was healing and I gave myself to it completely. If I had felt any violation, I would have responded immediately. But, I was feeling the wonder of the old story being cut out of me. I am so grateful," Laura said. "Everything moving toward healing. A miracle."

Augustine could not remember the tune of the whistle, only the light in the body and his certainty that he knew what to do. It was not African music, but American jazz, an idiom he didn't know. Playing jazz with the dead. I saw the ivory keys again and played them in my mind. Ivory. Elephant. Ally. Ancestors. I have been writing a book called *Doors: A Jazz Novel*. Augustine and I had wondered if we would meet "over there." We had met in the book. In the music of it. In the mysterious place that is being revealed to us about the relationship of music and healing.

And then it was time to walk up the hill to be with the *Ambuya*, who, as always, told us that she had dreamed that night that we were coming. In the dream, she had gone out to the river to get water in a pitcher. We heard the dream and then Wilderness bowed before her and offered the tiny silver ewer on a chain, already in her hand, that she had brought from Massachusetts as a gift. We filled it with water, as the *Ambuya* had done in the dream and we were all together in that world that is the Ghost River.

22

Masvingo. The old ruin of the colonial empire of the Shona people. The end of an empire. The end of ambition, power, militarism. When Patricia was here, she asked Augustine and Michael to lie down in the Cave of the Kings and we saw the spirits of the kings enter into them. They looked stunned; what had entered them was greater than they could carry. Afterwards, they spoke of the required benevolence of the king and the effort that it took to care for everyone within one's domain. They did not speak of power, but rather of capitulation.

From this citadel, the king surveyed all his lands to see what was required to protect them. As part of the initiatory process, Chuck and Wilderness were asking themselves what it would mean to carry regal spirits on behalf of the community that they served back home. There was no ego here, but rather the opposite, a great reticence to take on the burden that was given to them. Goodbye personal life, say the king and queen who are being called to gather everything they have learned, everything they have, everything they have ever dreamed and wanted for themselves to make an offering of it so they can give themselves entirely to the world. They had come to Africa to celebrate their twentieth wedding anniversary, and this demand was the *gift* given to them by the spirits.

In silence, we walked from the rondavel of the *Ambuya* to the entrance of the Great Enclosure of the Queen. We had taken everything from Wilderness so that she would know that she was being initiated as the queen. Purse, jewelry, everything but her simple clothes were taken from her. Her long silver hair fell like a mantle down her shoulders. Only later would we know the great sorrow that was welling up in her, that she thought then was the inevitable sorrow of any regent whose obligation it is to carry the grief of the citizens of the land. Inside the enclosure, she lay down on the ground and sobbed wordlessly as I cut her hair, but only a snippet, though she had expected I would take it all when she yielded to the sacrifice as a sign of her commitment. Then she got up and straightened her shoulders, as behooved the stately being she had become, and walked alongside Chuck up the mountain to the Cave of the King where he would undergo his own inner ordeal and take his own private and silent vows.

What is a king? What does he owe the people? Once he is king, he is indebted to the people and the land. How does he protect the domain that is now and until his death, in his hands? Robin and Michael went with them. Augustine went off to be by himself and Laura and I remained behind for she was also sobbing. Nearby some workers were restoring the wall that surrounded a tall broken tower whose apex had been toppled halfway from the base as was clear by the angle of its ascent.

The exposed and entangled roots of a great tree formed a kind of throne and Laura sat upon them weeping her heart out. Like Wilderness she would give no words to the grief, could find no words for her broken heart. Just a few moments before, a woman selling pottery by the *Ambuya*'s rondavel had embraced Laura fiercely and had whispered brokenly, as Augustine translated, the story of the death of her young child a few weeks before. It was as if the woman's grief represented all women's grief, the woman's loss all women's losses of their children, the accident of the child's death becoming all premature deaths. We had walked down to the Great Enclosure carrying the weight of her pain, world pain.

And so Laura and I stayed behind and mourned the end of worlds before the broken Shona tower with the dark stains where the pinnacle had been. Then we began a ritual of healing, slowly and deliberately. "Offer up everything, absolutely everything, that stays in the way of your healing. Whatever may have contributed to cancer in your life, give it up. Whatever you have done and whatever was done to you, separate yourself from it, so that disease will have no place to cling in your body or your soul. Whatever beliefs or activities led to cancer or disease, that hurt you or others, let them go. Pray now that they will not continue. Pray for a new story and a new path." This was Laura's task. It took her an hour. She kissed the earth and consumed it. Then she slowly circumambulated the mound of earth that was the *omphalos*, the ritual center, the holy place of the Shona people.

Then she was done. Sorrow still with her but hope also. We walked slowly, still in the processional mode, to the rectangular opening in the wall of the Queen's Enclosure. Above the wall, in the distance we saw the citadel. Before us through the opening a green meadow. Spring was just beginning in Zimbabwe and the earth was covered in new green. "When you step out," I said, "you will be out of the old story that brought you to your knees in illness and despair. You will be in a new story. You won't know it yet, but it is a story that carries kindness and forgiveness and is free of disease. In the next weeks and months, you will learn the dimensions and the ways of the new story, but now you need know only that it brings health to you, your kin and everyone you encounter."

The photographs we have tell the story. The broken tower. The *omphalos*. The throne of the tree. Laura praying for her life. The way she paused in the opening in the wall. And then the way she walked through and opened her arms to the sky, threw herself into joy, a cartwheel despite or in defiance of the broken rib, arms out, turning and turning, a child in the afternoon light.

When we came to the place we had agreed to meet the others it was about four-thirty in the afternoon. Once again, we came upon the woman who had lost her child. She was coming down from the rondavels and, again, as if I wasn't there, she threw herself in Laura's arms and wept inconsolably until Laura wept with her in equal grief. We gave her what money we had in our pockets for the rites of the dead and then we sat down to wait for the others.

And here they come. Robin, ecstatic, from having danced in the sacred place and Wilderness and Chuck equally joyous from having made the kind of marriage vows one makes when Spirit is calling a couple forth to do the work of the sacred together. We find Augustine and enter the car so we can return to Bulawayo. Only here come the *Ambuya* and Zou and we offer to take them toward their house and this takes time. It is getting dark. We stop at the crossroads where people are selling Shona sculpture, fabric and animal carvings. But we do not have the heart to buy anything. Something is pulling at us and we must get home. The women gather around our van, pulling at us. In the background, someone is ululating. A child has just been killed, run over by a car. It died on the way to the hospital. We are surrounded in grief again.

Given all these interruptions, we must set out immediately for Bulawayo or we will not get home tonight. But Laura insists we return to the hotel by the ruins so she can make a phone call. The phones have not been working in Bulawayo and she has not been able to call her husband. She needs to arrange for her circle of women to meet her as soon as she returns so that she will remember the path of healing before the habits of her life undermine everything in their hegemony. She is absolutely adamant though it means we will not return home until well after midnight. Her insistence feels irrational.

We ask the clerk at the hotel desk to assist us in calling the United States. "Oh," he says, "you are calling about the bombing." We do not know what he is referring to but we put the phone down and all of us go into the empty bar where he turns on the television for us with exquisite but mysterious sympathy. And then we see it. The broken towers. The collapse of empire. The dead. The World Trade Center collapsing. The attack on the Pentagon. Laura's brother works here. The brother she had fully forgiven. Is he alive?

At the time we began the rituals, Laura and Wilderness were both consumed with grief at the foot of the broken tower in the Great Enclosure of the Queen in Masvingo, the ruin of the great empire of the Shona people; it had been 3:15 p.m. in Zimbabwe and exactly 9:15 a.m. at the twin towers of the World Trade Center in New York City on September 11, 2001.

*   *   *

Dream:

Standing in the corridor as the train comes to a stop. Three or four black children call to me. They put a dying body in my arms. It is small as a child. I carry it in my arms into the train. A man boards saying, "Girl, get that away from me."

Horrified, I refute him, "This is a *man*."

The man dies in my arms and I step off the train and bury him, but not properly. I place the tiny bundle of a human being on the ground under a picnic table, dig a very shallow grave and cover him with earth. There is no time to do things right. I get on the train again.

This is my sacred work, traveling on this train, caring for, receiving the dead and dying. We need to have a record. There must be witnesses. Someone should photograph this. I meet Valerie in a small store, far from our homes. We embrace. She is reassuringly solid. It is her intent to photograph the dying on the train. This is our work together.

No matter what I imagined, I didn't expect to spend the rest of my life burying the dead.

The Tower. We watch CNN as do most of the people in the world who have television. Over and over. We watch the towers crumble. But we are watching this in Africa and so we are watching it also from an African perspective and after fierce initiatory work that has broken us down, each of us, in our own way.

The Tower is an image in the Tarot. It is one of the Major Arcana. Number 17. It signifies one of 22 archetypal moments of life. Most commonly, the Tower is depicted just before it collapses after being struck by lightning. There are people jumping out of the tower so as not to be in it when it is consumed by fire. The Tower card has come to life before our eyes.

We stay in Masvingo. We do not know if Laura's brother is alive or dead, only that she forgave him. We learn that our families are okay and that my son who is often on the two flights that went down is grounded and safe in Las Vegas. It is Tuesday night. Our initiatory time is to come to an end on Friday night. Naïve pilgrims who think they can orchestrate initiation as if it were a workshop or a planned vacation, we do not know what is going to be asked of us or what the words that we have been saying to each other might really mean. But we know that we, like everyone else in the western world, are being tested. We do not know what it may mean to be healers in this world. We do not know what it may mean to walk as peacemakers in a world on the brink of war. We do not know if/when we will be able to leave Zimbabwe.

We will soon learn that Laura's flight to the U.S. will be postponed indefinitely. While she can fly to Johannesburg as scheduled, there are no hotels left in the city and hundreds of people will be camping out in the airport waiting for the flights to resume the following Tuesday. Pooling all the American dollars we have, we manage a miracle and get her the last seat on the planes Robin is taking to Toronto via London. In London, in defiance of a supervisor standing nearby, a second gatekeeper cuts her exceptionally high fare in half. Laura will be able to get to Connecticut for her next chemotherapy appointment. When she will get home, her X rays will reveal a small crack in her rib but no cancer, and the lumps in her breast will be benign. Michael and I are scheduled to fly to Egypt with Augustine and Simakuhle on Saturday on Egypt Air. We will soon learn that airlines from Arab countries will be prohibited from entering the United States for at least a week. Wilderness and Chuck will soon learn that two passengers on the first plane that hit the tower are in their kinship network. We do not know what further tragedies may occur. We do not know if or where or how our country will respond. We do not know if war will break out or if someone's deranged version of Armageddon is about to be enacted.

*   *   *

These are the ways the Tower card is often interpreted. According to the Waite deck:

"The Ruin of the House of Life when evil has prevailed therein. A House of Falsehood. 'Except the Lord build the house, they labour in vain that built it.'"[45]

Liz Greene and Juliet Sharman-Burke, who created *The Mythic Tarot*, recognize in the Tower the collapse of old forms, of the inner and outer structures that we build to defend ourselves against life and its fearful truths. The Tower, they say, represents the facades we create in order to hide what is unacceptable. It represents the collapse of what is false and outgrown, the social and political constructions, the tired ideas or perspectives that are no longer viable or relevant to our current lives. The Tower represents the necessary breakdown or collapse of existing forms so that something new and vital can emerge. If we can, they say, dismantle these false edifices we may save ourselves a lot of grief as "the Tower will fall anyway"; it has come to the end of its time. It no longer serves us or the community that erected it.[46]

I feel the terrible truth of this. A coincidence of the exoteric and the esoteric. We are in a story. An old story coming to an end. An old regime. It had not occurred to us that we might be the old order, the ancient regime that must inevitably come to an end and all efforts to prevent its demise might be the final, violent gasps of an imperial rule that no longer serves the world. We had thought we were the future. We didn't imagine that we were what the future would see as decadent and rigid. We imagined ourselves the revolution living according to our original history; we didn't imagine that we had become the counter-revolution.

Everywhere we go, we are greeted with sympathy and concern, in southern Africa and then in Egypt. But everywhere also, people indicate that they understand the motivations of the attack. We Americans have not used our power well. In only considering our own economic welfare, we have done great harm in the world. The tower of affluence and globalization has fallen. The task, we understand, is not to build it back up again but to understand the causes of its collapse and to make amends. Our influence is everywhere and the people and the animals and the natural world are dying of it. It is time to begin again. How could we have come to this? We were once children and now we have become what, as children, we were taught to fear.

The card that precedes the Tower in the Tarot is the Devil. We try to understand the story we have been thrust into. What led up to this attack on the Tower? We cannot project the Devil on others. This is our story. Even this devil. Our collective story. Our national story.

According to The Mythic Tarot, "The Devil implies the necessity of a confrontation with all that is shadowy, shameful and base in our personality."[47] The way I would state it, is a confrontation with all that is held to be shadowy, shameful…. Historically, the figure of the devil with its cloven hoofs derives from Pan, the wild, goatish earth spirit, the great flautist, who introduces us to the irresistible call of music, or from Dionysus, the passionate, resurrecting god who carries the life force. A Puritan society like ours with its fear of the earthy and disdain for the earth, erects the great towers to protect itself from the uncontrollable natural forces and elements that it calls devilish and holds as crude or brutish when it finds them within itself. With the devil, we are at the heart of what plagues us. A dualistic society creates devils and angels, good and bad, dark and light. Eventually we are crucified on these arbitrary attributions and our structures fall. There are also other aspects of the Devil who is the quintessential image of what tempts us away from Spirit and from heart, the Faustian demon who entangles us in our greed, our materialism, our love of violence, our love of death.

And the card that follows the Tower? The Star. The part of us which, despite disappointment, depression and loss can still cling to a sense of meaning and a future that might grow out of the unhappiness of the past.

I think it was Spirit that planted the idea of "radical hope" in my mind. The necessity of carrying a belief in a future. "What are the far implications of the work you are doing, the story you are writing or telling?" I ask my students. Does it have a future? Star Wars does not have a future, but the forest does. When I visited the Death Camps in Eastern Europe, I meditated at the mass graves and before the ovens until I could see something, a light, a possibility, some transformation. Perhaps it was just the growing seed of compassion in my heart. Perhaps it was the light that enters through the heartbreak we must all experience. Hope is often associated with the will to live but I associate it with the will to life. Hope, in these times, comes from the insistence that life will continue and flourish, that the natural world will survive despite our violent attacks upon it.

Having made a pilgrimage to the ocean on the night that I finished the second draft of this book, I closed my eyes to hear the thunderous roar of the waves, trying to understand, again, what the water spirits are. I remembered a repeated dream I had had about a tsunami. Listening then to the awesome sound or song of ocean, I recognized that the dream tsunami was not warning me of danger, but was rather a gift – a vision of an awesome, indomitable spirit making itself visible. The tide came in and receded in its patterns of delicate lace and it seemed to me that I heard the whisperings of hope: *Do not be afraid. No matter how ignorant and violent you are as a species, you will not destroy the sea. You will yourself perish long before you can destroy it fully. The sea will remain and from its womb some fragment of life will begin again.* This was enough hope for me to continue, to bear witness, to call forth those who will find another way to live in harmony with the elements and the natural world. A hope that has the energy to create another story in which the sea remains alive and full of joyous creatures. A hope that has a future. A tower falls and the sea, as a consequence, continues. The tower falls and the sky becomes clear and the star is visible. Hope.

Every story has a beginning and an end, but where you locate the beginning determines the end. What you consider to be the components of the story determine its content. None of this is obvious, neither the beginning, the elements, nor the conclusion.

Where is the beginning of the story that ends with the collapse of the towers in New York? A creation story shared by all those who are warring against each other. Humans given dominion over the animals. Woman created out of a rib and made subordinate. Prohibition against wisdom. A doctrine created from all of this regarding an original sin and a taint that is passed on from generation to generation. Chosen people and people who are not chosen. A god who refuses the offerings of the field. A god that is crucified. Prophets who demand war on behalf of the Holy One.

Slaughter. A passion for conquest and a god who blesses war. Those who will be saved and those who will be damned. Absolutism. Totalitarian thinking. Self-righteousness. A vision of Armageddon. Holy wars.

But what if we do not insist that this is the beginning of the story? What if we do not imagine that these are our origins? What if we begin our story elsewhere? What if we locate ourselves elsewhere? What story will emerge? Where will it lead? What may come from a new and different story?

When we returned to Bulawayo on September 12th, the spirits insisted that we go immediately to Siloswane, the Bushmen cave that has been in continuous use for approximately fifteen thousand years. It was to this sacred arena that we were called in order to speak with the animals and the ancestors so that we might be guided to another ending, to other possibilities, to what might heal the devastations of this time.

We climbed the steep whaleback rock in silence to the cave that opens like an amphitheatre onto beauty. The women still dance across the ceiling among the animals, the hunters and the shamans who live in the dream between this world and the other world. A boulder centrally located at the entrance serves as an altar and we imagine that it was placed there ages ago for the same sacred purpose. From below we hear the tinkle of the donkey's bell in the fields of the Ndebele people. One can imagine that this is the beginning of the world and that we can go on and live this way without coming to harm. That we can be engaged in present tense, that there is enough to occupy our minds and souls with the mystery of existence; we do not have to destroy the fabric that sustains us.

Of the nature of hunters and gatherers, of our ancestors, of the indigenous people of Siloswane and similar sites across the globe, of the Pleistocene from which we all come, Paul Shepard says the following:

In non-Western, un-industrialized and largely illiterate societies, power is plural, societies are egalitarian, and leadership is not monopolized but changing and dispersed. Although there may be said to loom a single creative principle behind it all, in polytheistic worlds there is no omniscience and no single hierarchy; no top-down authority that frames what one is to believe and how one is to live. And still these people have a beautifully fluid yet stable culture that remains intact through climatic and other earthly mishaps. The cement that bonds primal peoples internally and inextricably – the paradigm and exemplar for this social discontinuity among human groups – is the array of natural species about them. Animals and plants are regarded as centers, metaphors, and mentors of the different traits, skills and roles of people. Insofar as they model diversity and the polythetic cosmos, the animals provide analogs to the multiplicity of stages and forms; they are interlocutors of change that is brought ceremonially into human consciousness.

....Gathering and hunting are the economic basis of an intricate cosmology in which epiphany and numinous presence are embodied and mediated by wild animals, plants, mountains and springs. Thinking is toward harmony in a system where people disturb nature so little that its interspecies parities seem to be more influenced by intuition and rites than by physical actions.[48]

Let us not think literally now. I am not advocating returning to primitive conditions. But I am asking where we deviated to follow something we aggrandized by calling it civilization. It brought us to unprecedented cruelty, poverty, discrimination, destruction of the natural environment and all the agonies and ills of the modern world. Under our sophisticated veneer are vast layers of barbarism and brutishness. Our ancestors knew how to live their lives aligned with the spirits and the natural world. We can reenter the earlier story wherein all people are free to walk in the world guided by the spirits and carrying a sense of the holiness of all beings. Because we are rooted here, all of us, in the old world, it is possible to be reinstated to a moral universe.

Archeologists Peter J. Uicko and G. W. Dimbelby say: "Some groups of Australian aborigines, despite their extremely limited, natural resources and their basically 'Stone Age' technology, have devised one of the most complex of metaphysical systems of belief held by any human group."[49] This cosmogony – how the universe became a moral system – is nothing like an Athenian skeptical philosophy but is a continual visionary, intuitive, poetic understanding, an ahistoric abiding. There is no quarrel with life. Their metaphysic assents to what men have to be because of the way their life is cast.[50]

We have come here to Siloswane twice in the last weeks. Once before September 11th and once afterwards. Both times we came to pray. The first time the Ndebele grandmothers came forth and took Elenna Rubin Goodman into another world of movement and light. This second time, we are bereaved and frightened for the world. Desperate, we have come to honor and appeal to the old ones.

The World Trade Center Towers have collapsed. This is our last ritual moment in Zimbabwe. We have come here to pray. We have come here to honor the ancestors. We have come here to express our gratitude to Augustine and Simakuhle.

Because we are in the presence of the old ones, Michael presents Augustine and Simakuhle with a cicada shell that he came upon when he was attending a Native American Sun Dance that is enacted each year for the renewal of the people. Chuck Madansky tells us the story of the cicada people:

> Once, long, long and long ago, in the time when stones were still soft, anyone could enter the Earth and be nourished and remember themselves in Her substance. No one had to know the way because everywhere you could lay on her soft breast and be healed. But as time when on, and creatures began to forget the one language, fewer and fewer beings could find their way in, could find their way back to the womb of forgiveness and memory, back to the place where all things could be. The Earth grew hard and harder through longing Herself for the touch of her children. So we who remembered were called to shift shape and live with the Earth for years at a time. Whenever the children's need was the greatest, we were called to the light and emerged with our singing wings calling and soaring. We entranced those who could hear, beckoning to them to follow us into the earth once again. To remember, to soften, to heal, to transform, to return and give life. The hard people call us Cicada.

Then Chuck and Wilderness give Augustine a fossil, again having had the perspicacity to bring such a gift of the old ones from the U.S.. Robin Wilds pours libations and dances the call to the animals, dances the dance of the animals as they dance it in their living. When she had first danced thus in Masvingo, alone, she thought, with only Michael present, his back to her, more than a dozen baboons had gathered and formed a semicircle around her. Her audience. Now she dances again, but as she has never danced. This professional dancer dances the dance for the first time in her life. This dance calling forth the entire history of dance, the beginning of dance, the call to the spirits, to the ancestors and to the animals. A dance learned from the animals as Robin learned it freshly in the days we spent in Chobe. First she dances the giraffe, then the elephants, then the lion who trance-possesses her so fiercely that Augustine must release her spirits before her body is consumed in their jaws. Then the baboon and, finally, when she flies before us as the eagle, she brings out Chapungu's feather from the tree in Chobe and presents it to Augustine.

From Robin's journal – the choreography of that moment.

The circling bird told me it was time. I laid out my gifts: shawl, feather, stones. Mask. I called the animals. Filled up with the energy of the place. Eagle flying. Bigger, bigger, stretch out. Fall to the ground. Lizard in, in, in to the stone. Let me In. Roar. Augustine spit water on me. Calm. Calm. Elephants. Old, wise, slow circling around in, in, in to the tight dark womb under-world, the black shell filled with blue/black void.

How do I not disappear? I feel the heartbreak tear my cells apart. How do I get out? Forever passes then. Follow the animals. Stretch. Giraffe. Eagle fly above. Gentle. See the scope of the worlds and in that pit – the belly of the world. That unbearable pressure transforms coal into diamonds. The jewels are found in the underground and one carries them out into the world.

Persephone, Queen of the underworld

Lost in the blue/black

Closed into the diamond pressure that transforms.

The entire time we were there, I was praying. Praying that the spirits of the old ones, the Bushmen shaman and wise ones, and the animals all enter into me, that I will carry them, that they speak through me, that I will be taught how to move from this beginning into actions that predicate a world that will survive.

It is almost dark when we descend. The moon is waning. Almost at the bottom, we hear the call of baboons. They have gathered and the old patriarch, the *sekiru*, the grandfather is moving in a circle in order to see us better. He perches on a great round boulder in a clearing between the trees and looks at us thoughtfully. We stand with him in silent communication. The monkeys gather in the trees. The dance and our prayers and our fear and our hope have brought us together.

23

Sinai. Now we go to Sinai. But it was not as I had expected. I went to Sinai to leave Sinai. We went to Sinai to pay our respects, to offer gratitude for the wisdom of Sinai and to turn around and return home, to the far home, that we have forgotten to our peril. Sinai is a point among many in a long story that begins in Siloswane and ends in peace.

Michael, Augustine, Simakuhle, I, and the baby, *Ka*Michael *kadikidiki,*[51] and a young Bedouin Muslim boy leading a camel climbed Mt. Sinai together on my 65th birthday which was also Rosh Hashanah, the beginning of the new year for the Jews, the first day of the ten Days of Awe. The boy took us by a back route so that until we came to the stairs that several hundred people would also climb that night to reach the summit, we were completely alone. Dark of the moon. Black sky except for the brilliant stars that lit only the narrow path we were to follow. We walked in silence following the iridescent shimmer of starlight that didn't ever illuminate the edge of the cliff or the dark stone walls of the mountain. Once, we fell on our knees before a tall cedar tree that rose up mysteriously out of the sheer stone floor and once we prostrated ourselves before a mysterious light that seemed to float on an improbable pool of water several thousand feet below us. Then we stopped to pour water along the crack of a great smooth stone where it is said Moses, seeking water, struck the rock in anger. The stars entered our stream of water as if it was itself a light. Sometimes Simakuhle was the torch, starlight luminescent on her tall body, clad in white. We followed her then. And when she disappeared from view we were led, again by the radiance of the stones that we clambered over, hour after hour.

*   *   *

We had wrestled that entire week of September 11, 2001 with whether we should go to Sinai as planned or whether we should remain in Zimbabwe and find some way home once the planes were flying again. I wondered if we should try to get home immediately so we could be with our grieving community. I worried about bringing *Ka*Michael *kadikidiki* into a potential war zone. I wondered if we would find ourselves marooned in an Arab country while the U.S. might be bombing other Arab or Muslim countries, as it was being threatened, "into the stone age."

"God can find me anywhere," I said, "I do not have to climb a mountain to find God."

And then since we were traveling toward Sinai and it was almost the time of the Rosh Hashanah when they were going to read the Torah portion regarding the sacrifice of Isaac by his father Abraham, I had to voice my concern again that we might be sacrificing the little one. Abraham had a right to sacrifice himself, I said, but in my view, he had no right to sacrifice Isaac, and equally as heinous, he had no right to sacrifice a ram. Saying this I moved further away from the holy book of my people and closer to an alliance with the animals who had already come forth in the last weeks to meet me eye to eye.

But then, after all the initiates had been assured of a safe journey home, it seemed as if we were being called to the Mountain by something beyond us and it was our holy task to submit. All the dreams and signs had indicated that this was the right action. On Saturday morning, September 15th, the five of us left for Egypt.

God can find me on any mountain, but in order to find God, I had to climb Sinai.

I had dreamed of returning to Sinai outside of scripture. A holy mountain is a holy mountain. A holy mountain is place where access to the Divine is possible. If you climb it, the veil is thin on the top of the holy mountain. Or the presence of God descends as one persists in the struggle to reach the place to which one is being called.

Before we began our ascent, Augustine reflected on Moses as a shepherd. Moses had spent some years alone with the animals in the wilderness. This was his exile and this, according to Augustine, was his education. First he had been educated by the priests of the pharaoh. There he had been taught the great Mysteries and magic. He had probably been introduced to the esoteric teachings of Tehuti. But this was not sufficient preparation to be Moses. The first teachings had enhanced him, but being in the desert had prepared him differently. Being in the desert had rendered him humble enough to meet the Presence.

Before our ascent, we met in an enclosure of great boulders that had fallen on each other so that they formed a temple. As everyone prayed, I wrote the holy letters on everyone's body, detailing as best as I could, the meanings of the letters, these building blocks, the most essential elements of creation. May all our actions be in accord with the Holy One. It was there that I turned to the set of holy letters that Moriyah Colaine had hand painted for me in the colors of twilight and sunset and shuffled them until a letter fell out. I hadn't known what question to ask but I knew that direction was required before we went up the mountain, before the moment of the initiation. "Please, God, Holy One, will you speak to us through the letters?" A letter fell out of the deck into my lap. ת Tav. A conversation with God. ת Tav, I understood, was for all of us. The final letter of the alphabet. The letter that contains all the other letters. God's seal. The sign of righteousness. The beginning that comes out of endings. The arrows of light that shoot out of the darkness.

The conversation that I had hoped to have with God was complete.

*   *   *

A series of dreams had opened the way to Sinai. Dreams of a peacemaker returning. Dreams of Chaminuka, the great hero, peacemaker of the Shona people. Everyone in Zimbabwe is waiting for the return of Chaminuka.

In the last dream, there was a small island in the middle of a river. Young boys had come to the island to become warriors to protect the spirit of Chaminuka who was going to enter the body of a healer. If Chaminuka entered the healer's body, it would mean an infusion of peacemaker spirits into the world. President Robert Mugabe, like all the other leaders, is on the hunt for the *nganga* who is carrying Chaminuka spirits. Like rulers before him, he wants to bolster up his kingdom through recruiting Chaminuka into his regime.

Chaminuka himself died like Christ, with a spear in his side. I light the candle before the Shona carving of Chaminuka that is on my desk. This is the question: How can Chaminuka reenter the world without bringing death in his mouth? My dreams insisted that I warn Augustine who has told us that if one carries Chaminuka spirits, one no longer goes by his own name, one is then forever called Chaminuka. "You may not become a martyr. If you carry Chaminuka spirits, you must do it quietly so that you will not be killed." Augustine began to have premonitions that Chaminuka might come forth at Sinai. This was another reason I was afraid of going to Sinai.

If Chaminuka is to land on any of us, let it be on all four of us, I pray, so the spirit of Chaminuka can be protected. The prayer begins to gather power around us. I do not think a single person is going to carry Chaminuka. I begin to imagine Chaminuka descending upon whomever wishes to be a peacemaker in the world. Chaminuka as mist. Breathe in peace. Breathe out peace. I am reminded of Thich Nhat Hanh's walking meditation: Breathe in peace. Breathe out love.

We have come to the end of the heroic time. This is certainly not the time for another great man. This is not the time for another man being taken for a god. This is not the time for martyrdom. The descent of such a spirit will spread quickly and infuse the world. We will never know how or where it entered. The spirit of Chaminuka will enter the world and it will be among us. Among us all. This is the prayer that we take up the mountain.

*   *   *

At 11:30 p.m., the hour that I was born, we will begin the ascent up the mountain so that we will be at the summit at dawn. Janet Mayhall had indicated that if I was on Mt. Sinai on my birthday, the focus of my entire birth chart would change, the journey I had been taking my entire life from the absolute light to the absolute dark would reverse, and I would walk toward the light until my death. She understands that writing my last novel, *The Other Hand*, was the descent into the absolute dark "that you embraced to its core – the death camps and the Bomb." Now, she says, I can go toward the light. Toward creation. As I listened to her read my chart, I thought: May the world go toward the light as well.

*   *   *

We arrived in Santa Katerina the evening before after having flown through the night and driven around the peninsula for the entire day. In the morning, we took a walk through the village, bought some juice, went to the bank. When we were walking back to the hotel, a white pick-up truck pulled up beside us and a young man jumped out of the car, calling my name.

It was as if we were all in a dream together. Five years before when Michael and I had been in Sinai, we had been befriended by a young taxi driver, Ahmed Keder, who had driven us to the base of the mountain. The next day, in the very spot where we were now stopped, he had driven by and called me by name. We had gone to the desert with him and then we had been invited back to his house to meet his mother. While waiting for her to arrive, her daughters, Ahmed's sisters, had dressed me in Bedouin clothes and Michael had photographed us together. When the mother had arrived, she walked toward me as if we had known each other for years and took my head in her hands and pressed our foreheads together. Inexplicable as it seemed then and even now, we had greeted each other like sisters. She had given me a silver ring and I who always wear two identical wedding rings, had given her my gold one. This young man who is greeting us now is Ahmed's younger brother Mohammed.

All of us are invited back to the house. Ahmed is there, as are his brothers, his mother and the many sisters, as well as a three-year-old girl named Dina. Ahmed's father had recently died and his mother put the wedding ring into the coffin with him.

"Our father died suddenly. One moment he was working in the garden and the next moment he was dead. My little sister thought he had lain down by the flowers to sleep and so she didn't disturb him. When we went to get him, he was gone. My world fell apart. I thought my life was over. When the planes hit the towers, we didn't know if you were alive or dead. We thought you must be dead and that we wouldn't ever see you again. And here you are."

Four years ago after we had been at Sinai, Michael and I had performed a wedding ceremony for Simakuhle and Augustine. They had no rings, and so we gave them ours. I gave Simakuhle my remaining wedding band and Michael gave Augustine his ring. Now, here we all were in the same room together in Sinai. Here in one room were the people to whom we had given our wedding rings. But it was something more than that. With the gesture of offering the rings, we had entered into a kind of marriage with them all. We had become kin. We had taken vows to love and honor each other. And now the families had been brought together.

On a shelf in this Bedouin house, there is a photograph of Michael and myself that had been taken when Ahmed had prepared a meal for us in the desert. On a similar shelf in the house of Augustine and Simakuhle is the very same photograph. Simakuhle and little *Ka*Michael *kadikidiki*, who is a year old, were seated under it alongside Ahmed's sister and her little boy separated in age only by days.

There is a lot of joy and laughter in the room though we scarcely share one hundred words of English. Understanding that Augustine is a healer, Ahmed's older brother prepares a potion of ninety-nine herbs, one herb for each, according to Islam, of the ninety-nine names of God. The herbs were gathered by Ahmed's grandfather when he was alive. Augustine leaves the family with a packet of healing herbs that he brought from Zimbabwe. We have entered into an unexpected exchange. We learn that one of the girls cannot sleep because she is afraid of her dreams. Augustine does not worry about the problems of cross-cultural communication. He moves quickly to do healing work upon her and then he drives dark spirits from another sister. I give our aspirin to the old grandmother who aches with arthritis and sit with the mother, hand in hand, in wordless wonder at our meeting.

*   *   *

It was Ahmed who decided that his young cousin would take us to the stairs that lead to the summit of Sinai so that we would climb most of the mountain the back way, alone, in silence and prayer, undisturbed.

We were the first to begin climbing that night and it is probable that I was the last to arrive at the summit. I was also the last to reach Santa Katerina in the morning as the monastery was opening its doors and crypts to the tourists who had come down from the mountain and had already breakfasted. A taxi was waiting for Augustine and myself after Michael and Simakuhle had made their way down, passing the young camel driver who had fallen asleep across a boulder in some shade he had found and could not be roused to give water or assistance. All in all, it had taken us seven hours to climb the mountain in the dark and four hours to descend in the blazing heat.

The ascent was difficult enough but the descent enflamed us all. Augustine, always agile and resilient, had twisted his ankle on the way up and had almost plummeted down the mountain as he missed the irregular steps carved from the rock. He had been trying to assist Simakuhle with the baby but now he could not walk without pain from the severe swelling. On the way down, little Michael would not stay with his father on the camel but insisted on riding on his mother's back. The sun that had risen hot was full on him for hours. I was afraid that we would lose *Ka*Michael *Kadikidiki* as his head lolled listlessly in the merciless heat. During the last hours we prevailed on Simakuhle, who was quite mad from the heat despite singing her water songs, to retreat into a shady niche in the mountain and nurse the baby. Then we put her trousers on her head with the white pants legs draped over *Ka*Michael *Kadikidiki*'s head, while Michael poured the little water we had remaining us onto the pants and on the baby's nappy hair as they descended together. In that week we had come to see that little Michael might be a divine child and it seemed incomprehensible that we had carried him up the mountain toward a baptism of light and still might then lose him on the way down into the Sinai desert.

Michael's feet were badly cut and infected from the heat and dryness of the wind and he was also staggering. I could barely walk with extreme pain and fatigue in every joint in my body and would not have survived if I hadn't been able to depend on the Ancestor's stick that Augustine had carved for me so that I might be supported on this journey. We were not the same ones who had been called forth toward the starry sky, so brightly and with so much hope hours before.

There is always the ordeal at the center of any initiation.

*　　*　　*

It was not at the summit that I found God, it was not when the sun rose over the stony waves of the vast and turbulent stone ocean that rises up from the sands of the desert that God appeared, it was not in a flash of light or the roll of thunder that God made God's presence known. It was not among the dozens or hundreds of tourists wrapped in rugs and blankets, flashing cameras, that we found God. But the Divine was with us and we were inhabited by or inscribed by its presence in the long, arduous, silent ascent – the arduous, silent assent – when we wandered uncertainly, up and up and up. When I stumbled and Augustine caught me. When Michael stopped to pray and make offerings. When Simakuhle walked steadily without faltering despite the great effort required, despite her heart condition and the burden of *Ka*Michael *kadikidiki* on her back. When the stars streamed across the dark sky, falling into eternity. It was there, without word or event that we were transformed without knowing then, but not doubting it afterwards, that we were changed forever and so praised the circumstances of our extraordinary and unexpected fate.

The long, long difficult climb up the mountain together and the agony of the descent was the time necessary for the spirit of Chaminuka to enter, imperceptibly, into the four of us, to align us to the heart and mind of Chaminuka, that is, to call us to the possibilities of peace.

*   *   *

Exhausted, we lay in the beds of small rooms, drifting. Outside the drawn curtains, the stark and glorious mountains of the Sinai range gleam in the brilliant light. That stone can carry so much light.

*   *   *

I cannot sleep so I live and relive the last six weeks that I have spent in Africa. This is not the first time the stars have led me. This is not the first time that the light from elsewhere has written its wisdom on my body and I have become its servant. It is not on this journey that the animals have spoken to me for the first time. This is not the first time that I have been taught by wind or informed by dreams. This is not the first time that I worked alongside Augustine or entered with him into mutual initiation or served the spirits, or listened to the ancestors, or healed the sick, body and spirit. Nor is this the first time that I traveled to the other world on behalf of the dying and came back with their souls, intact, in my mouth. But this is the time that I cannot pretend any longer that the spirit world is an invented country in my imagination or that the imagination is not a real world. Or that the human world, its bibles, priests and orthodoxies, its laws and assumptions, its beliefs and assertions, have hegemony over the path and revelation that may, at different times, be offered or imposed upon us by the invisibles. And this is the time that I learned that I had to give up the canon of wisdom that is the accumulated thinking of men in order to follow the inaudible voices and invisible presences that are the inscrutable faces of the Holy One. This is the time when I know that I have to tear everything out of my body and soul that allows war to be holy, that sacrifices sons and daughters to the gods of the fathers. This is the time. This is the time.

*   *   *

"The peacemaker comes in the middle of chaos," Augustine says soberly as we huddle around the television set in the hotel lobby, wondering if the world will soon be at war. "Don't be distracted. Take on whatever you must take on."

When I return home, the spirits come in my dreams and say: *Don't let the war distract you from the work you have to do. Put the forms in place so that the stories that were leading to death will change and the stories will lead to life.*

*   *   *

I am sitting here writing. How will we return to the way of beauty? At this moment when I look at the eyes of Chaminuka in the Shona sculpture, I see an image of a man or a spirit whose grief and compassion are continuous, like Christ, like Rachel weeping for her lost children, like Kwan Yin. Where I might have seen eyes once, now I see tears.

*   *   *

Friends must coordinate elaborate efforts to bring us home from the airport that is cordoned off because of another bomb threat. Armed guards with machine guns are everywhere. Tension and great confusion. Finally, we are home. Amanda, Kate Noonan, Valerie and myself are sitting together in my living room. "I dreamed," Valerie begins, "I dreamed that Chaminuka came to me and said that you, Deena, were to pull a card from the tarot deck, *The Book of Doors*. And then we would understand everything. I asked if I could pull the card since you were in Egypt, but Chaminuka said you must pull the card." Valerie hands me the deck. I shuffle the cards not knowing what is being asked. Then, as happens, a card falls out of the deck. I turn it over. Af-Neteru. The only card that has four Neters on it. They are a team of demi-gods who serve the greater spirits. They show the way for the dead in the *Duat*, the underworld. As representations of the four directions they prepare the individual for entry into higher consciousness.[52] I understand then that Chaminuka is returning and he will enter the heart and soul of anyone who is willing to carry him. We have entered the Ghost River and Chaminuka is among us.

*   *   *

One final miracle. We were driving north from Sinai toward the Suez Canal when I remembered that I had wanted to bring back stones from the sacred mountain. I look at the stones by the side of the road and none of them resemble the stones of the holy mountain itself, though we are in the mountains and we are in a world of stones. I am afraid that I have lost the opportunity to gather what I want. I pray to God that we be led to a place where we can gather the last stones. Within seconds, I stop the car by the side of the road. In this wilderness of stone, there is a hillock of green vines several hundred feet above us protruding out above the mouth of a cave. It is the only green we have seen for miles, the only such green we have seen in this mountain range. An astounding green. An unearthly green. There is no evident stream that feeds this mound of Venus. We move toward the entrance of the dark cave beneath it, and two doves fly out of the cave, perch above us and then fly inside again. Within we are in the body of a woman. Utter beauty in folds of rosy sandstone, wave upon wave. Sweet vaginal dark. Simakuhle drops to her knees and sings praise in her remarkable voice. Augustine and I know that once more as with the Ambassador we are in the presence of God.

We return to the car with stones, drive a few feet, take a bend in the road. The stone mountains are behind us and we are traversing a vast dry plateau. Several hours from now we will cross the Suez Canal. Then on to Cairo and home.

24

*S*unday, *January 06, 2002.* Epiphany. Today the first draft of this manuscript is completed. Tonight Michael, Michele, Amanda and I will come together to journey, celebrate and honor our meeting three years ago with the Ambassador. At this moment Jami Sieber is playing cello with the elephants in Thailand. The wolves, Akasha and Blue are bounding through the fields outside. We pray the whales and dolphins will soon be joyful in the sea again. Healing and Story – the same. The gathering together of all the elements in a harmonic order. Song. Wolf, Whale, Elephant, Lion – they are among the great singers and musicians of the natural world. Resonance. Daré emerged within weeks of our remarkable meeting with the Ambassador. There are Darés now in Santa Cruz, California, British Columbia, Washington state, Boulder, Colorado and more beginning. Elenna has started a Daré in Oakland, and Chuck and Wilderness have started one on Cape Cod. Each is original in its own way, each creating its own form of beauty, healing, council and community. The needs of the community met by the gifts inherent in the community and the gifts offered to meet the needs. The wisdom of the community and the wisdom that the community needs emerging from the field of stories that we tell each other as we sit in council. All the stories becoming one story that guides each of us in our own way. Daré, like Story and healing, gathers the elements together in collaboration with Spirit to create a harmonic order. A field of relationships that are alive and dynamic. As Michael noted, "A story must carry a body of energy, an organic presence. If it isn't alive in this way, it is a golem."

*   *   *

I am beginning to understand. What matters is the story that one tells. And the way one organizes events and acts accordingly. What matters is where one locates the beginning and how one understands the sequence of events. What matters is how one recognizes and identifies a pattern or cause and effect. What matters is where one refuses to be afraid.

What happens when one is initiated? The obstacle between oneself and Spirit is dissolved. Which spirit? The particular spirits that come to each of us. The dance between the story we are living and the spirits of that story. They come forth in a language of gesture and meaning that each of us will understand. Like story, like healing, initiation is totally original in each moment.

I understand now what transpired in Africa. I was initiated in Siloswane. My prayers were answered. The very, very old ones came forth, the ancestors of the ancestors, the Bushmen spirits, the ancient ones. The spirits of the most despised people anywhere came forth as the exalted ones. Despairing for the world, I had prayed for this and it is as if they are in me, guiding me, teaching me. I came home.

There is a meadow outside my home in Topanga, green after the rains, otherwise golden up to the foothills. Sometimes I stand here as the sun is going down and watch the changing light that imbues the land with the essential liveliness of creation. I imagine that the mastodons, wooly mammoths and saber-toothed tigers cavorted here and then padded down to the creek and down to the ocean so many thousands of years ago. When Gillian went to visit Angus in Toronto, she was compelled to stop at the museum where she stood mesmerized before a mastodon. And in the last weeks, Valerie and I have also been drawn to the La Brea Tar Pits to stand before the sacred bones of these ancient ones. History is right here, the past, the present, the future intermingled in our hands. "At least," Valerie says, "we did not cause this extinction. We can be in right relationship with these ancestors."

In African culture, some time after the death of a family member, one makes a place for the ancestor in one's home. From this place, the ancestor can do the sacred work allotted to such a spirit, can protect the living and the community. We, who call ourselves the civilized ones, we have abandoned the old ones. They did not ever leave us. But without their wisdom and guidance, we have gone astray. We are lost and endangered. Everything is endangered without them. Still, the old ones are out there waiting for us to call them home.

*   *   *

Imagine, then, that Siloswane is the center of the world. Imagine that this is the beginning. Imagine the first story that leads us gently to kindly moments of vision. Imagine that the forms that have been oppressing us have crumbled and we are now free to begin again, with the old ones, the animals, the spirits, God. Imagine that our lives can be redeemed.

"Those who have the elephant as totem usually find themselves in a position to reestablish powerful family and societal ideals." This is what Ted Andrews says in *Animal-Speak*.[53] I write a letter to Katherine Metcalf Nelson who received the elephant skull from a Randili warrior she met in Kenya and then gave it to me. I tell her I tried to return it to the elephants but they seemed to believe that it needed to be here so we could heal with it.

I am obsessed with Daré. Daré turns us all into elephants. Gives us elephant heart. *Mandlovu* mind. Makes real healers of us.

It is a great thing for a human being to be able to yield to the intelligence of another species. To make an alliance. To bring healing to the world through such music.

If we had moved forth from Siloswane rather than from Eden, we might not be where we are. If we had stayed with the sacred knowledge that is coherent with the natural world, we would not be destroying life. We have to return to the sacred world and step forth again. We cannot do this as we are – greedy, arrogant, power-hungry, separate and alienated. But we can do this in relationship with the other beings, visible and invisible.

Here is the Tree of the Sun and here is the Tree of the Moon. Between them flow the waters of the Ghost River. Once you step into this river, you never need leave it. You carry the wisdom of the ancestors with you wherever you go. They are in you, of you, as long as you make a sacred place for them. And they guard your life and the life of all the beings who are among us now. Let us go now then into these healing waters so we may live among the ancestors and the healing spirits.

*   *   *

This manuscript has come to an end. Do you see now, how all stories come together to make one story? Do you see how stories circle back to each other, and the circling creates a vortex, and from that a certain whirl of light emerges that is the exact shape of the larger story that holds them all? Do you see the way the stories come together and create little worlds? Each story a world and the stories together, another world. Configuring and reconfiguring. Do you see the pattern? Are some of the forms in place?

I could not have written this alone. I didn't write this book. This book comes out of what we call Daré mind or *Mandlovu* mind. If you want to know the truth, Elephant, the ancestors, wrote it.

In a few hours, we will drum and journey to meet the elephants again. We do not know, cannot know, what will come of this meeting but I can say that the writing of this manuscript and its completion at this moment is the offering I bring.

May this story have a future. May healing come. May the world be restored. May we live in the Spirit and the Heart.

Deena Metzger
Topanga and Pine Mountain, California
Sunday, January 6, 2002
Wednesday, February 27, 2002
Friday, June 7, 2002

AFTERWORD

by Michael Ortiz Hill

Some say we come out of the dream and return to it, or that the path through the dream is the same path along which we walk the sacred through a tortured era. The truest words in this book are, "I want to break your heart." But they are only true because the book itself is a cry from the heart and invocation of beauty.

It was beauty that called me to Africa so many years ago – coming radiant and indecipherable in the form of elephants. I dreamt of sitting in the grass alongside a huge river next to a small altar with bright yellow flowers and an African man in skins, dancing. Beyond him in a field, elephants, chalky white, much larger than life, dignified in bearing and majestic in beauty. I awoke puzzled. I knew nothing of Africa, had no curiosity whatsoever about African traditions. And elephants, so awesome in the dream were, in my waking life, objects of a very distant affection, which is to say, quite irrelevant. And so I did what one does – placed the dream on the shelf among other exotic artifacts passed to me through the dreamtime. Nonetheless, nine years later, I arrived at the doorway of Augustine Kandemwa. The evening we met, Augustine began initiating me into the way of the ancestors, the *midzimu* who meet at the crossroads of animal, human and spirit.

I can smile now on the white man's delusion that persisted unseen until near the end of my first initiation in spite of all evidence to the contrary that I was in control of the story I was living. I did not know what Augustine meant when he'd say, "People cannot initiate other people. It is the spirits that do initiation," until the fated evening that the elephant spirits arrived.

We were driving through the night just south of the Zambezi -- Mosiyatunya, "Where the Stones Thunder" – Big Falls. Three elephants crossed the road, chalky white in the headlights. My "exotic artifact" fell from the shelf into my hands. It was suddenly clear that we were approaching the circumstances of my dream, that neither he nor I were in control, that the initiation ahead was both unpredictable and benevolent.

The following afternoon, Augustine and I walked along the Zambezi to a place a dream led him to that he regarded as holy. Together, we made an altar of grass and bright orange flowers that grew along the trail for the elephants.

I tell this story as a small praise song to the elephant – to *Mandlovu* – that great mind that moves within the vibrational field where the craft of kinship is realized. The logic of *Mandlovu* is kincraft – like seeing in this case across the boundaries of race, colonial and neo-colonial violence, and in deep alliance with the animal other. Augustine and I made an altar to elephant; by day's end we called each other *mapatya* – twin brother.

Not a small part of the ritual elegance of this book is that stories are arranged as if each carries a quality of intelligence made fully lucid as they are heard within the vibrational field created by the other stories – no doubt inclusive of the stories the reader carries as well. I spy in this arrangement the lazy circles of elephants independent and related to each other as they browse the veldt. The invitation is to climb into the text and offer your own story within which the possibility of kinship is invoked. Yes, that the heart be broken. Yes, that the cry from *Mandlovu*'s heart be heard. And yes, that we might gather here in the eye of the storm with our original kin to hold council while "civilization," rogue, maddened, lives by war and the destruction of the natural world.

Here is both a cornucopia of stories as well as an esoteric text on the nature of story: the story within the story folded into fate, fate into the illumination of possibility.

Follow the circles of these stories, for the oldest story is here limning the edges of the telling. The oldest story is improvised fresh from indigenous mind and the circular telling is a way of ritual invocation. The place we sit now is the cave at Siloswane. The animals, shamans, the women gathering herbs, the ecstasy of the dance painted on the walls by the Bushmen and through them hundred of thousands of years of those who tended the fire and told stories. This is the way culture is created. There has never been another way. This is the way culture can be recreated.

A narrative thread in the book is cast from Siloswane to Sinai. Not quite the path of progress from the "primitive" to the "civilized," but four friends carrying prayers for peace from a sacred cave in south central Africa to a holy mountain in the Muslim world.

Islam, like all monotheistic traditions, has an understanding of the incomprehensible Presence of God as revealed to humans, limited as we are and so often blind. In Catholicism, the saints mediate; for Jews the angels are messengers. In Islam, the ninety-nine names of God connect the Nameless One to the named. Is it always the case that one must be shattered before one concedes to the one called Ar-Rafeeq, the hand of God, so gentle? Or Al-Kareem, God the kind? Of course, the rites of shattering belong to initiation and we were all shattered when the World Trade Center collapsed. On the evening of September 16th, we flew north towards Cairo: Augustine with his dreads tucked under a black Snoop Doggy Dog knit cap gazing over the clouds ecstatic alongside Simakuhle – their first flight. Little Michael hungry at the breast. Deena and I raw, vulnerable, easily angered. Were we out of our minds? The bitter volley of recrimination and self-recrimination. With more confusion than bravado and no clear picture of how exactly the decision was made, we were on our way to the Muslim world on what seemed like the cusp of a world war. I didn't sleep that night – facing the specter of a meaningless death born of a choice made by four confused people.

In African medicine when one walks into the village of one's enemy, one pays close attention to the spirit one meets at the threshold. "Deena, is that you?" said Mohammed as we arrived in Santa Katerina at the foot of Sinai. He recognized us from our trip five years previous and was just looking at the small album of photos we'd sent his family. His father had died recently and when he saw the World Trade Center collapse on TV, he was afraid that maybe we were dead also. As keeper of the threshold, Mohammed opened the door, conscripting his cousin to lead the camel to walk us up the back trail to the top of the mountain.

Long before the reign of conquest, long before the natives were Christianized or Islamicized, long before the encampment of Moses and his refugees fresh from enslavement, Mt. Sinai was the sacred mountain of Sin, the moon god, son of the Queen of Heaven, Inanna. From the Great Mother, Tiamat, he received the tablets of the Law. "In the 12th century BCE the Babylonian heaven was ruled by a trinity consisting of Shamash, Sin and Ishtar, represented by the sun, moon and stars," writes Barbara Walker.[54] I dare say, it was this Sinai that we climbed, the moon dark and the stars bright beyond telling. It was here that Augustine saw Moses as a

Bedouin, a keeper of goats not unlike his people – the goats running in the distance, the holiness of stone – it was here the peacemaker without name came upon us in the night. I suppose one could imagine high drama – the thin trail of tranquility buffeted on both sides by the fires of apocalypse. After all, the faith shared by George Bush and radical Islam is redemption through apocalypse – the final drama in which the world is purged of Evil and a new world order, by the grace of God, descends. One could also imagine the Law burnt into the heart, lightning to stone: that drama. That violence. Nothing of the sort happened.

What happened that night was true for its gentleness – Ar-Raqeem. The desire for the cosmic vision left at the foot of the mountain.

At this point I understand the vision best through my father's language – Buddhism. The Buddha of the future, it is said, is Maitreya. But Maitreya is not a person, but the quality of friendship that is, in fact, an aspect of enlightened mind. The Law (the dharma) is realized and fulfilled in the activity of friendship in all of its many levels. Kairos, the inbreaking of Maitreya, the future breaking as it must into the present moment. Spirit descends, friendship is inspirited and the spirit of friendship reveals the Law: Thou Shalt Not Make Enemies Any More. Live by this.

My arm around Simakuhle or on little Michael's back wrapped in a towel and tied to his mother. Ahead of us Deena and Augustine hand in hand, steadying one another on the dark trail. Sometimes visible, sometimes nearly transparent. Often only the starlight visible. Maitreya. Ar-Raqeem. The Nameless Peacemaker. After hours of walking the sky goes dark cobalt blue to lighter and lighter still. We arrive at the top of the mountain with the pinkening before sunrise. Now here we are at Sinai. Now, we hold council.

GLOSSARY

Ambuya Shona, grandmother.

Ambuya Buwe Buwe Shona, Spider Woman.

Ananke Greek, goddess of necessity.

bodhisattva Sanskrit, a being who from compassion refrains from leaving this world until all beings have achieved enlightenment.

Chaminuka Shona, a heroic figure who is seen as a spirit, peacemaker.

Chapungu Shona, Eagle.

Daré the Shona word for council.

golpé Spanish, strike, blow; the coup d'etat enacted by Augusto Pinochet against the elected Chilean government of Salvador Allende.

Indra from Hindu, the interconnection of all things.

Maat Egyptian deity or Neter. The Neter of the cosmic law or order.

Mambokadze The queen, the great mother.

Mandlovu Ndebele, female elephant.

mindfulness the quality of conscious awareness of the present moment.

mojo from the African *moco'o*, medicineman, a magical power, hence your talent or skill.

mystes Participants in the Eleusinian Mysteries. Those who enter the underworld with their eyes closed.

Ndlovu Ndebele, elephant.

Nganga Shona, a medicine person or shaman.

Ngoma Shona, literally a drum, but also the ritual circumstances of calling the spirits.

Njuzu Shona, water spirits.

omphalos Greek for navel, a central focal point.

rondavel a little round cabin, adapted from indigenous housing of the Shona and Ndebele people.

sadza mealie meal or corn meal grits, the staple of Zimbabwe.

Sangha Sanskrit, a community of people gathered to embrace spiritual practice.

Sekiru Shona, Grandfather.

Tatenda Shona, thank you.

Tehuti An Egyptian Neter, an esoteric intelligence similar to the Greek Hermes.

uroboros the snake eating its own tail, a symbol of the eternal cycles of life and death.

Appendix I

I Ching reading, September 30, 2001 by Stephen Karcher.

Michael and returned from Zimbabwe and Egypt to the United States on September 22, 2001 in time for Daré the next day. It gratified us that the community had met in our house on the 11th in order to face the grave circumstances of that day. We were praying in Masvingo and they were praying here. The council question we addressed on September 22nd was: What do we individually know about peacemaking and what is being asked of each of us as a peacemaker? Stunned as everyone around us was by the attack on the World Trade Center, we held the question in our minds each waking moment. Then we learned that Stephen Karcher was in Los Angeles and that he would consult with us. These are excerpts from a reading related to the circumstances of the terrorist bombing of the Towers and the Pentagon and our concern about the form and extent of American retaliation. We all felt that the crisis is real, the circumstances grave and we wanted guidance as to how to proceed. Besides Michael and myself, Michele Sang O'Brien was present at the reading.

These are the questions we formulated:

1. What is the way – path – to a change of mind [that will allow the planet and all living beings to survive, thrive and flourish]?

2. How can we facilitate this change of mind?

Stephen Karcher was working from his unpublished text *Myths for Change: The Total I Ching* (forthcoming 2003). He graciously allowed us to copy some of the text for the purpose of collectively addressing and contemplating these questions.

The first hexagram was:

49 Skinning/Revolution *Ge*
Strip away the old; let the new life emerge; revolt and renew; molting, melting metals; animal transformation, calling the bright spirits.

Skin/Revolution. *Ge* Take off or change the skin, molting; smelting, melt and cast bronze; revolt, overthrow, change, renew; radical change of state; prepare hides, skin, leather and bronze armor, soldiers; eliminate, repeal, cut off, cut away, plumage, feathers used in ritual dances that invoke the bright spirits; human skin, change the skin, renewing the generations, the next generation; "change heaven's mandates, reject the decadent and renew the Way." The ideogram portrays an animal skin stretched on a frame of three branches.

There is an expression in Chinese: "Fire in the Lake: Change Heaven's Mandates." A major shift. A revolution between dynasties. Fire in the lake. A time of transformation that involves basic images. It includes animal transformations, such as a snake changing its skin or the annual changes of form all animals were thought to undergo, symbolized as the change from bird to fish. It focuses on ritual transformation that occurs as the Wu, the technician of the sacred, puts on the animal mask to call the spirits and change the time. These sorts of dances occurred at Spring's Beginning (New Year) when the *Fang-xiang* or exorcists, dressed in bear skin and wearing a bear mask with four golden metal eyes, would drive out the old year animals, pushing them over the edge of the world into renewal and change. At this time, the people too wore animal masks, men dressed as women, men and women came together and the things of the old year were destroyed. Everything moves into the liminal state, the fertile chaos called Change. The Queen Mother, Lady of the Beasts, and the Moon Goddesses are called for transformations. Perhaps the most dramatic and secret of these rituals are the dances and ceremonies that lead up to melting the metals to cast a new Vessel or *Ding*. The Vessel is a ruling image, a sort of grail that establishes the time and connection to all the various spirits. It is also the founding sign of a king, a dynasty, a culture.

So the time of skinning is great indeed. It is a time when the basic images of our lives go into flux and renewal through that mysterious quality called *Yi* or Change, a time when the world we experience is renewing itself. We cooperate with this by "making the time," going through the imaginative preparations. We call on the animal powers and put on the mask, moving into their powerful, creative state. We skin away what is past and done with, challenge our old ideas and experiences. We go into solution, into the liminal zone. When change occurs, we accept the transformation and welcome the new time.

Deena: So, it is a time of real serious ritual activity.

Stephen. Yes, it is a time of serious ritual activity. It is a time of renewing and changing basic images. Basic, real fundamental changes. You are asking a big question so this is a big answer.

Skinning: On your own day there comes a connection to the spirits.

Source of success: Advantageous trial.

The cause for sorrow disappears.

The situation is being mediated by the *Wu*. Those are the intermediaries, spirit mediums and shamans. This is a time when Spirit reveals itself in the omens, speaks and spreads joy through the intermediaries, the *Wu*.

In this situation, one looks toward Elemental change.... This is Metal over Fire: changing inner awareness melts and skins away obsolete outer form. The Realizing Person reflects this by establishing the rites and rituals that elaborate and clarify the new time.

Yin, energy is activated or activating in the inner world. She is the figure, fate, that will power revolution, will announce the change in heaven's mandates. This Fate that is entering the inner world.... this shock, this anima lady, lady of fates is bringing something in, but it is entering the inner world and this is almost like saying, the fate that is being – *kaboom* – announced, let it resonate, bring it into the inner space, let it resonate there.

Fate. The power to realize what you are meant to be, your destiny. It makes you individual but it also connects you with the ancestors. Right at the mystery point.

The outer world, the outer operator or energy is Return, or Returning, going back to a source, going back to begin again, the return of Spirit or energy usually after a bad time.... Energy and Spirit return after a difficult time; renewal, re-birth, re-establish, new hope.

This is a time of rebirth and returning energy after a difficult time. Go back to meet this new energy in order to begin anew. Return to the source. Restore the original purity and feeling. This will bring success. Returning to the way is the root of virtue and power. Mark yourself off from others and nurture the returning energy.

....Like a shaman in the skin mask, you begin the change of aware-ness. You cannot act yet, but nothing can tear you away from this connec-tion. Be open to the impulse when it comes.... Don't be afraid to act alone. You are coupled to a creative force. Use it well.

A crisis. Gather all your force. Don't be afraid to act alone. Hold on to your ideals....Don't be identified with collective norms.

What is the way to a change of mind? Here is the change of mind. Here is the revolution.... Do the ritual work. It is ritual work, imaginative work. It moves in the imagination and then moves the imagination.

Here is what can we do to facilitate this.

60 Articulating/Crossings *Jie*
Sense the right time; measure, limit; articulate speech and thought; Chapters, intervals, music and ceremonies; loyal and true.

Articulate, *Jie*: Distinguish and join things; express ideas in speech; section, chapter, interval, unit of time; rhythm; months of the year, signs of the zodiac; limits, regulations, ceremonies, feasts, rituals; measure, econo-mize, moderate, temper; firm, loyal, true; degrees, classes, levels. The old character shows two bamboo sprouts, each providing a different opening in time from which streams flow.

The basic image is the nodes in bamboo or the joints in time, the *kairoi*, or openings, the critical moment in time through which things can be affected and movement harmonized with the Way. The root is bamboo: A node or joints on the plant, the strips of bamboo used for books, a bam-boo flute, a natural measure or interval. It means a chapter, a paragraph, an interval, a key or significant detail, a tablet attesting a mandate. Joyous words are organized and put into forms. It also refers back to articulating time symbolically, so that the experience of time becomes not that flat tra-jectory but a series of symbolic events, sensing the right time, you facilitate it one way by sensing the right time and moving through it, measure, limit, articulate speech and articulate thought. A joint or juncture in time. Chapters, intervals, music, and ceremonies, loyal and true.

Articulating describes your situation in terms of the relations between things. The way to deal with it is to articulate and make the connections clear. Express your thoughts. Separate and distinguish things. Make chap-ters, sections, and units of time. Create a whole in which each thing has its place. This is pleasing to the spirits. Through it they will give you success, effective power and the capacity to bring the situation to maturity. But don't harm yourself or others. Limitations and rules that are bitter and harsh will prevent you from putting your ideas to the trial.

The hexagram figure shows expression articulating the stream of events. Above the mists is the stream. Take the situation in and provide what is needed. Things can't simply spread out. They must be articulated. Articulating means holding things in. Cut things to size and calculate the measures. Think about what realizing the Way means before taking action. Articulating is pleasing to the spirits. Through it they will give you success, effective power and the capacity to bring the situation to maturity. Apportion the supple and the solid. Keep the strong at the center. Harsh limits will prevent you from putting your ideas to the trial. Your Way will be exhausted. Express things, take action and take risks. This is the right time to articulate your situation. Correct excess, stay in the center and communicate with others. By using articulating to shape the measures and the times, property will not be injured and the people will not be harmed.

Articulating… is also a *kairos*, a critical moment in time through which things can be affected and movement harmonized with the Way.

The first line change indicates the first step:

Articulating the Juncture
Don't come out of the inner door and chamber.
This is not a mistake.

Stay inside. Not a mistake. This means knowing when to interpenetrate and when it is blocked. Stay in your place within. Contemplate what is important to you; this is not a mistake. You are facing a dangerous situation. Take things in. Be open and provide what is needed.

The second changing line – the next step:

Articulating the Juncture
Not coming out of the outer gate and chamber,
Trap! The Way closes.

Leave your habitual ways of thought. Enter the new. If you don't, you will surely regret it. The way will close and you will be on the outside looking in. Direction: A new time is beginning. Give everything a place to grow. Strip away old ideas. Be open and provide what is needed.

The third changing line – the final step:

Articulating the juncture.
Sweet articulating. Wise Words! The Way is Open.
Going on like this brings honor and reward.

Stay in the center of the situation. Express yourself with sweetness, grace and delight. The way is open. You meet with honor and esteem. This is a significant time. A significant connection approaches. Something important returns. Be open and provide what is needed.

Stephen: When the gate opens, you have to walk out of the gate, that symbolizes walking out of your school of thought, out of your political party, walking out of your habitual or theoretical stances, whichever they are.

Deena: Walk out of your own mind and out of your own ideas.

Stephen: You must become an individual – in a time of crisis. It has something to do with Great Traverses. A time of considerable strain. It is not standing alone in a blissful time. It is standing alone in the midst of great trouble. That means not identifying with or being carried away by any stream (including your own voice and thoughts).

What can we do to facilitate or articulate the situation? Write a very sweet book. Persuasive speech. Step outside your usual ways of doing things and ways of thought and concentrate on the sweetness of it. Persuasion but with the quality of sweetness. Sweetness, grace and delight.

Appendix II

Dennis Kucinich, a United States Congressman from Cleveland, Ohio, delivered this speech on the weekend of February 17th at the Southern California Americans for Democratic Action at the University of Southern California, Los Angeles, California.

A Prayer for America.

I offer these brief remarks today as a prayer for our country, with love of democracy, as a celebration of our country. With love for our country. With hope for our country. With a belief that the light of freedom cannot be extinguished as long as it is inside of us. With a belief that freedom rings resoundingly in a democracy each time we speak freely. With the understanding that freedom stirs the human heart and fear stills it. With the belief that a free people cannot walk in fear and faith at the same time. With the understanding that there is a deeper truth expressed in the unity of the United States. That implicate in the union of our country is the union of all people. That all people are essentially one. That the world is interconnected not only on the material level of economics, trade, communication, and transportation, but interconnected through human consciousness, through the human heart, through the heart of the world, through the simply expressed impulse and yearning to be and to breathe free. I offer this prayer for America.

Let us pray that our nation will remember that the unfolding of the promise of democracy in our nation paralleled the striving for civil rights. That is why we must challenge the rationale of the Patriot Act.

We must ask why should America put aside guarantees of constitutional justice?

How can we justify in effect canceling the First Amendment and the right of free speech, the right to peaceably assemble?

How can we justify in effect canceling the Fourth Amendment, probable cause, the prohibitions against unreasonable search and seizure?

How can we justify in effect canceling the Fifth Amendment, nullifying due process, and allowing for indefinite incarceration without a trial?

How can we justify in effect canceling the Sixth Amendment, the right to prompt and public trial?

How can we justify in effect canceling the Eighth Amendment which protects against cruel and unusual punishment?

We cannot justify widespread wiretaps and internet surveillance without judicial supervision, let alone with it. We cannot justify secret searches without a warrant. We cannot justify giving the Attorney General the ability to designate domestic terror groups. We cannot justify giving the FBI total access to any type of data which may exist in any system anywhere such as medical records and financial records.

We cannot justify giving the CIA the ability to target people in this country for intelligence surveillance. We cannot justify a government which takes from the people our right to privacy and then assumes for its own operations a right to total secrecy. The Attorney General recently covered up a statue of Lady Justice showing her bosom as if to underscore there is no danger of justice exposing herself at this time, before this administration.

Let us pray that our nation's leaders will not be overcome with fear. Because today there is great fear in our great Capitol. And this must be understood before we can ask about the shortcomings of Congress in the current environment. The great fear began when we had to evacuate the Capitol on September 11. It continued when we had to leave the Capitol again when a bomb scare occurred as members were pressing the CIA during a secret briefing. It continued when we abandoned Washington when anthrax, possibly from a government lab, arrived in the mail. It continued when the Attorney General declared a nationwide terror alert and then the Administration brought the destructive Patriot Bill to the floor of the House. It continued in the release of the bin Laden tapes at the same time the President was announcing the withdrawal from the ABM treaty. It remains present in the cordoning off of the Capitol. It is present in the camouflaged armed national guardsmen who greet members of Congress each day we enter the Capitol campus. It is present in the labyrinth of concrete barriers through which we must pass each time we go to vote. The trappings of a state of siege trap us in a state of fear, ill equipped to deal with the Patriot Games, the Mind Games, the War Games of an unelected President and his unelected Vice President.

Let us pray that our country will stop this war. "To promote the common defense" is one of the formational principles of America. Our Congress gave the President the ability to respond to the tragedy of September the Eleventh. We licensed a response to those who helped bring the terror of September the Eleventh. But we the people and our elected representatives must reserve the right to measure the response, to proportion the response, to challenge the response, and to correct the response.

Because we did not authorize the invasion of Iraq.

We did not authorize the invasion of Iran.

We did not authorize the invasion of North Korea.

We did not authorize the bombing of civilians in Afghanistan. We did not authorize permanent detainees in Guantanamo Bay.

We did not authorize the withdrawal from the Geneva Convention.

We did not authorize military tribunals suspending due process and habeas corpus.

We did not authorize assassination squads.

We did not authorize the resurrection of COINTELPRO.

We did not authorize the repeal of the Bill of Rights.

We did not authorize the revocation of the Constitution.

We did not authorize national identity cards.

We did not authorize the eye of Big Brother to peer from cameras throughout our cities.

We did not authorize an eye for an eye.

Nor did we ask that the blood of innocent people, who perished on September 11, be avenged with the blood of innocent villagers in Afghanistan.

We did not authorize the administration to wage war anytime, anywhere, anyhow it pleases.

We did not authorize war without end.

We did not authorize a permanent war economy.

Yet we are upon the threshold of a permanent war economy. The President has requested a $45.6 billion increase in military spending. All defense-related programs will cost close to $400 billion. Consider that the Department of Defense has never passed an independent audit.

Consider that the Inspector General has notified Congress that the Pentagon cannot properly account for $1.2 trillion in transactions.

Consider that in recent years the Dept. of Defense could not match $22 billion worth of expenditures to the items it purchased, wrote off, as lost, billions of dollars worth of in-transit inventory and stored nearly $30 billion worth of spare parts it did not need. Yet the defense budget grows with more money for weapons systems to fight a cold war which ended, weapon systems in search of new enemies to create new wars. This has nothing to do with fighting terror. This has everything to do with fueling a military industrial machine with the treasure of our nation, risking the future of our nation, risking democracy itself with the militarization of thought which follows the militarization of the budget.

Let us pray for our children. Our children deserve a world without end. Not a war without end. Our children deserve a world free of the terror of hunger, free of the terror of poor health care, free of the terror of homelessness, free of the terror of ignorance, free of the terror of hopelessness, free of the terror of policies which are committed to a world view which is not appropriate for the survival of a free people, not appropriate for the survival of democratic values, not appropriate for the survival of our nation, and not appropriate for the survival of the world.

Let us pray that we have the courage and the will as a people and as a nation to shore ourselves up, to reclaim from the ruins of September the Eleventh our democratic traditions. Let us declare our love for democracy. Let us declare our intent for peace. Let us work to make nonviolence an organizing principle in our own society. Let us recommit ourselves to the slow and painstaking work of statecraft, which sees peace, not war as being inevitable. Let us work for a world where someday war becomes archaic. That is the vision which the proposal to create a Department of Peace envisions. Forty-three members of congress are now cosponsoring the legislation. Let us work for a world where nuclear disarmament is an imperative. That is why we must begin by insisting on the commitments of the ABM treaty. That is why we must be steadfast for nonproliferation.

Let us work for a world where America can lead the way in banning weapons of mass destruction not only from our land and sea and sky but from outer space itself. That is the vision of HR 3616: A universe free of fear. Where we can look up at God's creation in the stars and imagine infinite wisdom, infinite peace, infinite possibilities, not infinite war, because we are taught that the kingdom will come on earth as it is in heaven.

Let us pray that we have the courage to replace the images of death which haunt us, the layers of images of September the Eleventh, faded into images of patriotism, spliced into images of military mobilization, jump cut into images of our secular celebrations of the World Series, New Year's Eve, the Superbowl, the Olympics, the strobic flashes which touch our deepest fears, let us replace those images with the work of human relations, reaching out to people, helping our own citizens here at home, lifting the plight of the poor everywhere. That is the America which has the ability to rally the support of the world. That is the America which stands not in pursuit of an axis of evil, but which is itself at the axis of hope and faith and peace and freedom.

America, America. God shed grace on thee. Crown thy good, America.

Not with weapons of mass destruction. Not with invocations of an axis of evil. Not through breaking international treaties. Not through establishing America as king of a unipolar world. Crown thy good America.

America, America. Let us pray for our country. Let us love our country. Let us defend our country not only from the threats without but from the threats within. Crown thy good, America. Crown thy good with brotherhood, and sisterhood. And crown thy good with compassion and restraint and forbearance and a commitment to peace, to democracy, to economic justice here at home and throughout the world. Crown thy good, America. Crown thy good America. Crown thy good.

Thank you.

APPENDIX III

The Story of the Porcupine

In Memoriam Hella Hammid

My friend Hella lay dying in a small tree house nestled into a great sycamore in the middle of a burning city at the moment of the Los Angeles uprising. On Wednesday night, afraid I would not be able to get to her in time, I asked her, "Are you dying now?"

She said, "I don't know. I have never done this before."

When I did arrive at her tree house, Hella was dying in Nora's lap within the flowered pink linen sheets she had bought when she learned she was ill. There were flowers everywhere, as usual. Except the petals were falling. Someone had forgotten to change the water. The amaryllis that had been open mouthed was drooping in the corner. The patio garden facing her bed was ablaze with color as if the final test would require her to relinquish what she loved most.

On the past Sunday, she had said she would hold on until her daughter Julia arrived. Now the morphine was flowing coolly into her veins as she waited. Soon we would smell the smoke from fires that would not be put out. Nora, her lover, ran her fingertips along Hella's face, the way one strokes an infant to turn her cheek. On the white cabinet stood Nora's gift, a Madonna, two feet high, carved by a Native American. She was holding out the infant Christ, an offering wrapped in white cloth. Hella lay in Nora's lap in the trance of her very slow, spacious breathing. Nora's father was curled up in his four poster bed in a palace in Mexico City that he had built to house his collection of religious icons. It will become a museum when he dies. Whenever she was awake, Hella resumed giving her things away: the baskets on the walls in her kitchen, the pewter bowls, the vases, her bracelets, her photographs and all the cobalt blue glass along every window.

Suzanne did not know what to ask for so she asked for a gift of the plants she had tended; she wanted to have something that would die.

When the Virgin Mary had come to her while I was counseling her, Hella wept first for the sweetness of it and then out of shock. She could not understand how she, a Jewish woman, lay in the arms of Mary, in the posture of the pieta.

On Christmas, it had occurred to me to take Hella to the *Sanctuario de Chimayo* to gather healing earth from the *posito* to rub on her body, but she was too ill. Whenever Michael and I go there, we bring little shoes for the *Santo Niño* who wears out the soles of his shoes each night as he wanders the fields blessing the crops.

In the thirties, Hella's father had traveled to Spain to establish shoe factories. One afternoon he called his wife in Germany: "Leave today," he had said, "leave everything behind, take only what you and Hella can carry."

The past Sunday, believing there was nothing we hadn't addressed in our years of work together, I still asked Hella if there was anything standing in the way of her dying and mysteriously she said, "The porcupine."

A week before on Thursday, she had looked young as she clambered up and down the stairs to find a gift for a friend. The life force gripped her and despite the pain she was suffering, we couldn't imagine that it would let her go. By Sunday, she was suffering more pain and was older. By this Wednesday, age had set in. Her photographer's eye was dimmed. This psychic who was accustomed to crossing vast and remote distances no longer looked outward or even into this universe. She was not aware of the smoke in the air nor the atmosphere of anger or desperation. For her, the world had contracted to the perimeter of her bed. Her skin pulled tight about the muscles of her face, the bones began to emerge. Now this Thursday, we watched her becoming an old woman as her skull began to take over her face. By midnight, her face disappeared into that of a old woman dying. She was indistinguishable from her mother who had been almost a hundred when she had died. She was not Hella, not even an old woman, she was Age itself, without name and without origin.

In the beginning, Hella had said that she would refuse to be in pain, that she would leave before she was disabled, that she would not consider being a burden, that she didn't want to suffer. In the beginning, she said she hadn't done her work yet, she had more to offer, she loved life so much, she didn't want to leave it. In the beginning, she said she wanted to live and she would fight to the death. Then she said, she didn't want to die and wouldn't. Then she was afraid to live as long as her mother had lived.

In the beginning, she couldn't imagine dying. In the beginning, she thought she could heal herself. Then she found the pressure to heal the body a burden. Then she knew the choice was hers whether to live or to die, and it surprised her that she could not make the decision. Then something in her was ready and this readiness dumbfounded her. Somehow she had found the courage not to live. At the very end, she said, she was ready to die, but now she had to wait for a sign.

From the beginning, we didn't know what healing was, or how we would recognize it, or whether it would come. Some say preparing to live again, healing oneself, is the same path as preparing to die a good death, and her death was the proof of it, as is the story she finally told of the porcupine.

The last day, Thursday, she had invited me into her room and asked me to close the door. Then between long spacious breaths she spoke of what she had never spoken before. More than twenty-five years ago, she had had a summer house which, one year, was infested with porcupines and so she determined to be rid of them. "We didn't know anything then," Hella whispered. "We didn't know anything."

"The porcupine," she continued in jagged sentences broken by interminable silences between the raspy inhalations and exhalations, "wouldn't die. And so we beat him and we beat him and for so long a time couldn't beat the life out of him. I can't forget the rain of blows."

Now, she said, the porcupine was with her and his quills were piercing her liver, but, also, she was the porcupine who couldn't die while the cancer beat her and beat her. "And every day of my life," she said, "I have been thinking of the porcupine."

The summer before when Michael, Pami and I had been traveling to Canyon de Chelly, we had come upon a road kill and stopped to pull a porcupine to the field to bury it among the pine trees. After we had said prayers, we took the quills, then said some prayers again and covered it with earth and pine needles.

When I told Hella's story of the porcupine to Pami, she made a necklace of quills and without knowing Hella's passion, added cobalt blue glass beads. I brought it with me to Hella, showed it to her with assurances of absolution and placed it by her bedside. When her son, Tino, returned from the airport with his sister Julia, he was startled by the necklace, for he, himself, had just recalled a story of porcupines.

When he was ten, in the year, or another year, of infestation, his mother Hella had put a shotgun in the hands of the boy who had never killed anything, and insisted he shoot the porcupine. And Tino shot it again and again and again until it died. The porcupine had been between them until this hour.

Late Wednesday night, there had already been smoke in the air. The helicopters hovered overhead and we did not know if and where the planes we were awaiting would land. The uprising spread. Hella's breath slowed down even more, the rhythm of it extending like the wail of the sirens disappearing in the night, and we lost ourselves in the sanctuary of her breathing.

By Thursday midnight, we were all gathered in. The son and the daughter and the father of the son and the daughter. The lover and the ex-lover and the lover of the ex-lover, those women. And a cousin and Michael and myself. Then a patch of darkness entered and hovered in the air just over her closed eyes and the death's head of her face moved up passionately to meet it as Hella reached back toward us with a flutter of her hands, in regret or embarrassment that she was leaving us now, so unexpectedly of her own will.

She let us see – insisted we watch – her spirit drawn into a point about her eyes and opened mouth while the weight of her, the limbs, bones, muscles, were sinking back into the bed, wrinkling in folds. Her body – what we had mistaken for her – was thrust aside, undressed, left as one leaves the hem of the skirt or the pants leg as one extracts oneself from the cloth falling away in a pile onto the floor.

She sent us away then. She took thirty minutes for herself, then summoned, she cried out with a violent gasp and intake of breath, calling us back, sitting up, startled eyes opened, as we gathered around her again. She breathed three gasps of air, and fell back across Tino's lap – the porcupine was no longer between them – giving herself for the first time fully into the arms of her son who, in that moment, was able to embrace her – that pieta. And she was dead. And young again. All the lines smoothed out and her skin glowing with the first sliver of moon.

Or it was a birth which we had been witnessing from behind as the intense and relentless pressure thrust her before our eyes down the birth canal of her body and away from us. An undressing of spirit, an unprecedented nakedness in her dying, and then being born – elsewhere – and so, of course, we wailed.

Nora, her young lover, keened bitterly and then reached out in a gesture of unexpected maternity and took Hella's frail, elderly ex-husband, perhaps fifty years between them, transfixed on the bed, himself as immobile as Hella, into her arms.

In the morning, the sparrow came in the open door downstairs, as usual. It hopped up the stairs – as it had so many times, led originally by the crumbs Hella had used to guide it – and into the room and across the pink sheets on the empty bed and out onto the patio and away into the gray brown sky.

I thought of what Hella had taught me. If one has violated the god of porcupines, one may contract porcupine sickness. That is because nature has been transgressed. And if one says, I don't believe in porcupine sickness, that does not protect one from porcupine sickness. So sometimes one asks forgiveness of the god of porcupines and sometimes one's son is of an age to ask or give forgiveness. It was astonishing to think that the woman who had loved her garden so much, who had lived in the arms of the sycamore tree, who had never put screens on her windows, who had, each day, fed the birds, had also once offended the porcupines and had suffered from this her entire life.

Hella died on Friday morning at 3:15 a.m. when the smoldering city was relatively quiet and we were all beginning to wonder if we could rise from the ashes. She had often said that the three years of cancer had been, by far, the best years of her life. And perhaps, if she were interested in speaking to us from the center of her dying, she might have said that her death was, itself, the high point.

Her son took the porcupine necklace into his empty hands. The Medicine Cards say, "If you were to observe Porcupine, you would immediately notice its quills. These quills are only used when trust has been broken between Porcupine and another creature . . . . When fear is not present, it is possible to feed a Porcupine by hand and never get stuck by its quills."[55]

The place of healing is a narrow place that we can rarely traverse alone. And we never know if the healing place is in the living or the dying.

APPENDIX IV

Invoking the Holy Letters for Peace and Tikkun Olam
An Esoteric and Exoteric Practice

In the ancient tradition of Kabbalah, the quality and spiritual energy of the Holy Letters can be invoked for the sake of Creation. To do this with a pure heart is to humbly pray that a door be opened so that the Divine can enter and suffuse the world.

These prayers or Invocations came to me the week of April 10th. At the time when Israel was embroiled in the horrors of war, I was taken by the idea of creating a Jewish esoteric practice of Peacemaking through the Sacred Letters. The Letters may indeed be the original building blocks of creation and if so we are given a gift and possibility by the opportunity to summon them on behalf of divine Creation. Approached with the profound humility and devoted Kavanah that these times require, these Invocations may be effective prayers for the sake of Peace and Tikkun Olam, the repair of the entire world.

A three-part practice, both esoteric and exoteric: Meditating upon, contemplating, understanding the meanings and potential of the Letters as the essential elements of Peace and Peacemaking. Invoking the Letters so that Peace enters the world. Living the Letters, meeting each situation and conflict with the wisdom and insight that the individual Letters and the Letters together imply. That is, becoming Peacemakers. All of this following from the understanding that if we want Peace, we are called to act on it with all our hearts and souls.

The call to offer these Invocations came to me after I realized that each one of the Letters, not only individual Letters, the Samech ס let's say, is essential to the peace process and that invoked together the Letters con-

293

stitute another energy altogether. Anything on its own may become a golem. The circle of Samech ס without the independence of Vav ו, can be smothering, and vice-versa, as can be the unceasing voice of Pei פ without the silence of א Aleph, as the brokenness of Hei ה is eased by the inclusivity of Tav ת. And none of the Letters can be what they are meant to be without the divine spark, Yud י, moving through them. This affirms the idea that the essential act of Peacemaking and the essential act of Creation are similar and related in their reliance on the equal inclusion of all beings and all possibilities, all the qualities and all the elements.

May these Invocations be a Blessing to you and to the world in these times. May Peace descend.

I wish to acknowledge with much gratitude, the work of Yitzchak Ginsburgh, *The Alef-Beit;* Lawrence Kushner, *The Book of Letters;* and Edward Hoffman, *The Kabbalah Deck;* as being central to the development to this work. The first lines of the Kaddish in English are from a new translation by poet Peter Levitt and Rabbi Don Singer.

א Alef

Eretz. The earth. The earth will be restored. The silence from which all sound issues. The All in the One. Let no one and no part be eliminated. Let no one and no part be eradicated. Alef is the silent blessing on all beings. A Holy name in which all beings reside is Elohim. All the names of God are the names of God. All the Gods are God. We relinquish the fire that consumes all for the fire that does not consume. The Burning Bush is the Tree of Life. All One, the Burning Bush and Creation. One. One. One. Alef invokes the unity of all beings in the One.

ב Beit

Everything is a house for God. Let no house be chosen over another house. Build me a Temple and I will dwell in them. We are two and cannot war against each other. Here we are aligned, enter us all and at once, Divine One, that we may be fertile with You. Now each moment is Beresheet, is In the Beginning as we return again and again to the original creation. We live in the house of God and the house of God is in us. That is the Blessing. The grass, every blade of it, the songbird, and the howl, these are great Temples. The one we think is an enemy is a Temple. Beit invokes the recognition that all beings are Temples.

ג Gimel

Lovingkindness takes us out of exile to Paradise. Lovingkindness heals the tortured. We have tortured and we cease and heal with lovingkindness. No one can redeem the deeds we have done but ourselves. Gimel comes to the battle and takes the two of us into its arms. For Gimel to exist I must exist alongside the Other and the Other must be present with me. It runs after us to give us the courage of reconciliation. Each of us is rich in gifts and we run to give what we have to the other. We are the rich ones giving to the poor ones with an open heart. The rich ones give to the poor ones. The rich ones give to the poor one. Instead of these great wars, we enter the gilgul, the wheel, the cycle, death and rebirth, transformation, the soul's journey. There is a great wave coming toward us. It is God running toward Creation; we run together toward God. Alone, I cannot accomplish it but if we are all alongside each other, redemption comes. Gimel invokes the lovingkindness of the soul's journey that is generous to all beings.

ד Dalet

There is a door. We open the door that seems closed. We go through it from one world to another. In the fourth world, adepts enact the miracle of the first world, the great Peace that passeth understanding. Blood will not be spilled. Da, we know before whom we stand. The Judge discerns when we carry peace in our hearts, and when we are carrying fear, hate or murder. This knowledge. The hidden place on the Tree of Life. Daat is a door that we must open. Only then, Devekut. We bind ourselves to You and You are everywhere as we, poor ones, receive you. All of us are poor and bend down before the Holy One. Thus our egos are finally nullified as our souls are lifted up and ignited. We ask assistance from the four elements, the four directions for all beings. We open the doors of the four worlds: invisible, animal, vegetable, mineral. We invoke the Tetragrammaton on behalf of Creation. After our selves are finally undone, Dalet opens the door to Peace.

ה Hei

Here we are. Everything is broken. We are broken into many pieces. We are shattered into all the tiny but Holy distinct pieces of Creation. Atomized. Each one of us is a part of the shattering. We shatter and we are shattered. Because we are different from each other, we are the holy sparks. God calls us each. What can we say? We search our souls. Hitbodedut. This is the time of soul searching. We must account for ourselves with each other and with the world. Does Creation proceed from us or do we annihilate it? Are we seeds or are we destruction? Is the earth green under our touch or is it burning to extinction? Are the animals free and abundant? Are the trees exultant in their great woods? We scrutinize each of the 5 levels of our souls. We hear the voice again. The breath repeating itself twice in the Name of God. Breathe now. Breathe again. Be still. The breath carries us to the moment of awareness. Again, we are called. It is time to say, Heenayni. Here I am. Behold. Revelation comes to each, human and non-human in our own voice and understanding and way. It is not for ourselves alone. Hei praises the sacredness and equality of all the small particulars that are life and calls us forth on its behalf.

ו Vav

Vav mediates between the worlds. Vav joins heaven to earth. The lightning bolt of illumination for every one to see. It is the holy light descending. Vav calls every connection to be upright and sacred. Vav joins each one to each one. Each one is unique and independent and we depend upon these differences. We do not annihilate the others but treasure them equal to ourselves for their distinct ways of living and knowing. Vav is the straight line and the hook, the separate and individual paths that are fastened to each other. The jeweled net of Indra. The network of all life. The web of inter-being. This is the sacred that Vav mediates. When we forget – Vidui, confession. We confess for each other. We strike our hearts with our fists in great remorse and act accordingly. Vav invokes the sacred, indisputable interconnections.

ז Zayin

Zayin creates the Sabbath for all beings. Zayin offers the world rest, the joy and relief of prayer and contemplation, the heart eased by the Presence. Zayin is the holy life undistracted by personal and human cares and lived harmoniously according to the divine law. Zayin enfolds the secular and the sacred, the mundane and the esoteric. Zayin is the returning light, the prayers rising upwards and gaining consciousness so that they are on behalf of all. Zayin is remembering. Remembering the ethical life and living it impeccably. Remembering our joys, giving thanks and offering them to the world. Remembering our suffering with compassion and refusing to enact suffering on anyone. Zayin is the sword put down. And here come the grandfathers, the old ones, the ancestors in all shapes and forms who have wisdom and sustain the living community of all beings benevolently and equally. Zayin is the crown, the return to the great light, the splendor, that rescues us from our own darkness and illuminates all things. Zayin invokes the Presence in the world so that all beings live in its great light.

ח Chet

Life, the holy of holies. The faces of God are the living faces of Creation. A warning to all of us regarding the destruction and desecration we are wreaking in the world. We are doing this. We are. A small group of people gathered in piety brings life, restores life, saves life. We can do this. We can. We take the marriage vows under the canopy that shelters new life. We enter into the sacred union. We recognize the forty-nine gates of wisdom and do the work to pass through them, wise enough to study Peace. Life, not destruction, flows from us. Chet is the gate through which the dreams pass. The dream is the word of the Divine, the teachings of the ancestors calling us to the Way and the sacredness of all life. Chet is life. Chet invokes life. L'Chaim. To life!

ט Tet

Tet is the vessel. A vessel containing the blessing of Peace. Nine months we are pregnant with Peace. In its good time, Peace will be born. The sefirah, Yesod, the vessel, the angel or the attribute of God that symbolizes Peace. Peace is the only vessel containing blessing. The staff became the living snake in Moses' hand. Nefustan, the great serpent, is a name of God. The caduceus. Healing. Transformation. The Nine lives of peacemaking. Tiferet. Beauty. We walk in Beauty. Tet invokes the goodness of God. What more need be said? It is good. It is good. It is good. Peace and Blessings.

י Yud.

God. The name of God. The hand of God. The essential Presence of God everywhere. The essence of God hidden in Creation and extended as the hand is extended. The initial point from which Creation emerges. The point and the pathway. Every letter, the tiny, infinite Yud in motion. Giving thanks. Two hands. The hand extended in friendship. The hand of God extended to everyone. To the Presence, everyone is a friend. Therefore, minyans, councils that contain the wisdom of each individual. In council, together, we resurrect all the peacemaking traditions. We gather in minyans for the prayers of peace. The ten Sefirot and the pathway they travel. The attributes and paths of Creation entering and creating the world, continuously. Yona, the Dove of Peace. Yud invokes the Presence of God everywhere and gathers us into the Holy councils from which Peace emanates. God invoking God.

כ Caf

Keter. Here God first touches the world and God's spirit flows in the 10 Sefirot for the sake of creation. We touch our palms together in gratitude, in prayer. The palm of God sustains us, is under every burden and the palm of God blesses all of us. We raise our palms to receive God's bounty. We bless and we pray: Bless the clouds, bless the rain, bless the air, bless the earth, bless the holy fire in all things. Honor. Honor all. Honor all things. Honor all beings. Honor the mother and the father, the old ones, the ancestors, the four legged people, the crawling people, the standing people, the swimming people and the flying people. Honor the stones and honor the fire of the hearth. Caf is the intent to restore God's creation. Honor all. Caf is the intentionality, the will power, the focus, the one-pointedness, the devotion to prayer. Caf invokes the honor due all beings and the intent of blessing the wondrousness of creation. Kavanah.

ל Lamed.

Learning and teaching. The teacher and the student stand before the agonies and the mysteries of our time and respond with the wisdom of the heart. The teacher teaches peacemaking and the student becomes a peacemaker. One calls the other into being. The small flame of the moon is a light in the dark night of these times. These are the days when we are learning again and again the meaning of the words, 'Thou shalt not.' The ability to say 'No.' The willingness to say 'No.' The heart to say 'No.' Thou shalt not kill. 'No, we will not kill.' Thou shalt not steal. Thou shalt not bear false witness. Thou shalt not covet. We agree, 'No.' No, killing. No theft. No coveting. No bearing false witness. Lamed invokes the Lamed Vov, the ones who secretly and tirelessly carry the suffering and righteous action on behalf of the world. Lamed invokes the heart. Lamed invokes the Lamed Vov here. In us.

מ Mem

Here are the deep waters of wisdom and redemption. Here is the underground stream and the flowing fountain of Holiness. Here we purify ourselves so that we may return to the original state of blessedness. We went away, far away, from wisdom and purity, and now we step into the living waters so that we may return. The fountain of wisdom is never ending, it flows ceaselessly from the heights, and we drink from it. This is the wisdom we need in these times and it is given to us in abundance. The secret knowledge bubbles up from the springs in the earth, we bathe in it and are refreshed. The waters of the earth are gathered and purified. The waters are cleansed from our toxins and the wells we have poisoned are clear. We go into retreat, we quarantine ourselves, we take the time we must take, for our minds and hearts to be transformed from one consciousness to another. We wander in the desert until we are other than we were. We enter the kingdom, Malkut, restored. Mem calls the wise ones to guide our spirits and we restore ourselves in the presence of angels. Mem invokes the desire to return to holiness and means to purify ourselves. Mem is the universal activity of midrash, the penetration of the story, in order to understand the deeper meanings, the sacred teachings. Mem invokes the Messiah in everyone so that the Messiah can be among us.

נ Nun

Nun invokes the Jubilee year when all debts are forgiven, all slaves freed, all contracts dissolved. After Nun, no one is enslaved or beholden. Outside of slavery, each one attends his or her soul. Nun is the recognition of the soul in everyone. All souls are freed from the terrible servitude of hunger, fear and oppression. There are forty-nine gates to wisdom, Nun calls us to pass through the forty-nine in order to approach the fiftieth gate which is Faith. We carry the faith of the existence of the Divine and we serve that Peace in each moment. Now the spark is in us. Nun follows Mem and serves the exultant creatures of the Holy sea abundant in their joy and their liveliness. Nigun. A sacred melody. The song that Blesses and Invokes the Presence of the Divine. Nun invokes the healing song that brings all beings through the last gate where Faith is constituted in the Presence of God.

ס Samech

The circle. The sacred circle. Everyone and everything is in the circle. No one and no one thing is above another and each are necessary for the completion of the circle. The circle is the wedding ring that unites each with the other. With this ring, I thee wed. We say this to each other, endlessly. Creation is the Holy Book that we learn to read and honor. The secrets concealed in the worlds of holiness are revealed to all of us for the sake of restoring Creation. The teacher supports and blesses the student, transmits knowledge and blessings, in the way that the Divine supports us and blesses us in the work of Peace. We offer ourselves to God. Semichah. Each one of us. We are ordained to carry the wisdom that the earth and Creation teaches. We learn the sacred stories. We carry the sacred stories of the elements, of the animals, of the trees, of the water, of the angels, of the spirits, of our peoples in us as maps leading us toward Peace and kindness to each other. We search out the stories of peacemaking. We are all, in our different ways and languages, the servants of the sacred and the endless cycle of life. Samech verifies the completeness we feel when we are dancing with each other. The endless cycle. The endless cycle of the Sefirot descending and ascending. The ways and shapes of Divinity entering the world and Creation rising toward Spirit. Samech invokes the future.

ע Ayin

Peace depends upon humility. What is great in any nation becomes greater with humility. What is arrogant, oppressive, imperial is undone with humility. We have lacked humility, and we humble ourselves. Ayin is an eye. Perception. Insight. We see the great harm we have done to others and to the earth and we take in these insights and perception with humility. We do not know how to proceed. We call upon the Sanhedrin, the ancestors, the council of Holy Ones to guide us. The Sanhedrin are composed of all the ancestors of all the peoples in the world. We call upon the names of God, the secret attributes of God, the many faces to inform us. Each people knows another name and face of God. When we bring all the names and faces of God into the circle, then the full nature of God as humans can know it is revealed. The eye of God is upon us. And the eye of God sees through us all. We worship together. The different colors that we are, the full spectrum we carry together become the rainbow that is the covenant that we first make with each other. The covenant that we broke is renewed. We restore the sacred groves, the rain forests, the forests, the woods, the olive trees of peace that we cut down, and worship there among them. Ayin invokes the Tree of Life.

פ Pei

The mouth. Words. Words that open the gates. Right speech. The words we are obliged to speak and the words we must never speak. The end of evil speech. The end of calumny and bearing false witness. The end of propaganda. The end of the lie. The doors that right speech opens. The power of prayer. Pei supports the power of prayer. Pei is the wisdom of all that is hidden from us. In dangerous times, one cannot rely on what is obvious or on the surface, one must find the wisdom that is concealed. The elephant. Wonder of wonders. We make alliances with the other animals of the world. We learn the languages of the beasts, the birds and the trees. We speak peace amongst all of us. Peace is carried into the world with the entrance of the Shechinah, the indwelling aspect of the Divine. We go to the Holy apple orchard, to Pardes, to meet Her. The miracle of the invocation of Pardes on earth. The simple truth. The simple heart. The simple prayer. Being present. Here. The ability and willingness to be here and to be open to what is present among us. Pei invokes the words of God as they come through all of us and open the gates to Peace. The Word. That miracle.

צ Tzadik

In the beginning, the Divine One withdrew for the sake of creation. Tzadik represents the sacred act of withdrawing to make room for others. The world emerges where we are not. Tzimtzum. Preferring Creation to ourselves. The sacred act of allowing each its place. Bending ourselves to the Higher Will. Offering Tzadakah. Hunting out what we can offer. The act of giving rather than taking. We have taken what belongs to others. We have taken what should not have been taken from the earth. We have taken more than we needed. Tzadakah, reverses this. We give everything we have to rectify the situation. We are defined by our giving. We become the bedrock of generosity. Righteousness. Hunting out righteousness. Hunting out the fallen sparks. The Tzadik. Tzadikim. The righteous ones. The Tzadik bring down the light of heaven. The great wisdom of the world of Atzilut, the world of Emanation is drawn down deep in our world through the activity of the Tzadik. Tzadik invokes the congregation of the righteous from everywhere on the planet, the elders, the teachers, the healers, the holy ones, the council or minyan of the righteous who become who they are in concert with each other.

ק Kuf

The great prayer in the face of death. The great prayer of mourning and praise. Kuf invokes the prayer, Kaddish, for all the wrongful deaths we have invoked. We claim all the dead as our dead and we mourn them all. All the dead are our dead and we say Kaddish for them. 'Yitgadal veyitkadash... May the Great Name whose Desire gave birth to the universe, Resound through the Creation Now'.... We raise the glass, we Bless the wine of life for all people, all beings: Sanctification. We make the great sacrifice, whatever is necessary so that peace will come. We give up whatever we must give up that stands between us and peace. We make of ourselves an offering to all beings so that what we do is sacred, so that our peaceable actions have the power of this sacrifice. Whatever Peace wants we offer to it as a Sacred offering, a Holy sacrifice. We welcome peace as the luminous face of the Sabbath Bride. Kabalat Shabbat. We make ourselves so small that we can go through the eye of a needle. We follow the moon through her nineteen years of cycling the sun. We do not have to be the great light. We are content to reflect the light. We take down the walls we have put up and what we surround, we surround only with love and holiness. Kuf invokes the Sacred. Kadosh. Kadosh, Kadosh. Holy. Holy. Holy.

ר Reish

The wind. Ruach. We pray for the wind. We clear the air from the toxins we have released so that the wind may blow through the world as a great spirit. Ruach. Spirit. Breath. We follow the breath. We meditate upon Peace. We honor the breath of life in all beings. When we breathe in we take in the spirit. Compassion. Have Compassion. Rachel, the great womb, the great mother, weeping for her lost children. We weep for all our lost children. We do not send our children to die in the war. We refuse to allow any children to die in war. All the children are our children. We are Rachel to all the children. HaRachaman. Rachman. The all Merciful. The all Compassionate one. We become healers. We ask what will heal the world. We invoke God so that God might heal through us. We are poor but we are not destitute. When we are rich, we make others poor. There are not enough resources in the world for everyone to be rich. The poor planet. We can all have enough if we are poor in goods and rich in spirit. So we bow our heads so that Spirit might enter into us. We begin again. We put an end to the path we have been walking that endangers the world. We begin again. And we begin with the Spirit. Reshimu, the impression of Holiness. Reish invokes the Holy Spirit. Ruach Hakodosh. It blows through us.

ש Shin

The flame. The Eternal Flame. The Eternal Light. We must change our ways. We have the power to change our ways and bring Peace wherever we walk. We have broken the sacred vessels. Shvirat HaKaum. It happened before but in the last years we have broken them again. We have done this. We must gather up the sparks. We must make Peace. Shalom. Not only for us, but for all beings. Peace to those whom we call enemy. Shalom. Salaam. Peace to them first so that we will not have enemies. Shanaim. Two. There must be an end to duality. Two together are not a division. Two together are the two candles of the Sabbath Blessing. Sound the Shofar. The animal opens the gates of Heaven and calls the divine spirit into the world. We can no longer sacrifice the animal. The animal is holy. Shin invokes the Letters of Flame. Shin is the Letter of Flame within the Letters of Flame. Shin invokes the Holy One. Shaddai. Shaddai. Shaddai. May there be Peace. Shalom. Shalom.

ת Tav

Tav completes the Invocation. It is complete. All the Letters are in this last Letter. All the prayers are in this prayer. Stamps, marks, signs, seals. We bear the mark on our foreheads of those who have killed their brothers. Repentance. Teshuvah. We do Teshuvah. We make amends. We repent. We make reparations. We return to holiness. We follow Torah, the Law. We follow the Cosmic Law. Prayer. We pray that God will bring Peace to the world. We speak the truth. We live in truth. Emet is the seal. Emet. Tikkun Olam. We do the work of Tikkun Olam. We rectify, we redeem, we repair the world. We live among all beings as equals and so we make the world whole. The world is redeemed. The world is made whole. Tav invokes Tikkun Olam.

ENDNOTES

1. From "Psalm," Alicia Ostriker, in *American Poetry Review*, Sept./Oct. 2000, Volume 29, #5.

2. *Poems*, Anna Akmatova, selected and translated by Lyn Coffin, Norton, New York, NY, 1983. p. 82.

3. *Roth* v. *United States, 354 U.S. 476* (1957) (SC+).

4. See my article, "Personal Disarmament: Negotiating with the Inner Government," in *Tree: Essays and Pieces*, North Atlantic Books, Berkeley, CA, 1997, pp. 239-252.

5. *Tree: Essays and Pieces*, [including *The Woman Who Slept With Men to Take the War Out of Them* and several essays on healing], *ibid.*

6. See *Heart Politics Revisited* by Fran Peavy, Pluto Press, Australia, 2000, also *By Life's Grace: Musing on the Essence of Social Change*, New Society Publications, 1993.

7. *The Book of Doors*, Athon Veggi and Alison Davidson, Destiny Books, Vermont, 1995, pg. 76.

8. See the forthcoming *Gathering in the Names*, part three of the *Mapatya* [twin brother] trilogy Michael Ortiz Hill, Spring Publications, Autumn 2002 for a detailed recounting of twinship and the healing tradition of the water spirits.

9. "The Buddha of the Beasts," poem, *Looking For the Faces of God*, Deena Metzger, Parallax Press, 1989.

10. *The Last Lords of Palenque*, Victor Perera and Robert D. Bruce, Little, Brown and Company, 1982.

11. *Intimate Nature: The Bond Between Women and Animals*, edited by Linda Hogan, Deena Metzger, Brenda Peterson, Fawcett Columbine, 1998.

12. From "Voronezh," from *Poems*, Anna Akmatova, p.53.

13. *Hope Against Hope, A Memoir*, Nadezhda Mandelstam, Atheneum Publishers, New York, NY, 1970, p. 297.

14. *The Book of Doors*, Athon Veggi and Alison Davidson, pg. 119.

15. *Looking For the Faces of God*, Deena Metzger, Parallax Press, Berkeley, CA, 1989.

16. "In Service of the Sacred, Education of a Healer," by Michael Ortiz Hill, *Whole Life Times*, Los Angeles, CA, February 2002.

17. *Coming Home to the Pleistocene*, Paul Shepard, Island Press, Washington, DC, 1998, p. 7.

18. *Ibid*, p. 173.

19. *Myths for Change: The Total I Ching*, Stephen Karcher, London: Little, Brown, 2003, (forthcoming).

20. *Ibid*, p. 200.

21. See *The Village of the Water Spirits* and *Capable of Such Beauty*, Michael Ortiz Hill, forthcoming, Spring Publications, for a full discussion of water spirit disease and its symptoms.

22. *The Elder Brothers: A Lost South American People and Their Message About the Fate of the Earth*, Alan Ereira, Alfred. Knopf, NewYork, NY, 1992, p. 163.

23. *Ibid*. See also, *Gathering in the Names*, by Michael Ortiz Hill, Spring Publications, 2002, for other such stories.

24. *Peyote Hunt, The Sacred Journey of the Huichol Indians*, Barbara G. Myerhoff, Cornell University Press, Ithaca, NY, 1974, pp. 166-167.

25. *Secrets of the Talking Jaguar: Memoirs from the Living Heart of a Mayan Village*, Martin Prechtel, Jeremy P. Tarcher, Los Angeles, CA, 1999, p. 173.

26. From "Walking With Neruda," *A Sabbath Among the Ruins*, by Deena Metzger, Parallax Press, Berkeley, CA, 1992, p. 99.

27. From "Cape Cod: Caitlin" from Shadow Letters: Self-Portrait of a Woman Alone, in *A Sabbath Among the Ruins*, by Deena Metzger, Parallax Press, Berkeley, CA, 1992.

28. From "Calling a Mother with Advice for the Duat," 1996, unpublished.

29. *Alef Beit*, Yitzchak Ginsburgh, Jason Aronson Inc., Northvale, NJ, 1995.

30. *Alone with the Alone, Creative Imagination in the Sufism of Ibn 'Arabī*, Henry Corbin with a preface by Harold Bloom, Bollingen Series, Princeton University Press, Princeton, NJ, 1969, p. 34.

31. *Writing For Your Life: a Guide and Companion to the Inner Worlds*, Deena Metzger, HarperSanFrancisco, San Francisco, CA, 1992.

32. *How to Use the I Ching, A Guide to Working With the Oracle of Change*, Stephen Karcher, Element Books, Inc., Dorset, UK, 1997, p. 56.

33. *Ibid*, p. 148.

34. *The Book of Hags*: a radio play in the form of a novel. Written by Deena

Metzger. Dramatized by Everett Frost. Produced for KPFK, Pacifica Radio, Los Angeles, CA, 1976. Published on cassette, Washington, DC, Black Box, 1977.

35. *The Book of Doors*, Athon Veggi and Alison Davidson, p. 207.

36. "The Elephant Cull," Gillian Van Houten, *Femina*, South Africa, December 1998.

37. *The Other Hand*, Deena Metzger, Red Hen Press, Palmdale CA, 2001.

38. Thai Elephant Orchestra, CD notes, Dave Soldier and Richard Lair, Mulatta Records MUL001, 2001, www.mulatta.org.

39. "Coming Home," by Deena Metzger in *Intimate Nature, Women's Bond with Animals*, co-edited by Deena Metzger, Linda Hogan and Brenda Peterson, Ballantine, New York, NY, 1998.

40. "Call to Readers, Animal Intent and Agency," *Earthlight Magazine*, ed. By K. Lauren de Boer, Summer 2001.

41. "An Act of Forgiveness Leads to Healing," Laura Bellmay, Letters to the Editor, *The Hartford Courant*, Saturday, November 12, 1999.

42. *The Alef-Beit*, Rabbi Yitzchak Ginsburgh, p.255.

43. *Ibid.*

44. *The Book of Doors*, Athon Veggi and Alison Davidson, pp. 119-123.

45. *The Pictorial Key to the Tarot*, Arthur Edward Waite, Rudolf Steiner Publications, Blauvelt, NY, 1971, pp. 133-135,

46. *The Mythic Tarot*, Liz Greene & Juliet Sharman-Burke, Fireside Books, Simon & Schuster, New York, NY, 1986, p. 67.

47. *Ibid*, p. 65.

48. *Coming Home to the Pleistocene*, Paul Shepard, Island Press, pp. 60-62.

49. "Introduction," in *The Domestication and Exploitation of Plants and Animals*, Peter J. Ucko and G. W. Dimbleby, Chicago, Aldine, 1969), p. xvii, quoted by Paul Shepard in *Coming Home to the Pleistocene*, page 62.

50. *Coming Home to the Pleistocene*, Paul Shepard, p. 62.

51. The very littlest Michael.

52. *The Book of Doors*, Athon Veggi and Alison Davidson, p. 166.

53. *Animal-Speak: The Spiritual and Magical Powers of Creatures Great and Small*, Ted Andrews, Llewellyn Publications, MN, 1988, pp. 267-269.

54. *Woman's Encyclopedia of Myths and Secrets*, Barbara G. Walker, HarperSanFrancisco, San Francisco, CA, 1983, p. 940.

55. *Medicine Cards*, Jamie Sams and David Carson, Bear & Company, Santa Fe, New Mexico, 1988.

The cost of this book reflects the cost of materials and essential labor undertaken by the community around Daré and Hand to Hand. We would greatly appreciate contributions to support the publication and distribution of this book. Make tax-deductible donations to Mandlovu-Hand to Hand c/o Social and Environmental Entrepreneurs (SEE). 20178 Rockport Way, Malibu, Ca. 90265-5340, Tel: (310) 456-3534, Fax: (310) 456-0388. As this book arises from and desires to meet the great need of these times, it is our hope that you will join us in all ways you can in our labor to bring the book to the community and to those who will be informed and sustained by it. Please tell your friends and your colleagues.

Hand to Hand is a community based endeavor that supports independently published works and public events, free of the restrictions that arise from commercial and political concerns. It is a forum for artists who are in dynamic and reciprocal relationship with their communities for the sake of peacemaking, restoring culture and the planet. For further information regarding Hand to Hand please write hand2hand@earthlink.net. For further information about Deena Metzger, her writing and work, please see http://www.deenametzger.com/ or write to her at theghostriver@earthlink.net or P.O. Box 186, Topanga, CA, 90290, USA.

This book is set in Caslon Book and printed on acid-free, recycled paper using soy-based inks.

FOR ADDITIONAL COPIES OF THIS BOOK:

Please contact Book Clearing House at:
(800) 431-1579
or visit their website at:
http://www.book-clearing-house.com
or visit your local independent bookseller.

ABOUT THE AUTHOR

Photo © Jessica Shokrian

Deena Metzger is a novelist, poet, essayist, storyteller and healer seeking to map the imaginal realms. She is an explorer of the deeper meaning and manifestations of Story. She and her husband Michael Ortiz Hill have brought the tradition of Daré to North America for the sake of restoring beauty and bringing healing to individuals, community and the natural world. Deena is the author of many works including *Tree: Essays and Pieces*; *Writing For Your Life: A Guide and Companion to the Inner Worlds*; *Intimate Nature: The Bond Between Women and Animals* (with Brenda Peterson and Linda Hogan); and the novels *The Other Hand* and *What Dinah Thought*. Her most recent books of poetry are *Looking for the Faces of God* and *A Sabbath Among The Ruins*. She is also known for her exuberant "Warrior" poster that illustrates the triumph over breast cancer. She lectures and teaches the ways of writing and creativity nationally and internationally, and has developed a training program for the 21st century in the creative, political, spiritual, and ethical aspects of healing. She and her husband live with the wolves Akasha and Blue.

Notes

Dare :

1) Call in Spirits
2) Telling & receiving Dreams
3) music

Notes

healing moments
- Borestone Camp - helping girl climb mtn